A LIFE WITH
GHOSTS

A LIFE WITH GHOSTS

TRUE, TERRIFYING, AND INSIGHTFUL TALES FROM MY FAVORITE HAUNTS

STEVE GONSALVES

with **MICHAEL ALOISI**

G

GALLERY BOOKS

NEW YORK   LONDON   TORONTO   SYDNEY   NEW DELHI

G

Gallery Books

An Imprint of Simon & Schuster, LLC

1230 Avenue of the Americas

New York, NY 10020

First Gallery Books trade paperback edition July 2024

GALLERY BOOKS and colophon are registered trademarks of Simon & Schuster, LLC

Simon & Schuster: Celebrating 100 Years of Publishing in 2024

For information about special discounts for bulk purchases, please contact Simon & Schuster Special Sales at 1-866-506-1949 or business@simonandschuster.com.

The Simon & Schuster Speakers Bureau can bring authors to your live event. For more information or to book an event, contact the Simon & Schuster Speakers Bureau at 1-866-248-3049 or visit our website at www.simonspeakers.com.

Interior design by Hope Herr-Cardillo

Manufactured in the United States of America

10 9 8 7 6 5 4 3 2 1

Library of Congress Control Number: 2023935216

ISBN 978-1-6680-0832-4
ISBN 978-1-6680-0833-1 (pbk)
ISBN 978-1-6680-0834-8 (ebook)

This book is dedicated to my parents for a lifetime of unconditional love and support.

And to my sister, the strongest person I know.

CONTENTS

CONTENTS

CONTENTS

SOMETIMES IT'S WHEN YOU LEAST EXPECT IT

AFTERWORD

ACKNOWLEDGMENTS

INDEX

A LIFE WITH
GHOSTS

INTRODUCTION

MY LIFE BEFORE GHOSTS

—

What I remember about my life before ghosts is basically family, Halloween, *Star Wars*, and cartoons! When I was growing up as a child of the eighties, the decade that's now peak pop culture nostalgia, ghosts were a hot-ticket item, including a long list of films featuring spooky spirits. Movies like *Ghostbusters* made me think, *God, that would be fun to do. Poltergeist* made me consider, *Okay, maybe it's not so fun*, and the *House* film series made me wish there was a spirit world ready to visit right then and there. The mainstream was lightning quick to jump on the paranormal craze. Television's *Unsolved Mysteries* dedicated entire episodes to ghosts. Time Life, along with other publishers, released numerous books that showcased the inexplicable . . . and many of those titles sold frighteningly well.

While all of them played a part in creating the ghost-loving—and ghost-hunting—person I am today, it was the 1982 movie *The Entity* that burrowed real fear and intrigue into my brain and started my path in the field. The film was scary for adults, but it was pure nightmare fuel for younger kids like yours truly.

My mom let me watch more age-appropriate movies like *The Goonies* or *Raiders of the Lost Ark* alone in our living room on weekend nights, but one particular evening I fell asleep on the couch just before *The Entity* came on. When I awoke, I had a blanket over me and the light was off—my mom had let me sleep, knowing I would shut the television off and go to bed when I was ready. Groggy and with heavy eyes, I sat up and looked at the screen to see a happy family about to eat a big bowl of ice cream. It seemed innocent, and the massive dessert had me excited. But then, just as the on-screen mom (played by Barbara Hershey) said, "Don't start without me," she was violently grabbed by an unseen force, thrown onto a couch, and brutally attacked over the next minute and a half. The mom's teenage son tried to help her, but invisible hands held him back as well. Then, out of nowhere, vibrant blue bolts of electricity hit the son, shocking him repeatedly.

I don't think I even breathed during that entire scene; my little heart clenched and cried out for me to run. But I couldn't move— I was scared out of my mind, especially since I was also on a couch and in the dark. I wanted to bolt out of the room but didn't dare put a foot on the floor for fear that the same unseen force might come after me as well. To make things even worse, the remote control had fallen off the couch during my slumber, making it too precariously close to the four-inch gap under the sofa, which I just knew *had* to be a hiding spot for supernatural trouble. I was stuck watching the movie, my legs pulled tight to my body and my blanket clenched in a death grip.

It wasn't until my bladder was ready to burst, when I knew that one more scare would make me wet myself, that I dared to think leaving would be safer than staying. (Though by that point I think I had watched almost the entire movie with my mouth agape, like a driver unable to look away while passing by some horrific accident.) That's when Mom suddenly walked into the room, her own sleepy eyes squinting from the glow of the television. She saw the fear on my face and immediately raced to hug me as I blabbed on about how horrible and scary the film was. Mom told me not to worry and that it was only a movie.

Trying to suck in a deep breath, I repeated what she said. However, my new mantra was quickly smashed to pieces when the words "The film you have just seen is a fictionalized account of a true incident . . ." appeared on the screen before the end credits. Panic-stricken, I made my mom look at the television; she just let out a sigh and reiterated that it was still only a movie and that Hollywood makes things up . . . but I could tell by the goose bumps forming on her arm that she was a bit uneasy as well.

As Mom held my hand and brought me to bed, my tiny brain was shooting off fireworks about those two words: *true incident.* I thought of everything I saw in the film—the horrific assaults, the moving objects, the electricity . . . and the scientists investigating the haunting. *That all happened?* I said to myself. *People really research ghosts, like in* Ghostbusters? This seemed rather bizarre but also incredibly fascinating to me.

My sister, my dad, and me on Halloween

Me and my mom

The Entity made me think not only about the paranormal researchers but also the real ghosts outside of books and films and television. Up until that point, I didn't take any of it too seriously, but those haunting words—*true incident*—changed everything. I remember them sticking in my head like a popcorn kernel wedged between your teeth that you can't get out no matter how much you floss. It became a constant annoyance that couldn't be removed. The idea that the events dramatized in that terrifying film *really* happened forever transformed how I saw the world.

Afterward, whenever I walked through my house, I was on the lookout for ghosts (as if they would just suddenly be hanging around). Whenever the temperature changed in my room, I wondered if it was a paranormal event. If I felt an unexpected breeze on my legs or heard a noise I couldn't place, I considered whether it was really a spirit trying to mess with me. *What if my own house was haunted?* It was a terrifying thought for a kid, and for a person of any age really. I hadn't had any significant life experiences to make me think this was the case, but post-*Entity* every creak and odd sound in my home was something that needed investigating.

There were nights when I would lie with the blanket and sheets pulled up over my head, as if they were some sort of magic shield protecting me from spirits who could be haunting my room. Sometimes I would get so scared that I'd race into my parents' room, jump into their bed, and curl up next to them, warm and safe as I looked around to see if I'd been followed. Thankfully—or maybe not so thankfully now—I didn't have any experiences in the homes I grew up in. Being five years older than my sister, Holly, I did my best not to scare or torment her with my ghostly thoughts, but it was hard to always keep them to myself.

One might associate being afraid of ghosts with a fear of the dark, a phobia many kids develop at a young age. That never happened with me, though, and I think I know why. Dad moved the family from Massachusetts to Pennsylvania, so that he could take a job as a district manager of a major jewelry chain. Shortly after that, I think Mom saw that living in a new state was a bit hard for me. So, one evening, she woke Holly and me out of bed and took us on a nighttime mission at the local shopping mall. I couldn't believe so many people were out shopping after my bedtime—I'd always thought the world shut down when I went to sleep. But here we were, pushing our way through dozens of people to stand in line at Hills Department Store.

When my mom got to the counter and asked for a Nintendo video game system, I screamed and hugged Holly. My parents were amazing (and still are); they made sure we always had what we wanted and gave us a great childhood, without ever spoiling us outright. But sneaking us out at night to buy the coveted item that every kid wanted—and without it even being a holiday or birthday—was absolutely mind-blowing. Looking back, there were several factors stemming from that very special evening that made me fall in love with the night: The after-hours surprise. The beauty of the lights reflecting in the rain that fell that evening. Seeing a world buzzing with life after I thought it had shut down. The association of elation and astonishment with a nighttime adventure. Since then, I've been drawn to the so-called witching hours. I love nothing more than being out in the dark, walking around and just enjoying the vibe the evening brings, whether I'm exploring the gloominess of an abandoned building or strolling around the Disney theme parks after sunset—being obsessed with the night obviously helps my career.

Meanwhile, my interest in the paranormal continued to increase. Though the film *Poltergeist* came out before *The Entity*, I didn't actually see it until about a year or so later, when it was broadcast on HBO. Back then, it was easy to sneak-watch movies at home that were geared toward adults; they ran all day and there was no such thing as parental controls on a television. If your parents were doing yard work, busying themselves in the house, or had simply fallen asleep before you, you could watch *anything* that was on . . . including *Poltergeist*.

I remember my mom was making dinner and my dad was still at work and there I was, alone in the living room and pushing the buttons on a big brown remote, changing the channels to find something to watch on our massive, 27-inch cabinet television. At that time, HBO was one of the first channels I would flip to, as there was always a movie on . . . and usually one that I probably wasn't supposed to watch. (The cable channel was a game changer back then, allowing home audiences to see movies uncut and uninterrupted by commercials.) There I saw a little girl kneeling in front of a static-filled TV screen. It was a position I knew very well, having taken it so many times myself while watching Saturday morning cartoons. I could also tell something ominous was going to happen.

Quickly flipping through the *TV Guide*, I saw that the film was called *Poltergeist*, and my heart started to race. I'd heard about how terrifying it was from other kids at school and around the neighborhood, and this was my golden opportunity to watch it. I realized that the middle of the film would cut into dinner, but *TV Guide* showed that it would run again that night at 11:00 PM—way past my bedtime. On occasion, I would secretly watch late-night movies on my bedroom television with the volume very low, sitting close by so I could shut it off if I heard my parents get up. I was ready to do that later with *Poltergeist* and catch anything I might miss during dinner—my backup plan was set.

An hour into the movie—which seemed like seconds as I clutched an orange-crocheted throw pillow to my chest—I was finally called to eat. Having just watched the rotting meat and maggot-filled chicken scene, I couldn't touch my plate. Mom asked if I was getting sick, but I told her I was fine, just not hungry. She was concerned, then slightly annoyed, as she thought I had snacked before supper, but eventually she let me go back to the living room—none the wiser about what I was watching—as long as I took a dinner roll with me.

Poltergeist had me enthralled. It was much more fantastical and big-budget than *The Entity* (even at that age, I understood that), and again my thoughts lit up with excitement and fear over the idea that an unseen force could manipulate our world. After the film ended, I brushed my teeth, kissed my parents good night, and went to my room . . . where

I immediately popped on my own television, turned the volume to a minimum, and got ready to watch the 11:00 PM showing in its entirety—I just had to see it again.

During that second viewing, I really focused on the team of scientists that investigated the haunting. I found that vocation simply fascinating, and to this day I'm amazed at how close that film is to my real life (minus any face peeling and evil clown dolls that drag people under the bed). The way those scientists looked for answers with a command center, their endless patience, the way they'd marvel in awe when they saw or experienced something . . . it's exactly what I do now. A seed was planted in the fertile soil of my mind, and thankfully, with such eighties entertainment as *Poltergeist*, it got regularly watered.

As the years ticked by, that little seed sprouted and started to reach for its own sunshine, which I'd often find at the local library and bookstores. When we made family trips to the library, I'd race to the "New Age" section, which I called the "Paranormal" section, as most of the books were themed around that subject. It was small, but at least they had one, and I took out *every* book there. When they didn't have anything new, I would simply read the same books over and over.

Although I knew about works by Ed and Lorraine Warren, Dr. Barry Taff, and others, the one book I read the most was *ESP, Hauntings and Poltergeists: A Parapsychologist's Handbook* by Loyd Auerbach. That was my bible, and I read it religiously. I studied every word and carried it with me everywhere I went. It was this book that made me realize that *I* could investigate the paranormal . . . and not only that, it told me *how* to do it too. It also taught me how to take the field seriously and focus my work on scientific structure, to respect the craft and the spirits, and to always be professional. It was an absolute life changer for me.

By the end of the decade, as my preteen years vanished, the seed inside my head had matured into a strong sapling that needed more than just books and films to help it grow. Like Audrey II in *Little Shop of Horrors*, it could no longer survive on drips of blood—it needed the real thing. So, when I was about fifteen, after having moved with my family back to Massachusetts a year earlier, I decided to start investigating on my own. At first, I did little experiments and explorations, but I never caught anything because the places I tried weren't haunted. As soon as I got my driver's license, though, I went to every place that I thought might be worth checking out. Yet even with my shiny new laminated license, there weren't many places that would allow a teenager to just wander around the grounds at night calling out to ghosts. So, I often ended up in public places, where I did my best to investigate in secret.

Now, aside from some friends with whom I would rabidly talk about the unexplained, I hid my love of the field. I hate that I had to do that, but back then I didn't want to have to defend myself from the people who thought my passion was odd, so I kept it to myself. If people found out that I "hunted ghosts" as a hobby, I was often subjected to criticism and mockery, or people would say dumb things like, "You don't *really* believe in ghosts, do you?" Of course, there were always the *Ghostbusters* comments and constant laughs at my expense. The real knuckleheads would yell out stuff like, "Hey, Steve, have you seen Casper lately?" and much worse things that aren't worth repeating here. I quickly learned to talk in hushed tones and feel out whom I could confide in regarding my dark and weird hobby. (Ironically, now that investigating the paranormal is mainstream and *Ghost Hunters* became a huge success, the same people who used to tease me ask for autographs and pictures. It's truly amazing how times can change.)

Worrying about crap like that made me so thankful that my parents were understanding about my passion and let me go out after dark to investigate, provided they knew exactly where I was going. I must give them credit—not many parents would let their kid go sit in a graveyard or an abandoned building at night, let alone not judge them or their desire to do that in the first place.

One night, I decided to follow in the footsteps of famed paranormal investigators Ed and Lorraine Warren, and I waited in a cemetery near where I lived, all night long, in the hopes of seeing something like they had seen. I'd visited this particular graveyard a few times before and hadn't experienced anything, but I was determined to keep going back until I did. Heading out after saying good night to my parents, I made my way across town and sat in the cemetery, which had headstones dating all the way back to the late 1600s. Having done this for a while, I knew to bring a flashlight, some water, a few packs of Pop-Tarts, and a lawn chair (sitting on damp ground wasn't much fun after a few hours). It was a bit cloudy, but I could still see rather well. It was so peaceful just sitting and listening to the crickets and tree frogs sing their nightly songs.

Hours went by and I almost nodded off a few times, but to my disappointment, I didn't see or experience a single thing. Then, as I prepared to leave, a wave of . . . *something* . . . ran over my body. Every inch of my skin felt electrified, giving me an overwhelming feeling that I had to leave, *fast*. It was as if my physical being knew something was wrong and it was screaming at the top of its lungs to get my brain's attention. At that point, it succeeded. I grabbed the chair by its scratchy nylon straps and ran, dodging headstones like an Olympian as I hurried to the exit, not daring to look back. With every step and leap I took, I could have sworn something was an inch away from grabbing my ankle and keeping me there for good.

By this point in my life, I had already sat in graveyards numerous times and never experienced a single thing. I had never gotten scared or felt fear or even the slightest worry. That made the overwhelming feeling I had at that moment mean so much more to me. I was certain that something paranormal had to have been close by or was trying to communicate or warn me. Looking back now, I'm still not sure what it was; it's possible that it could have been more environmental or physiological than paranormal. It didn't matter, though . . . the sapling in my brain instantly grew into a tree that night.

It was a pretty lonely tree, though. One of my good friends, Ken, was also really into the paranormal. The two of us would talk about ghosts and that field of fringe research for hours—but I was needing much more. Unfortunately, back then there were maybe seven to ten paranormal teams across the entire country—numbers that a single town can have today—so I didn't have a group of like-minded investigators to work with. The closest one I could find was called RIP (Rhode Island Paranormal Society), which was almost two hours from home. It was run by Jason Hawes, a serious but warm investigator. Jay (as I would later tend to call him) and I chatted frequently and became fast friends, but we were just too far apart at that time to work together regularly. So, when I was twenty years old, I started my own group: New England Paranormal.

We were small at the start; with the internet in its infancy, it was hard to get the word out, but we were able to build a solid team of investigators. I quickly set up a set of stringent protocols and procedures, and all members had to do a series of trainings to ensure that everyone followed the same methods in the same way. This type of consistency helped us to know that any evidence we collected and examined could be trusted. At the same time, I was developing a reputation for being well-read in paranormal theory, to the point that I earned myself a teaching position at the Boston Center for Adult Education, where I lectured on the paranormal.

• • •

Whereas movies showcased paranormal research here and there, unless you were a full-blown scientist with a grant, the concept of making a living in the preternatural world wasn't even a thought in any of our minds. (Besides the Warrens and a tiny handful of other investigators, there was pretty much *no one* who actually made a living doing it.) In fact, back then we lost money on every investigation. Before digital photography, we had to take photos with film cameras; on any given night, we would burn through ten to twenty rolls of film, each of which cost around seven dollars to buy and another four dollars to develop. Most of the time, we were eager to find out if we'd caught anything on film, so we would go to the sixty-minute photo centers and pay extra for speedier service. Those kinds of places loved people like me, as I was a steady source of their income.

It was an expensive hobby, which meant I had to make extra money to support my passion. Throughout those years I taught classes, worked in a restaurant, and went to school to become an EMT, with a long-term goal of becoming a police officer. At one point, Dad asked if I'd be interested in helping him with his growing jewelry business, so I went to New York City's Gemological Institute of America and became a diamond grader and GIA-certified appraiser and designer. I was a regular jack-of-all-trades. Balancing two budding careers on top of speaking at the Boston Center was exhausting and took away from my free time to investigate the paranormal. I was good at designing jewelry, but I excelled at appraising and selling diamonds. I enjoyed working with Dad, but the corporate sales world didn't sit right with me and I couldn't see myself doing that for the rest of my life. Plus, I certainly didn't enjoy wearing a suit and tie every day, so I eventually made good on my original plan and got hired by a local police department, which sponsored me to go to the police academy. (Unlike a lot of states, in Massachusetts you need to be hired first by the police department in order to attend the academy.)

Not long after, I was sworn in as an officer and started patrolling the streets of western Massachusetts. Serving the community and helping those in need was amazing and rewarding, but it could also be extremely stressful and emotionally taxing at times. Seeing someone hurt and in need of protection or being at their worst, not knowing what could happen during any given shift . . . all of it weighed on me. Thankfully, I had a small music career on the side, as a drummer in a local band, and my passion for the paranormal as an escape when I was off duty. Plus, I'd still work for my dad occasionally, picking up shifts when I needed extra cash for my expensive paranormal passion.

To be fair, even though being a cop was a trying occupation, I really did enjoy it. In fact, I thought I would live out my entire life as a cop with a hobby of doing paranormal investigations and playing gigs with my band. But all of that changed when Jason Hawes met Grant Wilson, and the two of them grew RIP, which eventually became TAPS (The Atlantic Paranormal Society). They started doing more investigations farther out, making it much easier for me to meet up with them. Whenever the three of us got together, everything seemed to click. We really had the same mind-set and ethics when it came to the craft, which helped us learn to trust one another almost instantly. We truly felt like we were starting a new method of investigating, where we focused on disproving or debunking things before anything else. (If you find out what caused something and it's not paranormal, that is *disproving*; *debunking* is the same thing, only with the intention of exposing fraud behind the claim.) It worked well, and despite our busy schedules and the distance between us, we started regularly investigating together.

In the early 2000s, after we'd gotten attention nationwide, producers from various TV production companies started to approach us about creating a show around ghost hunting. I was both surprised and thrilled that producers were taking the concept seriously enough to take it to that level. Then again, the collective memory of ridicule for being passionate about the paranormal was deeply ingrained in all of us. Besides, most of our clients wanted to remain private, as they didn't want anyone to know their house was haunted. So, the team declined all the offers for a show. Eventually, though, the producers at Pilgrim Media wore us down, convincing all concerned that the show would be done aboveboard and that they would not make light of the craft.

While Jason and Grant were the founders of our group, I was considered an integral part of the team, which meant I would be a major part of the show. The team and the producers all wanting me to appear on-screen was a genuine honor. It meant that I was trusted to represent our field and the team on a global platform. I'll always be grateful to Jay and Grant for wanting me to be a part of the group. At the time, I was still a police officer and making jewelry but was able to move my busy schedule around enough to film the show . . . which turned out to be a rude awakening. Sure, I was good at being a jeweler who became a cop who also studied the paranormal, but I didn't know television at all. Filming the first episode was truly a unique experience.

By the time production on *Ghost Hunters* started, Jay, Grant, and I had done close to a hundred investigations together; we were in sync and knew what we were doing. Now, suddenly, there were strangers accompanying us—a film crew and producers, as well as the ever-seeing eye of a camera that was always focused on us instead of any spiritual activity. It made me uncomfortable, though mostly because I worried that it would take away from the work. At one point, I wasn't even sure if being on television was the right fit for our work. Ultimately, we all agreed that showing how we investigated would, we hoped, start a conversation about the field in a larger, more productive context, so we pushed forward.

Since all of us were worried about a Hollywood crew telling us what to do and that they wouldn't legitimize our work despite their promise, we made a pact to present the field in the best possible light. This was our collective life's work and we didn't want anyone trashing it. Besides, none of us thought the TV thing would last long anyway, so we wanted to make sure that when we went back to our normal process of investigating, our reputations would remain intact. We were a bit uneasy, but by the end of the first week of shooting, we were pleased to see that the crew really only wanted to observe us. Other than occasionally stopping us to explain things here and there, it was almost like they weren't around. No worst fears realized.

The first time I had to sit and talk in front of a camera was weird and off-putting. I had never done it before, unless you count that one time a local news station interviewed my third-grade class about our pinecone self-portraits. I had hosted dozens of lectures and classes, yet I couldn't help but wonder why anyone outside the paranormal field would want to watch or hear from me. Little by little, though, I realized that every time the camera was focused on me to speak, it was an opportunity for me to talk with people at home who might not get to investigate on their own or perhaps didn't even know that what we did existed. So, I ignored the camera and producers, and I thought of the lens as a fellow paranormal enthusiast. To this day, I still think that way.

Another tricky part, not only for me but also for the entire team, was getting used to making sure the camera could see us when we talked among ourselves. It's natural for people to circle around or huddle up to look at something, but that doesn't translate well on television. We had to learn to be "open" to the camera, meaning we had to face it whenever we talked as a group or showed something. We had to stand next to one another so the cameraperson could get a good shot. It took some getting used to, but it became second nature quickly enough.

During our first filmed investigation, in Altoona, Pennsylvania, I was impressed by how much the crew stayed out of our way—it was rather easy to pretend that they weren't there. The few times they accidentally hindered us or made a noise while I tried to listen to some audio, they'd quickly apologize or speak up that it was them, so we wouldn't misinterpret anything. This method is called "tagging," basically noting anything that isn't paranormal so we don't misinterpret it later. Any time I felt a bit distracted by them, I reminded myself that our entire investigation was being documented for the world to see, which was a rare opportunity (at that time at least). Not only that, but we also had the added benefit that their cameras and sound equipment might actually pick up things that we didn't. As the night wore on, the film crew and the investigators found a way of almost dancing around each other. The crew quickly learned to anticipate how we moved and found the best places to stand in a room while we did our jobs. It became a very synergetic relationship;

once we got to know the crew, it felt like they were a part of our team, as they were also invested in capturing evidence.

After that first investigation, we were all amped up and excited to see what would become of the show. At most, I hoped we would get a handful of episodes, and maybe a few people would watch it and become inspired to take up paranormal investigating themselves using similar protocols and procedures. I remember that the first episode premiered the day after we finished filming the first season. In fact, the crew was still in Rhode Island, so Pilgrim set up a unique viewing party for us. Jason and his wife had infant twin boys, and like any good father he didn't want to leave them to go to a wrap party. Hearing this, Pilgrim rented a blow-up movie screen and set up an outdoor party in Jason's backyard, complete with fire barrels, food, and lights. As we sat watching on the big screen, with the fires crackling next to us, we cheered and laughed while the opening credits rolled; it was a bit awkward watching myself on-screen, but we were all thrilled to see that the producers stayed true to their word. They really showcased what we did, and they even high-lighted our personalities. It was a surreal experience, and the second the end credits rolled I wondered if *Ghost Hunters* would be a onetime thing (especially when many new shows are canceled before there's even any discussion of having a second season).

Boy, was I wrong. As the season went on, *Ghost Hunters* became a surprise hit, with over 3 million people tuning in every week. And it just kept growing. Before we knew it, the network wanted us to do a second season. We all saw how the show was helping the paranormal commu-nity rapidly grow and expand, so we were more than happy to oblige. However, between the investigations and filming schedules, there was simply no way I could continue working as a police officer, a jeweler, and a weekend musician. I was faced with the decision of leaving a band I loved, a secure career with my dad, and another career as a cop to take a chance and follow my passion on a show that I thought would be lucky to last another year.

The pressure to make such a life-changing decision weighed heavily on me, so I turned to my parents and had a heart-to-heart talk with them. Unlike many parents who wouldn't encourage fantasies over a steady job, Mom and Dad both agreed that I was still young and didn't have much to lose if I stayed with the show. Dad even noted, "You have to do this; it's awesome." He wasn't a big believer in the paranormal, but he saw the potential both in the show and in his son. I think he understood the importance of following dreams, and he knew how dedicated I was to the field of paranormal study. I trust him so much that if he'd said no back then, I know for certain I would have turned down the show and followed a different path in life.

Leaving my law enforcement career behind was definitely a risk, but thankfully it worked out great, as *Ghost Hunters* became an international sensation. At its peak, it was one of the highest-rated reality shows in history and aired in over 150 countries—and it was a big hit in all of them. It was surreal. We were in magazines and on talk shows. *South Park* was parodying us. Fans suddenly started to show up with shirts and signs wherever we were investigating. I felt like a real-life Ghostbuster, which was great but would sometimes leave me wondering if I too was going to be hired to work birthday parties when the TV phenomenon was over. I'd experience bouts of imposter syndrome, where I just didn't feel like the success was real or that I deserved any of it, despite putting in so much time and effort. Fortunately, I'm happy to say that after almost twenty years, four different shows, eighteen seasons, and hundreds of episodes, the team and I are still investigating together, representing our field in the best way we know how.

At this point, I have done investigations in well over a thousand locations across the United States, completed countless hours of research, studied and consulted with some of the greatest minds in the industry, lectured, and accomplished a lot in the paranormal field. I couldn't be happier or more grateful to be a part of such a vibrant, enthusiastic, and welcoming community of like-minded people. This field has afforded me an amazing life, one I'm thankful for every day.

· · ·

In this book, we'll travel throughout the United States to some of my favorite large-scale investigations, the ones that have given me the greatest paranormal and personal experiences. Believe me, it wasn't easy narrowing down such a huge list, but the investigations I've selected here have truly left an indelible impression on me. I'll also admit that despite the insane experiences my colleagues and I have shared together, we haven't been able to prove beyond a doubt the existence of ghosts. We've collected dang good evidence and encountered things that I believe can only be attributed to the paranormal, but there will always be people who think ghosts aren't real. Until we can gather solid, irrefutable evidence, those skeptics will remain just that, and that's fine with me. It's not my mission to convert anyone; the paranormal is personal to me, and what matters is finding the truth for myself, for those I work with, and for the clients I help. I didn't get into this field to change the world or even anyone's mind. I simply wanted to satisfy my own curiosity . . . and maybe see a ghost.

And speaking of which . . .

There are a ton of terms we tend to throw around: *Ghost, spirit, entity, apparition*, *haunting*, *spook*, *phantasm*, *phantom*, *soul*, *specter*, and others are all used rather interchangeably, even by people in the field. However, for myself and some of my closest colleagues, we differentiate the words to help us be more specific. As an example, a ghost is technically only a ghost when we know the *name* or identity of the entity with whom we're interacting. Although we have these definitions, for the sake of variety—and so you don't get sick of that one word or have to try to recall the definitions—I'll use the terms interchangeably within these pages.

In addition, please note that in most of the locations I'll refer to in this book I was accompanied by my TAPS teammates Jason Hawes and Grant Wilson, and my best friend, Dave Tango. While there have been numerous other vital team members over the years, these three have been my ever-present companions. Though Grant moved on to other ventures a while back, Jay, Tango, and I have been through just about everything together. However, my goal with this book is to share my experiences with you in the most personal way I know. Therefore, even though you'll hear their names thrown around here and there, most of the time you'll read about what I personally felt, saw, and thought.

I hope you enjoy reading about my experiences, and that they inspire you—regardless of your level of interest in the paranormal—to find the answers to your own questions, get a few goose bumps, or just simply enjoy the journey.

NOT JUST ANY HOMETOWN HAUNT

THEODORES' BOOZE, BLUES, AND BBQ
RESTAURANT/BAR AND SMITH'S BILLIARDS
—
SPRINGFIELD, MA

OPENED 1902

In 1902, businessman Fred Smith opened a billiards academy in Springfield, Massachusetts, to teach the game of pool to all levels of students. Renting one floor of a five-story building, the school quickly became popular. With the number of people showing up for lessons and games, the facility was quickly expanded to offer additional entertainment. At one time, the building housed a bowling alley above the billiards floor and a two-floor bar below it. Although the billiards and bar never closed, the bowling alley was eventually shut down due to newer venues with more lanes being introduced in surrounding areas.

Theodores' and Smith's has enjoyed constant business for over a hundred years, yet very little history about this New England location has been recorded. Thousands of stories, laughs, fights, and tragedies that occurred within its walls have been lost to time; only whispers and rumors about gambling bets and Mafia involvement remain. Stories of fingers being cut off for not paying debts, pool cues being broken over heads, frequent

Front entrance of Theodores'

players disappearing forever, and organized-crime figures hiding out in the attic have all been told without any verification. Though the true tales have faded, both the owners and employees claim that some of those who frequented the location are still there . . . despite the fact that they have long since passed on.

While cleaning up in daybreak, some workers have heard the sound of a bowling ball rolling down the old wooden floor in the abandoned alley above them, then what sounds like a strike followed by mumbled cheering and happy voices. In other instances, employees have ventured into the old, dank basement and discovered that items have fallen off their shelves, and not due to poor placement. While attempting to restock the goods, the employees have passed through temperature fluctuations and cold spots that chilled them right to the bone. On more than one occasion, workers have responded to a voice, only to realize that no one was there. But perhaps the most disturbing claims of all are the numerous sightings of a little boy sitting on top of a pool table, looking forlorn and expectant, as if waiting for a parent to scoop him up and take him home.

The claims at Theodores' and Smith's are consistent and frequent, but with the bar open for hours on end most days, the loud and exciting atmosphere makes it difficult to verify these experiences. Who knows how many times these apparitions could have been seen by patrons, only to have them brushed off as other customers?

• • •

There's no bar I feel more comfortable being in than Theodores' Booze, Blues, and BBQ restaurant/bar and Smith's Billiards, colloquially known simply as Theodores'.

I grew up just a few miles away; the blues and barbecue joint has been a part of my life since the day I turned twenty-one. When I'm not traveling, hardly a week goes by when I don't visit at least once, as it's my go-to place to have dinner or a few drinks. In my early twenties, I was the drummer for a band that often booked gigs there; I have to say we'd pull in a good crowd and typically sell it out. I enjoyed the vibe and people there so much that it felt like a second home. It still does. And even though I'm a regular, the paranormal activity at Theodores' adds a layer of intrigue that just can't be beat.

Long before I became known as "that guy from that show," the staff and owners found out that I was into the paranormal. Mind you, I didn't talk about my passion openly; as I mentioned earlier, I was careful to keep such conversations to a minimum, and only with like-minded people I trusted. Yet I was always so comfortable in Theodores', I guess I didn't realize that one employee was listening intently to a discussion I'd been having with a friend. I could certainly understand why they wanted to listen, since the subject of my conversation was none other than Ed and Lorraine Warren.

The Warrens are arguably the greatest paranormal team in history. Today's generation of moviegoers know them as the main characters in the *Conjuring* cinematic universe that's based on their cases, but for me while I was growing up, I knew this husband-and-wife duo from their books and their work on the legendary Amityville haunting. The Warrens truly dedicated their entire lives to investigating the paranormal and collecting evidence of the supernatural. Along with Hans Holzer, there was no one bigger in the field. They frequently appeared in the media, interviewed as authoritative figures on various shows; wrote numerous books; and were even called as expert witnesses in trials.

With the Warrens based in Connecticut and me living just over the border in Massachusetts, I was lucky enough to go to many of their local lectures. When I was younger, my parents would actually drive me to their appearances—my mother loved the stuff too, but she thought it was important for me to have my independence, so she always graciously dropped me off. When I was old enough, I would simply drive myself anywhere the Warrens were scheduled to appear, even if it was hours away.

At the conclusion of one lecture in Connecticut that I went to with my friend Ken, I wiped my sweaty palms on my pants and mustered the courage to make my way to the front, introduced myself to the Warrens, and joined a few other attendees in chatting with them. I was a bit timid, so I couldn't believe I was actually talking to them, not to mention having a good conversation about all sorts of paranormal topics. Then, out of nowhere, Ed announced to the small group that he and Lorraine were heading to the Union Cemetery, which was part of the White Lady investigation and the subject of a book they had just released called *Graveyard: True Hauntings from an Old New England Cemetery*. At first, I thought that was his way of saying they were leaving for the night; I was a bit disappointed that my face time was up but still happy that I got to talk to them at all. Then Ed continued with: "It would be all right if a few of you wanted to join us." I looked over to Ken and saw that his mouth visibly dropped before I realized that mine had as well.

Not even a half hour had passed before Ken and I found ourselves standing smack in the middle of one of New England's most haunted cemeteries, side by side with the one and only Ed and Lorraine Warren—a dream come true. Ed had gotten permission from the cemetery and the police to investigate the location. Seeing that ethic early on was an important factor in my learning to respect property and locations in this field. I was so nervous and excited, I'm surprised I didn't faint, crack my head on a gravestone, pass on, and turn into a spirit right then and there. Thankfully, I didn't cross over, and I joined the group in doing some casual investigating. Those of us who kept flashlights in our vehicle glove boxes, which included me, grabbed them and led the way to check out the grounds. Taking slow steps, we asked questions into the air while the Warrens told us stories and pointed out where they'd had encounters. We also spoke about some of their most famous cases, ranging from the Amityville haunting, to their experiences with the haunted doll Annabelle, to theories on the afterlife and, oddly, cheeseburgers. They were incredibly kind, welcoming, and more than happy to hear our opinions just as much as they offered theirs.

When the night was over, I couldn't believe what I had just experienced—the two most famous people in the field invited *me*, some kid with a passion for the paranormal, out on their investigation. For a budding young investigator, that evening was the definition of a mind-blowing experience, and it really cemented my love for what I do.

I kept going to their events and eventually, a few years later, they gave me the number to the New England Society for Psychic Research, which they ran. I kept the number in my desk drawer, but despite having their blessing, I just couldn't bring myself to use it, at least not right away. At that point, I was taking my investigations very seriously, but I didn't want to reach out to them until I came across a situation for which I needed help, which came about quicker than I thought. I was working on a case in which I concluded that a person, rather than a location, was haunted. I hadn't come across this in the past, so I pulled out the Warrens' number and started dialing. My stomach turned; I had no clue if they would even remember who I was, let alone be interested in helping me. No one picked up, but after hearing Ed's gruff voice on the answering machine, I left a message. To be honest, I didn't expect a call back.

An hour later, the phone rang, and it was John Zaffis, their nephew and fellow investigator. He asked about the case, and I gave him all the details. After taking notes, he told me to stay by the phone and hung up. For the next two hours I hardly dared go to the bathroom as I sat staring at the phone. Thankfully, Ed and Lorraine themselves called back. I lost my breath so rapidly it was like I had taken a punch to the gut. The way Ed spoke, the fact that he was treating me as a fellow investigator, put me at ease and got me talking about the case. Over the next hour, Ed asked questions—as did Lorraine, who had been listening in the background—and I answered them as best I could. It was so thrilling; at that moment, it felt like my interest in the paranormal was becoming something so much more. Toward the end of the call, Ed and Lorraine asked if I would pass the case on to John. I immediately said yes, then realized that I was cutting myself out of something I'd been working on for weeks. Thankfully, before I could speak up, Ed said, "Great, I'll have you talk to our nephew, John Zaffis. You can coordinate with him so you can help us out and be there for the initial investigation."

Looking at all of the Warrens' books on my shelf in that moment and then having Ed Warren tell me that *I'd* help *them* out . . . that feeling was indescribable, unforgettable.

Over the next several weeks, I worked with John, a world-renowned investigator and demonologist. I can't provide any real specifics about the investigation here—it was a private matter and is not my story to divulge—but I can say that what impressed me the most was how much John and the Warrens cared for the client. They genuinely wanted to help the person first and get the evidence second. While their expertise certainly helped shape my own career, I think I was most influenced by their heart and their kindness. Not only did they take me, some random teen with very little experience, under their wing, but they truly did everything they could to help the afflicted person. Thanks to them, whenever and wherever I investigate a case, I make sure that the client always remains my main focus.

Over the years, I'd go on to spend a decent amount of time with the Warrens, and every moment with them was an invaluable experience. Not only did I get to work with my idols but I also made a trusted colleague in John Zaffis; the two of us still work together to this day. I see him at a few conventions every year, and we even appeared together alongside Josh Gates on *Larry King Now*, and John also did an episode of *Ghost Hunters*. Try telling that nervous teen with sweaty palms sitting in the audience at a Warrens' lecture that one day he would work alongside these paranormal icons, and he couldn't have fathomed any of this.

In later years, the Warrens would come under scrutiny, with some of their detractors declaring that evidence and cases were exaggerated and possibly fabricated. People can say whatever they want, but there's no denying what the Warrens did for the field. They brought the world of the paranormal to a new level of popularity and gave people like me much-needed support and encouragement. And let's face it—with blockbuster movies about their cases starring fictionalized versions of themselves regularly released in theaters, seven decades after they first started, I don't think Ed and Lorraine's legacy is going anywhere.

So, that all being said, you could understand why telling my friend about my experience with the Warrens might attract an extra listener or two at Theodores'. In this particular instance, it was one of the bartenders who overheard me and got excited about it. Before I knew what was happening, the whole staff suddenly wanted to talk to me about the paranormal—and they were dead serious, embracing what I did. They told me all about Theodores' history and stories about the location, and they even gave me a tour of the basement, long before I was known as a paranormal investigator, simply because they knew the history of the place would interest me.

The staff's kindness and the experience that evening always stuck with me, so when our team began planning out Season Four of *Ghost Hunters* I recommended that we should investigate Theodores'. It was rather ironic that I'd spent years investigating locations all around the country but never the one place where I'd enjoyed so many nights. At the same time, it was nice waiting until we had a full crew and were in a position to properly document such an investigation.

• • •

Even though the bar was open seven days a week, Theodores' closed exclusively for us so we could investigate without any interruption. I'd known and frequented the place for nearly a decade, but with five full floors, there were entire areas that I'd never seen. Fortunately, unlike the abandoned buildings we sometimes found ourselves in, setting up in the restaurant was easy. There were already bright lights, power outlets, and plenty of places to secure the cameras. If only all our investigations could run so easily.

Tango and I started our investigation on the fourth floor—the old bowling alley that was now a barren, somewhat-cobwebbed chamber used for storage. Every step we took on the hundred-year-old wooden floorboards registered a wailing creak beneath our feet. We tried to make as little noise as possible so we could listen for the sounds that many of

Theodores' patrons and workers had claimed to hear—like the bowling ball rolling and pins getting knocked down. Those aren't unusual noises in a bowling alley, mind you . . . except this one had been closed for decades. It was operational long before automated alleys came into play—that meant men were poised at the end of each lane, waiting to roll balls back to bowlers and set up the pins by hand after every set. I wandered around, trying to picture what that must have looked like: sharply dressed individuals pitching marbled globes down lanes under the dull glow of gaslights. It was pretty much the same game across the years, yet the mood and atmosphere were drastically different from what one experiences in the music-thumping, neon-glowing alleys of today. Back then, it was considered a man's game (though women were allowed to play together on certain days and at certain times): cigar and cigarette smoke permeated the air, bets were made, and legs were sometimes broken if debts weren't paid.

My train of thought was interrupted when I found something via my flashlight beam around some boxes stored near the end of the lanes. At first, the quick flash of a light color made my heart beat a bit faster. As I moved the beam back again, I saw this shape that instantly made me think of Disney's *Silly Symphonies* skeleton dance, in which things were far from scary but they were certainly spooky fun. There, standing in front of Tango and me, was a human skeleton.

Tango and I were awestruck and confused. We kept our lights on it as we walked over; we could tell right away that it wasn't some plastic Halloween prop or even a replica. It was a legitimate human skeleton, like the ones used in medical schools. In the past I'd heard workers say that there was a real skeleton stashed away somewhere in the building, but until that moment I hadn't believed it was true. I never discovered

the reason why a skeleton would be there to begin with, but one employee speculated that it was used for an old promotional display back
in the 1930s. We did some research but couldn't find anything specific at
the time. The idea that these bones once belonged to a living, breathing
person may feel a bit surreal and macabre for some people, but since
medical skeletons typically come from companies using donated bodies,
we had no reason to believe any paranormal activity was at play here.

Bones are a vital part of our physical structure and we can't live
without them (obviously), yet for centuries skeletons have been associated
with death and used to scare or warn people. Throughout history, bones
have adorned pirate ships, castles, and other objects and locations as a
warning for those who come near. Since bones are the only things left of
a human after passing on, some of you might think that spirits would be
attached to them (especially if you've watched shows like *Supernatural*,
where usually the best way to stop a vengeful spirit is to "burn the bones").
Personally, though, I don't think spirits tend to attach themselves to
bones as much as they do to objects and places that someone treasured.
Also, why would you want to stay with your bones? Wouldn't you want
to be in a place you loved? It's not like we see our bones or think about
them much . . . at least not until we break one.

Some find bones creepy, but I personally find beauty in them and
I have my own collection—as I'm a horror fanatic and ghost hunter,
what do you expect?—and currently, I have seven skulls, five mandibles,
a skullcap or two, and a few full skeletons on display in my house, but
they're all ethically sourced from reputable dealers who get them from
museums, medical supply chains, and such. If you ever decide to buy
some yourself, please make sure you do your research beforehand—the
last thing you want is something that ends up having been stolen from

a loved one's body before or even after they were buried (sadly, this atrocity still happens).

And for full transparency, I have never experienced anything paranormal with these bones in my home. I just find them beautiful and stunning to look at—the patina that forms naturally as they age, and the uniqueness of each one. Skulls are ominous, thought-provoking, Halloween-esque, and constant reminders that we'll all end up like that one day. Each skull and bone has a story to it, and I can't help but be curious about whom the people were behind them. Some of you may be thinking I'm a little morbid, but trust me, I give these bones a good home—I say hello to them, admire and respect them, and don't treat them just as grim ornaments. In a way, I try to keep their spirits alive . . . which, to me, is better than just having them rot in the ground. To me, I am honoring them and still giving them a purpose and meaning.

Almost fifteen years after our experience at Theodores', while doing research for this book, I finally found out the truth, and a bit of mystery, behind the skeleton. Stopping by to eat dinner and to chat with Keith, one of the owners, I asked about the skeleton. Come to find out, it was a medical display used at the University of Massachusetts, which is only a thirty-minute ride away. How it ever got to the bar they don't know. I find that part a bit intriguing myself, as a medical-grade, fully articulated real human skeleton costs upwards of $8,000. That the school would have gotten rid of one in perfect shape does not make sense. The only thing I can think of is that it was no longer needed and passed through several hands until it finally landed there. Keith said it was used for window displays for some of the other properties in the building over the years. Since our initial visit, I found out that the skeleton's name is Mr. Bones. But what I found most interesting . . . the skeleton has now disappeared. Keith said that just a few years ago someone noticed Mr. Bones was missing and they have not seen it since. Obviously, it's worth money and an attractive item to steal, but walking out of a bar with a full-size skeleton would be a tricky feat. I'm not sure if knowing the truth of Mr. Bones has appeased my curiosity or if I am even more curious now, knowing that he is gone.

While at the time we did not know the purpose of the bones at Theodores', Tango and I didn't have long to ponder over it—a few moments later, something flew past my face and shot toward the ceiling. I pointed my flashlight up toward the rafters and expected to see a bat. Almost instantly, I felt a slight panic; bats don't freak me out like spiders do, but I still don't want to get in the way of one of their flight patterns. The last thing I wanted was one of them flying down at my face and attacking me, causing a spontaneous Tippi Hedren reenactment from *The Birds*.

I hunched over a bit, pulled my hat down to protect my face, and began to sweep my flashlight back and forth, trying to find the black mass that I saw darting around. Tango also pointed his light up toward the ceiling and moved it about. When it became clear there was nothing present anymore, I stood up, calmed myself, and checked our thermal-imaging camera. I was surprised that it didn't pick up any heat signatures to show there was a bat. Which meant . . . there was no bat. It had to be something else. After a few more minutes and no further sightings, Tango and I shut off our flashlights and focused our attention on the rest of the area.

While we stood there in the darkness, I realized that what we'd just experienced echoed several accounts already made by Theodores' employees—reports of dark masses zipping around the building and disappearing before anyone could discover what they were. As Tango and I started to discuss the similarities, the darting movement occurred again, and we switched our flashlights back on. A strange, dark shape scurried around the rafters. Its movements appeared similar to those of a bat, but it was more graceful, floating like some underwater creature in a nature documentary. I tried to get a better look, but the second my beam was on it, it would change direction and avoid the light. I've had many experiences with creepy, crawly critters in my career, but I can tell you there weren't many that were as fast as whatever this thing was.

Between the darkness in the room and the speed of the anomaly, our cameras were unable to catch any concrete footage. Tango and I shared some theories, but ultimately we couldn't come up with any solid explanation for the experience. After a while of no further movement or sightings, we decided to take our investigation downstairs. I was a bit disappointed that we didn't hear any bowling sounds, but I was also rather happy that we did experience for ourselves one of the staff members' other common claims. Experiencing something unexplainable like that was exhilarating. To this day, it is hard to know if it was a spirt or an energy. If you think about why a human spirit would be darting around a rafter, it doesn't make much sense, which leads me to think it was something else. When you're investigating, it's always important to consider the intent of an experience. It might not give all the answers, but the thought process of why something happened could lead you down the right path.

• • •

Tango and I made our way down to the basement, where employees reported that items often spontaneously fell off shelves or that they'd sometimes walk into strange, drastically hot and cold spots. Several times we felt slight temperature changes as well, but they weren't anything dramatic that couldn't be explained by simple science. For instance, when an empty room with little airflow sits stagnant, hot air rises and cold air lowers to the floor. When a person enters the room, the sudden movement stirs and pushes the still air around, and that person can feel like they've walked into a "cold spot." That being said, it's worth noting that it's only a cold spot if the air actually *isn't* moving; otherwise, it's just a breeze or a draft, which tends to always feel colder when it hits the moisture on your skin. This issue causes a lot of confusion with new investigators, who might sometimes mistake a common draft for a paranormal cold spot.

When I'm in a location and we suddenly feel a significant rise or drop in temperature of more than a few degrees, we pull out our thermal cameras to check the actual levels. Most of the time, we'll see some slight variations, which is expected; other times, we'll register temperature readings that don't make sense via normal science, so we'll investigate further. Sadly, while we could feel some temperature differences at Theodores', we just couldn't detect any variance significant enough to warrant pursuing the matter further.

Later that night, we investigated the main dining area. The pitch-black room and its complete silence were in stark contrast to the vibe I always associated with the bar, where I'd enjoyed so many delicious meals. Though the deafening quiet was eerie, it was also quite peaceful, and it was arguably the most "at home" I ever felt during an investigation—a part of me even wished I could order some barbecue while I was there.

I was about to note something to Tango when I heard a voice I didn't recognize behind me. It said something that I couldn't make out. I clicked on my flashlight and turned to see who was there; other than Tango, who was in front of me, I was alone. Even though I couldn't discern what it said, the disembodied voice sounded rather clear, so it couldn't have come from the street or even another room. Truly excited by what this meant, the two of us stayed put and did a recording session in the hopes of capturing the sound, or EVP (Electronic Voice Phenomenon). Unfortunately, we didn't hear anything again that night; our audio recordings picked up only minor oddities, but nothing that could be clearly pinpointed as being paranormal.

• • •

Although Theodores' was far from ranking among the most active places I've ever investigated, I do believe that the claims its employees have been making over the years are legitimate and that there is *something* going on there. And regardless of whether I ever experience any paranormal activity there, the food, the atmosphere, and the people will always make Theodores' my favorite "hometown haunt."

MY TIME SPENT

ALCATRAZ
—
SAN FRANCISCO, CA
BUILT 1847
OPENED AS A PENITENTIARY 1934

The word island usually evokes images of a tropical paradise. Alcatraz Island, however, does anything but. Murky, cold waters surround wet, drab land that contains a background of pain and torment spanning centuries . . . all the way to when indigenous people banished individuals to the island to die among the "evil spirits" they believed inhabited the land. Since then, Alcatraz's history has been one filled with countless imprisonments, torture, boat crashes, and more . . . including claims of the supernatural running rampant.

With its proximity to San Francisco, the twenty-two-acre "Island of the Pelicans"—the archaic Spanish translation of which resulted in the land's more widely recognized name: Alcatraz—has housed lighthouses and military installations since the mid-nineteenth century.

In the early 1930s, when there was no longer a need for a military outpost, the Department of Justice bought the island and converted it into a federal prison. The plan was to utilize the location's remoteness to build an

Alcatraz Island as seen from San Francisco Bay
DARREN PATTERSON

inescapable jail that would contain inmates who were deemed too dangerous or difficult for other facilities to handle. By 1934, the cells were ready, and shortly after, 130 prisoners arrived by ferry, chained and escorted by FBI agents and U.S. marshals to their new home, Alcatraz Federal Penitentiary.

During the prison's years of operation, America's most hardened criminals spent time behind bars on "The Rock"—murderers, gangsters, and robbers, ranging from Al Capone to "Machine Gun" Kelly (this one didn't rap . . . that we know of). Yet despite its foreboding presence, the reputed "inescapable" structure didn't last long; after less than thirty years, operational costs and constant erosion from the surrounding salt water forced Alcatraz to close its doors forever. Though the prison was open for only a brief time and six decades have passed since its closing, Alcatraz remains the most famous prison of all time, inspiring more movies, TV shows, and books than any other jail in the world. And when it comes to the paranor-

mal, claims of countless spirits lingering throughout the penitentiary have cemented Alcatraz as one of the most sought-after locations to investigate.

It's easy to understand why: Phantom noises—from bloodcurdling screams and echoing gunshots to the faint, soothing plucking sounds of a banjo—reportedly have been heard throughout the property. Inexplicable smells of soap and sulfur reportedly pervade specific locations. Among accounts of inmates being forced into isolation holes, completely naked, it's rumored that one such prisoner died in cell 14-D, after shrieking all night long about "red eyes" trying to kill him. Did the inmate go mad or was there really something malevolent inside the cell with him? And of course, famous spirits like the Birdman of Alcatraz, a convicted murderer with an avian obsession, and the Butcher, a Mafia hitman slain by a fellow prisoner in the laundry room, are believed to wander the halls.

The long list of experiences at Alcatraz centers mostly on the penitentiary and its inmates, though many have suffered and died on the island throughout its history. No one is sure why this location has so many active spirits, but one thing is certain: The claims of Alcatraz being inescapable seem to be true, as these ghosts have never left the island.

• • •

Pulling up to a location for the first time is always one of my favorite experiences. No matter how distracted I may be, I try to center myself and take in the building or home that I'm tasked to investigate. There are often winding roads, trees, or mountains that block the view before you round the corner and see the location sitting there in all its glory, giving it a grand reveal of sorts. For me, it's like arriving at Walt Disney World's Magic Kingdom in Florida: You already anticipate Cinderella Castle as you enter the park, but you can't see it fully until you round

A typical cell in Alcatraz
LIBRARY OF CONGRESS

the corner on Main Street. As soon as you do, the majestic towers and spires are in front of you, and it takes your breath away. I love that feeling, whether it's at Disney World or inside an insane asylum.

Going to Alcatraz was an entirely different affair, however. There are no roads to travel, and since it's an island, the team had to take a boat for the "grand reveal." Instead of rolling up to the location, we had to "boat up" to the island's dock and disembark.

From our small ferry, I could see a tiny brown dot off on the horizon. It seemed so insignificant in the distance, but it didn't stop my stomach from bubbling up with excitement. Dramatic theme music rose in my head as the boat sped over the cold, choppy waves toward Alcatraz. I think it would be nearly impossible for any male my age not to think about the 1996 Nicolas Cage/Sean Connery cheesy action flick, *The Rock*. Of course, folks my dad's age would be more inclined to think of Clint Eastwood in *Escape from Alcatraz*.

As we approached the island, I got a much better look at the structures; they were all brown, deteriorating, and *very* intimidating. They were also surrounded by rocks that were jagged and sharp, like the crooked teeth on some monster. Climbing out of the boat, I think the whole crew was excited to be on land—I know I was. And poor Tango . . . the water had sloshed the boat up and down so violently it made him feel sick. I looked over my shoulder to see just how far away the mainland was, and immediately understood why Alcatraz had earned its reputation as the most inescapable prison in the country. Trying to swim one and a quarter miles from the island to the mainland in frigid, raging waters would be a nightmare on a clear day. But at night, amid rocks impossible to see, wearing a prison jumpsuit, while fleeing from armed guards? The fact that any inmate even dared to try to escape blew my mind.

With my feet now on solid ground, I experienced an exhilarating and slightly hesitant feeling that I didn't normally get before an investigation. Though I had been to numerous prisons in the past, I had never gotten that sense before; I'm not sure if it was caused by seeing the world's most famous penitentiary in front of us, or the fact that we were dependent on a motorboat that looked like it was about to capsize. Whatever the reason, the feeling I had was electrifying and hyped me up for the hunt. Doing my best to stay focused, I listened to our guide as he gave us a historical tour while pointing out the active locations and hot spots.

I was fascinated to discover that Alcatraz's military history had spanned over 150 years. Meanwhile, the prison, which operated for just a fifth of that time, seems to be the only thing there that interests people. All the hauntings and tours are focused solely on the prison; I mean, that's also why TAPS was on the island. Yet there was another over-120-year span of artificial structures being on the island and the countless decades that indigenous people used the land, and I hadn't realized that there was so much more to this place.

With the prison being so massive, we had brought along extra investigators, though I'd spend most of my time with Tango, my usual partner in crime (no pun intended). When we entered the main building, I was filled with awe and wonder. The main cellblock looked just like one might imagine—long rows of cells, stacked one level on top of another. Maybe it's because of my love for movies, but I couldn't help but imagine seeing the inmates reaching out through the gaps of their cell doors, pacing around, hitting the bars with their steel drink cups, and throwing things in a rambunctious manner.

I listened intently as the tour guide told us of claims about the loud banging noises and phantom gunshots heard in a section of the prison he took us to, called Broadway. Though he briefly touched on the incident, I remembered from my research that back in 1946, inmates had taken over the penitentiary and locked themselves in that area. A two-day standoff ensued, ending with five people dead, over a dozen wounded, and two inmates who were eventually executed for their participation. It was such a massive ordeal that a whopping *five* movies were made that featured a storyline about this "Battle of Alcatraz." Standing in that very spot, I could practically picture the events happening before my eyes.

Our tour continued over to solitary—the area known as "D Block" or the "Treatment Unit" for disciplinary cases, which is the locale that's believed to have the most hauntings.

The stories vary, but so many of them are downright bone-chilling (and *not* because of the San Francisco Bay waters). In one account, as mentioned earlier, an inmate in isolation screamed all night long that he saw red eyes in his cell . . . and the next day he was found dead, mysteriously strangled. Some insist that the cause was demonic in nature, but honestly, it's much more plausible that being confined practically twenty-four seven (inmates could go out in the yard for only one hour a week) in an incredibly small cell (averaging nine feet by five feet by seven feet high in this block) would be enough to drive someone to end their own life. In another story—one that occurred after the National Park Service took over and turned Alcatraz into a tourist destination—

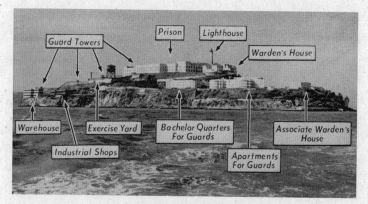

A 1962 diagrammed view of Alcatraz Prison
THE GOLDEN GATE NRA, PARK ARCHIVES

a visitor entered one of the empty cells and suddenly felt a hand on his shoulder, then heard, "*You're mine*," whispered into his ear. The TAPS team could only hope for such an experience.

Next up on our tour was the prison's Citadel, a basement-level cellhouse area that was constructed over a Civil War–era fortification. And that was more my speed. As the oldest part of the building, it used to hold the kitchen, the bakery, storerooms, and some jail cells. Being so old, the basement literally looked like a dungeon (as it's commonly referred to), with arched brick ceilings and poor lighting. The Citadel was also originally used for solitary confinement cells, but the state quickly deemed it too cruel to keep prisoners in a wet stone structure with no lighting. In this dark, cavernous area, the most common claims were centered around hearing screams. Other accounts ranged from phantom smells to voices and full-body apparitions.

After getting the full lowdown on the entire place, Jason Hawes, Grant Wilson, and I were told that a park ranger would always be on hand to open any areas we wanted to explore, to answer questions, and to help us navigate around the prison, which was a bit of a maze. Knowing that TAPS had full, unrestrained access to the entire island, and that Alcatraz was shut down exclusively for us, felt exhilarating. In fact, from what we were told, this was the first time the National Park Service had ever shut down the prison for a paranormal investigation (technically, since it's a state park, it's almost always open for tourists). If you told twenty-one-year-old me that I'd one day get to investigate The Rock itself with unlimited access, I probably would have choked on my popcorn.

While the team ran wires and set up their equipment, I wandered around the solitary block, looking for a good place to position a thermal camera. I entered one of the cells to see if I could place it in the back corner when something suddenly came over me. Slowly, I turned around and looked out of the cell, then grabbed on to the tool-proof steel bars, took a deep breath, and, given my law enforcement background, started to think about what might lead someone down a path of crime, especially to the point where they would end up in this godforsaken place. It didn't take long before I thought of an inmate on whom I had done a bunch of research. . . .

Robert Stroud, also known as the Birdman, was arguably the most notorious prisoner in Alcatraz's history. There are dozens of stories about how psychotic and cruel he was, yet with his heightened intellect I can't help but wonder if a different upbringing might have motivated him to do so much more good in life.

Running away from an abusive father, Stroud became a pimp at the age of eighteen. By the time he was twenty, he'd killed a bartender who attacked one of his girls and was sentenced to spend the rest of his life behind bars. Stroud was eventually transferred to Leavenworth Federal

Penitentiary in Kansas, where he killed a guard in a fit of rage when his visitation privileges were rescinded. It was only after he'd been placed in solitary confinement that things changed for him; while in isolation, he found three injured sparrows that he decided to nurse back to health.

For the next several decades, Stroud studied birds and raised over three hundred canaries in Leavenworth and in the process became a respected ornithologist. He wrote books about canaries that were well received within the scientific community, and he even developed a cure for a family of diseases that had plagued birds. At first, the prison provided Stroud with equipment to continue his studies, then stopped doing so when they discovered he'd been using some of those materials to manufacture alcohol and run a side business. In 1942, Stroud was shipped to Alcatraz Island, where he wasn't allowed to care for birds (which makes his "Birdman" moniker somewhat inaccurate). His story is quite sad, really; with his incredible knowledge and academic contributions, Stroud could have lived a drastically different life, had he been given the opportunities at a young age.

Alcatraz mugshot of Robert Stroud
NATIONAL PARKS GALLERY

Thinking about Stroud in that dank cell also got me mulling over my days as a police officer. What might have become of some of the people I interacted with? What might they have become under different circumstances? I don't subscribe to the belief that people are born evil. We're a product of our experiences. My own life could have gone a thousand different ways; I could have become a jeweler, a chef, or a traveling musician. Heck, at one point I wanted to create monsters like one of my idols, makeup and special effects guru Tom Savini, but life took me on a different path. Thankfully, I was aided by amazing parents and a great upbringing . . . but what if I didn't have that? What if Stroud did? The man was a genius with specific passions and drive; he could have easily contributed so much more to the world. Instead, life led him down the wrong path, where he was forever deemed an "extremely dangerous and menacing psychopath" by the system that confined him.

I let go of the bars and turned my attention back to the tiny cell. All that remained inside was an old steel frame where the cot used to stand, just inches away from the toilet. I couldn't get over that this is considered a typical cell that's "home" for over 2 million people in the United States alone. For me, someone who enjoys life, movies, theme parks, concerts, bars, traveling, video games, nature, food . . . the idea of having all of that taken away and being forced to live in this tiny space, day in and day out . . . it's utterly horrifying.

Thankfully, I didn't have to think about that for long. My name suddenly crackled over the radio; one of the team members was checking to see if I had finished setting up. The callout startled me, but it also helped me clear my head . . . long enough to get a momentary, static feeling that someone was in the room watching me. I knew it was probably just part of my primal gaze detection system that is built into all of our DNA, but it still got my senses working overtime.

I wasn't scared, but I did wonder that if something was present, could it sense what I was thinking or perhaps feel some sort of solace that I understood the pain it might have endured? Having nothing to investigate with, however, I was forced to leave the room and start my long night on The Rock.

• • •

Tango and I made our way to the prison's hospital wing, where Robert Stroud had been kept in isolation. Records state that he was separated from the other inmates because he was "too difficult." Based on what I read, though, the difficulty stemmed from his silver tongue; he could talk other inmates into doing anything or rile them up, which the guards didn't appreciate. Knowing Stroud's love for birds and the fact that he was rather intellectual, Tango and I decided to offer him a feather we'd found outside earlier, to see if it would bring out a reaction. We set it on the edge of a short wall, making sure there was no breeze to disturb it, and we spoke out loud to make sure Stroud knew the feather was for him. An item used like this is called a trigger object. The concept is to take something that would have had personal meaning to the suspected spirit when they were alive and offer it to them in the hopes that you will have a paranormal experience. With someone like the Birdman, something innocuous but essential like a feather could do just that.

Tango and I sat on the floor and placed our EMF (electromagnetic field detector) between us. The device read a flat .2—a very low and normal reading for the type of structure we were in. The meter didn't fluctuate at all, which meant there was no current electrical interference. However, as we started to ask questions aloud,

"Do you miss your birds?"

"What was your favorite soap?"

"Why did you love to shower so much?"

"Do you think you deserve to be here?" the EMF suddenly jumped up to 1, then to 1.9—nearly ten times our original reading. This was a very significant spike and worth paying attention to because it's usually indicative of being near an electrical current or due to an unknown fluctuation in the field.

Yet the device hadn't moved closer to anything electrical . . . something seemed to be manipulating it.

Suddenly, we heard a loud banging noise in the hall. Tango and I raced into the corridor to figure out what it was when I noticed a bathroom across the way. The two of us quickly discussed how Stroud was notorious for taking daily showers and washing obsessively, so we looked inside the bathroom for something that could have caused the noise. Nothing. After trying various doors and windows, we ventured down a flight of stairs to see if the sound was coming from below. It took a while, but we finally found a heavy cell door that re-created the noise *exactly*. This door closed rather easily, but not so much that the wind could have slammed it shut. Someone or something substantial would have had to have pushed it to generate such a sound . . . and no one else was down there at the time we heard it slam. (We keep constant track of the team's whereabouts for reasons like this.) Being that none of this occurred near Stroud's cell, we didn't attribute it to him, but Tango and I were still in awe. The fact that a door so heavy could start slamming on its own following our attempt to make contact was incredible.

We returned to the Birdman's cell about ten minutes later. Just outside that particular door, Tango and I caught a whiff of a soapy smell, one that was incredibly strong and fragrant. The unique scent hadn't been there earlier, and this was so fresh smelling that it was as if someone were actively showering right outside the bathroom. We took a quick look around to ensure there was no soap in the bathroom, though both of us knew there wouldn't be, since the prison hadn't been in operation for decades. Sure enough, we were correct, but we *did* discover that when either Tango or I pointed our nose an inch in another direction, there was no smell; when we turned back, that distinctive soapy scent filled our nostrils. The smell was only in the direct walking path from Stroud's cell to the showers, and there was absolutely no source for it.

Detecting this phantom scent was astounding. It was almost like Robert Stroud had heard us discussing his showering habits a few minutes earlier and wanted us to smell the soap to confirm that we were right. But the phenomenon also left me a bit puzzled—if Stroud's presence was powerful enough to manifest an odor, wouldn't he be able to communicate with us in ways that were clearer or more obvious, like moving an object or speaking, or perhaps even touching us? Why choose a smell that we could confuse with someone just having washed their hands? I doubt we'll ever figure out why, but there was *no* doubt that Tango and I experienced something that wasn't there before.

Phantom smells seem so simple in concept; we smell things all the time, so walking through an area with a certain scent is normal. However, there was nothing around the cell area to create such a strong aroma, so as far as we know, what we perceived was scientifically impossible. It's pretty incredible to smell something that isn't there: How is it created? How can a ghost make us smell something? Or maybe it isn't a ghost but something else that's tickling our noses with these supernatural scents? Regardless of what it was, some people in our field believe that when they are dealing with a ghost, phantom smells are usually more pleasant, like flowers, detergent, perfume, or other scents in line with the human experience. However, if they smell unpleasant odors, like feces, rotting flesh, urine, or sulfur, they typically suspect that they're dealing with something that is trying to make them uncomfortable or compel them to leave the location. I understand this theory, but personally I think a smell is more about the incident that occurred and not about the good or bad of the phenomenon causing it. With this clean smell appearing minutes after Tango and I talked about how Stroud loved his showers, and in the exact spot where he would have bathed, it's almost impossible not to think that it came from the Birdman himself. It was an exhilarating moment.

While we were there, Tango and I also tried out a newer piece of equipment at the time called a BumbleBee-Tablet. It's a spectrum analyzer that measures a variety of continuous wave bands like Wi-Fi, Bluetooth, and other electronic waves that are sent through the air. The concept is pretty simple: Once you get a steady reading of the waves in the room, you can watch to see if the wave interface fluctuates on the handheld device. In theory, whenever the wave interface fluctuates outside of the already-recognized patterns, there is a slight possibility that there is something worth paying attention to. In one respect, the device does not produce evidence in and of itself, but it does give us information that allows us to look at certain aspects and to guard against contamination from outside sources. Since Alcatraz was known for having a lot of unexplained audio phenomena, we thought it would be a great place to continue the tablet's testing phase.

When we used it at the prison, it was still rather new to us, so we were getting used to how to interpret the data and weren't able to pick up any fluctuations that could lead us to any possible evidence. After that investigation, we started to figure out how exactly to use the BumbleBee to our advantage. When we were trying to communicate and build some rapport with whomever or whatever might be there with us, we started asking some questions and noticed a few distinct patterns indicating that there might be something there trying to communicate with us—or perhaps just a disembodied sound without a conscious thought behind it somehow traveling on a frequency to our ears. According to science, everything in the known universe can be measured by energy, frequency, and vibration, so in theory, the BumbleBee could be picking up a voice or sound that is traveling via a frequency or that maybe is itself a frequency.

We used the BumbleBee for a while after that investigation event, but we could never completely count on its data or our interpretations of its findings. It did work to an extent, but the amount of time put into the device was not worth the results, so we stopped using it. Although in the end the BumbleBee just didn't help investigations enough, it is always important to push the boundaries in this field by trying out new equipment, theories, and techniques, as it is the only way to advance the field. Every advance in technology and new piece of equipment is an opportunity for us to find the answers we are seeking for our clients. And who knows, our drive to push the field's boundaries through new technologies and understanding might one day help us get closer to understanding life's existential questions, such as is there life after death and what does it all mean?

• • •

Ours wasn't the only experience within the prison. Other TAPS members were investigating a disembodied voice that first spoke to Jason Hawes and Grant Wilson. They had heard a different loud bang on their own and asked if whoever was responsible could repeat the sound. Seconds later, a loud, clear voice replied, "No." That was crazy enough, but the best EVP we caught on Alcatraz—and one of the clearest I have ever heard in all my time investigating the paranormal—was a voice saying, "*Harry . . . Brunette . . . three . . . seven . . . four.*" While researching the prison records, we were shocked to discover that there was once a prisoner in Alcatraz named Harry Walter Brunette, a Depression-era bank robber who was involved in a forty-five-minute shootout with J. Edgar Hoover and the FBI. Even more astonishing, his inmate number was 374.

Some of the TAPS team also saw and heard movement down various halls throughout the prison, such as a shadow blocking out a light or the sounds of footsteps. They also recorded a few EVPs that sounded like a woman saying "*no*" and "*hello.*" Why a woman's spirit would have been in a men's prison we weren't sure; maybe she was a staff member or a visitor? Then again, as I mentioned earlier, Alcatraz Island has a much, much longer history than just the prison. It's possible that this feminine presence could have been a spirit tied to the land and not to this notorious construction.

• • •

After several days of us exploring the prison, our investigation ended and we headed back to the mainland. From the boat, I watched and smiled as the island grew smaller in the distance. I had experienced a true paranormal phenomenon—a phantom smell—and certainly the most profound one of my life there. Personally, I didn't have many other strong paranormal encounters there, but it was enough that I would go back to Alcatraz anytime to investigate further. Just having the opportunity to spend so much time wandering through the most infamous jail in the world was unforgettable . . . an opportunity that I was fortunate to have because my parents gave me a good foundation toward the right path, one that I followed in life, leading me there.

EVIDENCE OF A MADMAN

CRESCENT HOTEL & SPA
—
EUREKA SPRINGS, AR

OPENED 1886

The town itself was founded on magic. Indigenous legends tell of the "Great Healing Spring" in what would become the city known as Eureka Springs. Over time, both natives and settlers believed that the warm water from the natural springs possessed magical healing powers. By the late 1880s, doctors were claiming the water could cure almost anyone of their ailments, prompting droves of sick people to flock to the city in the hopes of being healed. Amazingly, many believed it worked. Some bottled the water and sold it as an elixir, while others set up health clinics, and the city thrived from all its newfound business.

The Crescent Hotel was built in 1886 as part of a calculated venture to capitalize on Eureka Springs' booming success and accommodate the thousands who visited the town in search of cures.

The opulent structure was erected high in the Ozark Mountains, where its stunning views and gorgeous Victorian architecture were intended to draw in the rich and famous. Over the next twenty years, however, as science evolved and people started to realize that the "curative" spring

Bird's-eye view of the Crescent Hotel
BEAU BREWSKY/ALAMY PHOTO

waters offered little more than enjoyable baths, hotel attendance dwindled. The Crescent quickly became unprofitable and unmanageable, forcing its owners to close its doors.

In 1908, the facility reopened as the Crescent College and Conservatory for Young Women, an exclusive boarding school that ran throughout the academic year and turned into a hotel for the summer to earn extra profits. This incarnation was also destined for failure, however, and its doors were shuttered sixteen years later. It reopened again in 1930, this time as a junior college, but met the same outcome only four years later. For a booming town with a unique market, many believed that the hotel was cursed. Though they didn't know it then, their beliefs would be realized in 1937 after Norman G. Baker became the location's new owner.

Baker had made his fortune wearing many hats, including those of a vaudeville performer, an inventor, a "shock-jock" radio pioneer, a publisher, a mail-order salesman, and a congressional candidate. Lawsuits and litigation followed him everywhere he traveled, however, and that would eventually include the Crescent Hotel. Baker vocally denounced the medical community and, despite having no formal training whatsoever, advertised himself as an expert who successfully developed treatments that could cure cancer and other life-threatening ailments. He repainted the Crescent in tones of purple and lavender, renamed it Baker's Cancer Curing Hospital, and used his formidable resources to convince thousands of seriously ill patients to make their way across the country and stay at his luxurious clinic.

Unfortunately for them, the self-professed "Dr." Baker's "cure" was nothing more than injections of alcohol, glycerin, brown corn silk, watermelon seeds, clover, and carbolic acid—a completely nonmedical concoction that often did more harm than good. Not surprisingly, his patients would grow sicker or develop nasty infections, so Baker's would charge even more to heal them. One of his costlier procedures consisted of cracking open a patient's head while they were still conscious, then pouring his watermelon water mixture directly onto their brain to cure them. Another gruesome "treatment" included cutting off a dead patient's arm and sewing it onto a living person, thereby giving them a "healthy new arm." Unfortunately, the newly attached arm—which hadn't been properly connected to ligaments, tendons, or muscles—would rot and cause infections that made the "healed" patient suffer horribly before dying.

The list of Baker's unethical and lethal procedures runs long. Not a single treatment was based on science or medicine, and every one of them was conducted under unsterile conditions by people with no medical training. Baker's unwitting patients, desperate for a cure, were drained of their money and tortured through fake medical procedures before they finally died inside the hotel. The dead piled up so quickly that Baker's staff had to come up with creative ways to secretly move them around the hotel, store dozens of bodies in the basement, and slip them out the back door so that any incoming patients wouldn't see them. Because Baker's Cancer Curing Hospital wasn't a legal medical facility with actual records, the number of people who died under Baker's care is unknown. What is known, however, is that Baker took home over $500,000 one year running his sham facility—roughly the equivalent of $10 million in today's economy. It was a fortune forged from the lies of a silver-tongued charlatan who had little to no regard for human life.

Baker's Cancer Curing Hospital operated for only three years. Although the facility boosted the economy in Eureka Springs, the federal government realized the danger that Baker posed and managed to bring him to justice on counts of mail fraud. Baker was sentenced to four years in jail, but he was never convicted of any of the heinous crimes that occurred at the Crescent; he never put his name on any legal documents, and he made his patients pay in cash. Following his release, Baker spent the next twenty years living on his private yacht in Florida until, in what many would consider to be poetic justice, he developed liver cancer. Opting out of his own watermelon cure and turning down all medical treatment, Baker suffered a painful death inside a sanatorium at the age of seventy-five.

Over the next sixty years, the Crescent would see numerous owners, a few fires, and finally its resurgence as the majestic hotel that stands today. In 2007, the Crescent became a member of the prestigious Historic Hotels of America, the official program of the National Trust for Historic Preservation. Yet even though the mountaintop hotel and spa has realized the potential for which it was built, the structure's walls, rooms, and ceilings cannot erase the sordid history that has earned the Crescent a reputation for being "America's Most Haunted Hotel." It is widely believed that many *of Norman Baker's unfortunate patients have never checked out and, in fact, remain there to this day.*

•••

Driving through the Ozark Mountains is like journeying through an artist's perfect painting; it's simply stunning everywhere you look. In the heart of this surreal landscape, Eureka Springs is a colorful town, with pink and teal roofs, countless art studios, amazing stores, bars, and restaurants, and plenty of natural spring stops all nestled together throughout hilly roads. The sight of the Crescent Hotel sitting on a mountain peak on the edge of town is enough to make your jaw drop. It's incredibly elegant, yet if you look closely, there is something ominous oozing from its architecture.

Walking through the doors of this "Grand Ol' Lady of the Ozarks" feels like stepping back in time. Usually, when the TAPS team does a large-scale investigation (meaning outside of a home), we often find ourselves in abandoned buildings with crumbling walls and port-a-potties out in the nearby fields. So, any time I get to stay in a luxurious place and not have to go anywhere to investigate it's a real treat, especially when something can happen even right where I'm sleeping.

With some places, it can be difficult to find any written history, and when you do it's typically conflicting information from various resources. A great aspect of the Crescent is that it has a vast and well-preserved background that allows investigators like me to research and dive deep into the building's past. There's even an entire room dedicated to the history of the location, and it's always open to the public. Containing documents, photos, and assorted items from the past, the room is like

1914 photograph of the Crescent Hotel atop a mountain made primarily
of limestone

a mini-museum. I can't think of another hotel that offers such an in-depth display.

It was during one of my many trips to this mini-museum when I learned that the Crescent was built primarily out of limestone, and that the surrounding mountains contained it as well, which is interesting because limestone can absorb energy. Entire books have been written on the subject. I have even worked with several physicists who do not believe in ghosts and yet taught me how limestone can absorb energy and release it under the right conditions. If this is possible, then is it also plausible that something paranormal could draw from this energy source somehow?

What's also remarkable is that the hotel is constantly finding more history and adding to its amazing showcase. In 2019, after coming across numerous old glass bottles buried on the hotel grounds, the management called in an archaeological team. Over a period of several days, archaeologists dug up more than *four hundred* glass bottles, fully intact and with some containing what looked to be human tissue. These bottles matched ones that Norman Baker used for a large display to entice people to come to his hospital. The display, which he featured in newspaper ads across the country, included a row of glass bottles that contained "tumors" he removed from patients whom he cured. The discovery of these new artifacts is fascinating, and new activity is bound to happen around them. Period items, particularly ones that have meaning, can often trigger a spirit or conscious energy's reactions. These bottles, if they did belong to Baker, could stir up a whole new wave of paranormal experiences.

Of course, the main reason most people visit the Crescent's history room is to learn about the insane story of Dr. Baker. (Though he wasn't a doctor, I may occasionally refer to him here as such, as that's what he considered himself to be.) His story is so unbelievable, it would be difficult for even the greatest horror writer to conceive of the sick, twisted experiments that happened within the walls of the hotel. Three years may seem like a blip in the building's almost 140-year history, but the depth and pain Baker caused inside the Crescent left permanent scars.

• • •

At the hotel, the team learned about claims of people seeing a doctor walking throughout the halls, a gentleman sitting at a table as if waiting for someone, and an angry spirit guarding the morgue in the basement. (Yes, there's an actual morgue in this hotel; more on that shortly.) There were also consistent accounts of a strange phenomenon in room 419, in which clothing has been folded and bags left against the door, as if someone wanted the guest to leave the room. In fact, before we even began our investigation, Grant Wilson, who was staying in that very room, had his own odd experience there—a ten-pound computer bag that he'd left inside somehow ended up against the door, making it hard for him to open the door from the outside. It's pretty much impossible to be able to put a bag like that right behind a door and then leave the room, making it problematic to reenter. Having something like that happen put us all on high alert and made the gang more than eager to begin investigating.

Honestly, when I think about the bag incident I am conflicted—it could have been a complete accident in which the bag just fell, or it could have been done by something intelligent. What I find interesting is that most of the time a paranormal movement caught on camera is incredibly subtle . . . a pencil or ball rolling, or a toy car moving slightly. Other times that are a bit more drastic, like a chair moving away from a table over the course of a night or a door closing slowly while someone sleeps, are generally noticed by time-lapse cameras. Most investigators agree that it takes immense energy for a spirit to move anything, which is why it's not a common experience. So, the idea that a spirit actually lifted and moved a ten-pound bag is unbelievable, and it makes me think that if it was actually moved and wasn't an accident, that spirit must be one hell of a powerful entity.

I'm not trying to cast doubt or rain on anyone's parade, but it is possible that it was just an accident, and the TAPS team needs to approach such incidents from every angle. Without experiencing what happened in person or having video evidence, we'll never know. The only fact we have is that a bag moving and at times being placed behind the door was a common claim in room 419, so it seems more likely than not that what occurred was indeed a paranormal event. And if we assume that it was, then we must also ponder the "why" of the activity. Why did the spirit choose to move Grant's bag, and why put it behind the door in order to bar entry?

With the paranormal, while we can hope to catch an EVP, there's no just asking why a spirit did something. They don't play by a set of rules and instructions, so everything we do is a guessing game based on evidence and experience. That's one of the things I love most about my job—there are no clear-cut answers. It's up to us to piece together these vague, unclear parts of a massive puzzle. I like to think that we are some of the last explorers. At one point, *everything* had to be discovered and figured out, just like we're trying to do today with the paranormal. I can only hope that when the puzzle is fully solved, I was able to place a few of the pieces together.

• • •

As the team rushed to set everything up, something internally urged me to slow down. I told the rest of the crew that I needed a quick break before we started, then snuck away and walked downstairs, not knowing where I was going. I wasn't surprised that I ended up in the lobby. Since I first entered the Crescent, I had been enthralled with its dark and rich Art Deco motif. If Edgar Allan Poe could create a sitting room for a hotel, I imagine that it would look like the one at the Crescent. I felt so at ease there.

Sitting down on an antique couch, I ran my fingers along its bloodred crushed-velvet cushions and watched the fire crackle in the hearth across from me. Then, without warning, I saw out of the corner of my eye a blurry image darting by. A second or two later, I felt the impact of four tiny, sharp-clawed paws on my lap. Before I could react, there was a quick meow that calmed me; the cat who just hopped on my legs motioned for me to pet her. Smiling, I obeyed her command and scratched the fur of the beautiful tabby nestled in my lap like I'd been her owner for years.

The story of the Crescent lobby cats is legendary. One of them had become such a mainstay that when he passed after twenty-one years, over three hundred people came to his funeral. (You can still visit his grave.) The hotel even has pictures and plaques up for the cats, as well as a specially built cat door that leads out to the back porch, where the felines can enjoy the view. I'm not sure if any of these things were a factor, but I just felt a world of calm in petting this adorable, loving tabby while sitting on a Gothic couch, and in front of a fire within a hotel lobby that made me feel like I had traveled back in time. It gave me goose bumps. I had never felt that way at any other location I'd investigated, and I did my best to let this magical feeling wash over me.

Unfortunately, the hotel's darker history kept resurfacing as I looked around. I could envision Norman Baker putting on a show in the middle of the floor, playing doctor and cutting someone's head open a mere few feet from where I sat. It made my stomach tighten, and I think the cat felt it too; she gave me a sharp meow, as if telling me to cut it out. With a deep breath, I gave my new friend a few more pets, then told her I had to get going and that I would find her later to say good night. I had a long evening ahead of me.

• • •

We started off our investigation of the Crescent heading to the place that everyone loves to gravitate toward: the morgue. Granted, the area had long since been repurposed into a maintenance room, but it was still largely untouched from the days of Baker's experiments. Regardless, I was stoked. Any time I'm about to investigate an overly creepy location, it awakens my love for horror movies and makes my heart speed up a bit. That said, I've typically found that most real morgues and graveyards don't live up to our Hollywood standards; in most cases, there tends to be very little activity in the places we think should be scary. The best stuff usually happens where people *lived*, not where the dead rest. As a result, even though my horror excitement level was high, my paranormal expectations were low.

Man, were those meters sure flipped.

We walked down a narrow staircase and ended up in a cramped room that looked more like a standard basement workshop than a morgue. Sure, with the lights off and its dingy walls, the room looked "old," but as someone who has spent countless hours investigating abandoned mental hospitals, I admittedly felt a bit of a letdown. If I hadn't been told it was once a morgue, I would have never thought it was anything but a workshop. Something that at first resembled a workbench was actually an old autopsy table, while other items throughout the room were immediately more recognizable as what you'd expect to find in a morgue: deep sterile sinks, lockers, and what appeared to be an old walk-in freezer. When I saw a lunch pail on the far end of the makeshift worktable, a part of me wondered if the maintenance guy ever stopped to consider the corpses that once lay where he was setting down his meatball grinder (what we call sub sandwiches in New England, by the way).

I still wasn't expecting anything in the room, but all that changed when the thermal camera Jay and Grant were using around some lockers suddenly registered a human-shaped heat signature. When they scrolled back through the footage, they couldn't believe what they saw: something that looked like a full person standing in front of locker number two.

With a thermal camera, you can tell the temperature of everything in a room; humans appear as "hot," meaning they'll glow orange, yellow, red, and even white if they're really warm. Typically, actual body temperatures also show up on the camera screen. The rest of the room usually reflects blue tones and registers temps that are much lower than those of something living. This thermal image we caught at the Crescent, where no one had been standing, was the perfect outline of a person for a solid few seconds. The only thing was, instead of reflecting warm hues, the outline was dark and its colors were all in green tones. No human would ever look like that on a thermal camera . . . unless they were dead. Almost everyone on the team took turns trying to repeat what we had captured earlier, but no luck. Nothing we did could perfectly create the shape of a human or what we all saw.

The thermal camera footage picked up something else bizarre: The locker number, two, was glowing *through* the heat signature of the figure, as if it was much warmer than the rest of the locker. The large number was blaring hot tones, mostly a deep red with an outline of yellow. It was weird; why would only the number glow? Plus, the number sat perfectly on the figure's arm, like it was some sort of patch. Paint can be reflective, so it's possible that the paint of the number could have been reflecting the heat that registered. It was a long shot, though, and one that we couldn't re-create. We even shined a flashlight on it for thirty seconds to see if it would replicate the glow (back when we were there, our flashlights didn't have LED lights in them, so they could get pretty hot); the number hardly got into the warm tones.

We stopped trying to duplicate the glow around the number and looked for a possible explanation inside the locker. We even did some historical research later to see if there was any significance about the number, yet we found nothing that would explain why it was highlighted. To this day, I wish I could have found the connection. What we caught was unexplainable and some of the best evidence we ever got. In my opinion, it's likely an apparition of someone who spent a lot of time at the Crescent.

Editing is a magical part of television. When you watch one of our shows, you're seeing only forty-two minutes that were put together from countless hours of footage. Editing often makes it look like we were at a location for one evening when, in reality, we're typically there for several nights to make sure we've thoroughly investigated the entire locale and collected as much evidence as possible. When it's a large place like the Crescent, we can be there even longer. For this particular investigation, since we did a few other things close to the hotel, we were there for two full weeks. And I can't tell you how much of that time we spent talking about that heat signature in the morgue. It blew our minds, and not just us investigators—*everyone* on the film crew was baffled by what they saw. All concerned watched the footage repeatedly and talked about it constantly during any downtime. Because it happened early into our stay, most nights when we weren't investigating, we'd find ourselves sitting down in the morgue throwing out theories, trying to re-create the original conditions and attempting to reestablish contact with what we strongly felt was a spirit. Yet nothing happened, which makes it even more amazing that we caught what we did. There's one thing about ghost hunting: If it's a residual haunt, it's all about being at the right place at the right time.

Over the past few years, the Crescent's management realized its history and further embraced the hotel's paranormal aspects by cleaning out the entire morgue and turning it into a tour attraction. Now it's just as it was back in Norman Baker's day, complete with pictures, medical equipment, and fancy lighting. (It's certainly much creepier now than when someone's lunch pail was sitting on the table.) They even have locker number two on display based on the TAPS team's finding, and encourage visitors to try to gather their own evidence.

• • •

Back in the late sixties, the Crescent had a fire that destroyed its entire roofline and caused immense damage. This was a traumatic event in the hotel's history and surely an isolated incident . . . at least, the owners hoped so. Ironically, one night during our stay there, at around 4:00 AM, a fire alarm started blaring, waking everyone up. Groggy and a bit annoyed that I'd been roused from bed on the only night we had off from investigating, I got dressed and made my way out of my room. I ran into the crew, one by one, and all of us evacuated the hotel. Once outside, everyone was shocked to see the smoke that was filling up the cold night air. There was an actual fire on the roof—the building had been hit by lightning. There had been storms all night, which for me added to the ambience of being a guest in "America's Most Haunted Hotel," but they weren't anything terrible; in fact, I slept through most of them.

I've been woken by fire alarms before, but they were mostly false alarms. This, however, was real and it was nerve-racking. Not just because we had all our equipment and personal items inside; those were replaceable. However, the Crescent itself wasn't. Everyone stood around, petrified that such living history would be lost. Thankfully, the fire was contained rather quickly, albeit a bit comically—the town was so small, no one could use the ladder truck because the only guy who knew how to operate it was off that day, so the firefighters connected hoses and ran them all the way up the building one balcony at a time using a little ladder.

Well over a hundred years old, and the "Grand Ol' Lady of the Ozarks" had never been struck or set on fire by lightning. Yet it happened while *we* were there, exploring the Crescent's dark past and trying to make contact with its long-lost madman. It felt like there had to have been some sort of connection or deeper meaning behind it. If I were a fiction writer, I'd craft a story about Baker making a pact with a demon for one well-placed lightning strike to burn down his old facility and, he hoped, claim a few more victims. Most likely, it was a billion-to-one coincidence, but part of me will always contemplate from time to time whether it wasn't.

Amazingly, what I recall the most from this potential tragedy was standing outside and seeing a fellow investigator, Dustin Pari, exit the hotel through a cloud of smoke, wearing nothing but blue boxer shorts and an old, beat-up baseball cap, as the firefighters rushed in. It was like something out of a comedy—this casually strolling, almost-naked man, who slept through the alarms, emerging from the smoke and delivering some one-liner about what everyone was looking at. To this day, I can't figure out what Dustin's thought process had been: *Fire alarm! Shoes, pants, shirt? Nah, I need a hat.*

• • •

Being in town for a while, we had heard about a local resident who considered himself to be a psychic and lived in a private house situated next door to the hotel. While we were having fun at the Crescent, we thought his story was interesting, so the team wanted to look into some claims he made about experiencing some paranormal activity in his own home.

I work with and have a lot of friends who are psychics, and I trust them and have seen them do some amazing things. Unfortunately, there are a lot of scam artists out there who give real psychics a bad reputation. Go to any tourist destination and you'll see neon signs for "Psychic

Readings, Palm Readings, Fortunes Told," and more. They put on a show for excited travelers looking for laughs, or for giggling teens who want to know whom they're going to marry. For ten dollars, they give you five minutes of their time and a generic reading that anyone with a bit of practice can dole out.

That day, I joined Jason, Grant, and Tango to meet the psychic—an older man named Carroll Heath. His residence was so close to the hotel that we simply walked across the street and onto the property. It was a lovable, large, and lavish Victorian home filled with opulent curtains and art at every turn . . . though what struck me most about the house was some odd dolls that were attached to the wall on each side of the living room doorway. They didn't feel out of place in the eclectic room, but man, they were *creepy*—so much so that I kept wondering if they were going to move like one of the animatronics at the Haunted Mansion in Disney World.

Until the Crescent, I had only had a few experiences with a medium or psychic that couldn't be explained. So, when I saw Carroll via the set-up thermal camera emitting some strange anomalies while he was doing a reading, I was completely stunned.

It started with Jay and Grant sitting across from Carroll and asking him questions. Jay then asked Carroll to give him a reading. Carroll quickly conducted a standard reading, with nothing out of the ordinary happening. Then it was Grant's turn. During his reading, there was a large *bang*, like a double *thump*. It ended up being one of the thermal cameras that I'd set up. I admit, it wasn't hooked on the best spot, but it seemed unlikely that it would have fallen on its own, especially since it fell at the exact time Carroll was asking Grant his questions.

While the readings were ongoing, Tango and I did our own little investigation of the reported activity in Carroll Heath's house. Before we could experience anything, we were called down to look at what was happening. The thermal camera had been going crazy on Carroll while he was asking Jay his questions. It was almost as if it were glitching . . . it simply couldn't settle on a steady color. Then, as Jay sat there, trying to purposely throw Carroll off with vague answers to the psychic's questions, a weird, globulus, Technicolor cloud started to surround Jay's body. The readings showed all different temperatures, which made no sense to us. Then, like an amoeba swimming in a petri dish, the cloud oozed itself away from Jay and floated right over to Carroll. It also seemed like Carroll was completely aware of it, because at that moment he raised his hand and literally swatted at something, like a bug. The second he did so, the colored mass dissolved.

Having used thermal cameras for decades, I've seen pretty much everything you possibly could on them. I know when I'm seeing a heat reflection or, in a rare case, a wind draft. . . . I've gotten to learn all the signs. But nature can't create cold—cold is simply the absence of heat, which *can* be created. There was no heat present in our camera footage, and the crazy fluctuations of temperatures we saw simply shouldn't have existed. I have never seen anything like it before or since. Carroll himself thought the camera was reading the energy that Jay was putting off. That sounded good in theory, but as far as science goes, the thermal camera is only supposed to catch temperatures. Is it possible what we found out that night was that psychic energy has its own thermal fluctuations?

•••

That experience with Carroll Heath, in addition to all the evidence we collected at the Crescent Hotel, was astounding, some of the best evidence we ever captured. I remember sitting alone at 5:00 AM, back in the lobby and next to the gorgeous fireplace, once again petting the feline friend I'd made and racking my brain about the footage we'd caught. What was that thermal image in the morgue, and why was the number two hotter than anything else? What was that aura around Jay during the reading? In the eyes of science, the thermal data we captured was as close to indisputable as you can get. The readings are right there; we just don't know how best to interpret them . . . yet. All I know is that some of the greatest moments I have ever experienced as a paranormal investigator took place inside "America's Most Haunted Hotel," and for that I feel incredibly fortunate.

IN THE DARK AT PENNHURST

PENNHURST STATE SCHOOL AND HOSPITAL
—
SPRING CITY, PA
OPENED IN 1908

"Every feeble-minded person is a potential criminal." That's what Penn-hurst's lead physician stated around 1918, quoting eugenicist Henry H. Goddard in a letter submitted by the board of trustees. Around this time, the government and physicians alike viewed people who were diagnosed or perceived as having mental disorders with disdain, distrust, and con-tempt. Massive facilities were built to house and confine those who were deemed mentally unfit away from the general public, to make certain that they didn't procreate or harm society. Chief among these structures: the Eastern Pennsylvania State Institution for the Feeble-Minded and Epileptic, founded in 1908 and later renamed Pennhurst State School and Hospital.

Pennhurst sprawled over a hundred acres of land, but it was an asylum that grew severely overcrowded within a few years of opening. New structures were rapidly constructed in order to contain the criminals, orphans, and immigrants whom the state didn't want in society. At its peak, nearly four thousand patients lived inside Pennhurst's wasteland of buildings, amid deplorable conditions and understaffing. By the time a lack of funding,

AMITY PHOTOS

overcrowding, and reports of patient abuse forced Pennhurst to shutter its doors in 1987, there were more than thirty buildings, consisting of over six hundred thousand square feet spread across fourteen hundred acres.

When pushed through the institute's doors, mostly against their will, patients—almost none of whom would be housed today for their disabilities— were mentally designated by the state under one of two categories: "Imbecile" or "Insane." Physically, they'd be classified as "Epileptic" or "Healthy," and their teeth would be categorized as "Good," "Poor," or "Treated." The intake was fast and confusing; most patients would never see their families again, nor would they ever step foot outside the grounds once they were admitted. They'd live their entire lives inside the asylum. Those who were able were forced to work for no pay until they were no longer physically able to do so. These enslaved laborers made mattresses, farmed, did laundry, baked, and performed other tasks as needed, all to keep the mini-city operating and, of course, to keep costs way down.

It wasn't until decades after opening that the real horrors behind Pennhurst surfaced—female patients were segregated to prevent them from being impregnated, while allegations of abuse began to seep into the mainstream. In 1968, local CBS correspondent Bill Baldini exposed the asylum's extreme, horrible conditions in a five-part documentary called Suffer the Little Children. The unsettling footage, which showed the squalor and horrors inside the institute's walls—adults in cribs, patients naked and filthy, rocking or pacing in overcrowded rooms—disturbed anyone who watched. In perhaps the most upsetting part of the documentary, a patient was asked what he wanted most in the world; he simply replied, "To get out of Pennhurst."

Though Baldini's damning report triggered public outrage and investigations, the thousands forced to remain within the miniature city continued to suffer for decades. In 1981, Time magazine once again exposed the atrocities at Pennhurst, calling it a facility "with a history of being understaffed, dirty and violent." A few years later, nine workers were criminally charged with abusing patients. Yet, inconceivably, it wasn't until 1987 that Pennhurst's horrific history finally came to an end; after nearly eighty years and more than ten thousand inhabitants, the institute was closed forever. Over the next thirty years, buildings were torn down, the property was added to preservation lists, and ownership of the property changed hands many times. In 2010, to the initial dismay of neighboring locals, the former administrative building was renovated and repurposed as PennHurst Haunted Asylum.

But what of the unfortunate souls who were condemned to reside there? The immigrants who ventured to America for a new start, only to be committed, coerced to work for free, and then die within Pennhurst's grounds? Epileptic people who, instead of living normal, productive lives, *were regularly beaten and forced to exist in unsanitary conditions? Or the Down syndrome patients who were made to wear diapers and live in adult-sized cribs amid their own filth? Nearly eighty years of pain, torment, and death have seeped into the walls and floors of Pennhurst. It is said that those who suffered, who were treated with no respect or human decency, who could never escape their constant torture, remain on the grounds. Now they wander the halls and reach out to those who visit . . . but are they reaching out for help or out of anger?*

• • •

It would be one thing if Pennhurst had housed only the sick or people with severe ailments, but that wasn't the case. This was, in effect, an entire city created to confine people whom some local socialites didn't want walking around their streets. It's hard not to imagine the disgusting behavior that happened there when you drive onto the property, which is practically isolated from the outside world. As you maneuver down the long, vacant, and bumpy road, you can see old train tracks that led to the storage buildings—that's right: Pennhurst was so big that trains used to deliver supplies to the place. Pulling onto that road, leaving the town and the rest of the outside world behind, one can't help but also wonder what it must have been like for a patient to be transported there, knowing that it was likely only a one-way trip.

When I first drove onto the property, I figured I'd see some massive creepy old asylum just waiting there for us to investigate. Instead, I was shocked to discover what looked like a dump. Not the building; I mean an actual dump, with mountains of trash and other items. I'd find out later that at one point the facility was rented out for garbage disposal, so the grounds, though beautiful in their deteriorated glory, were also piled with mounds of trash, machinery, and tons of medical devices. I was surprised at first, but it certainly added to Pennhurst's eerie history. Looking at old, decaying contraptions on the grounds and knowing this place was a "medical" facility made me really think about how quickly some of us throw aside things—devices *and* lives—and leave them to rot.

Thankfully, it's no longer like that. I went back a few years ago and was pleasantly stunned to see how much the property had been cleaned up. The place now has amazing historical tours, ghost hunts, and a killer haunted house event during the Halloween season. There's even a yearly paranormal convention on the grounds, called Pennhurst Paracon, that draws thousands of people. I have been a guest at it and had a fantastic time, though it was held in the summer and was as hot as hell; in all the pictures I took, the convention patrons and I have beet-red faces (they've brought in better air-conditioning since then).

I parked the TAPS van next to a building that made me immediately feel intimidated by how massive it was. The structure stood four stories tall, with dark, glassless holes where windows once were. . . . they looked so ominous, like pitch-black, gaping mouths. It didn't help that I was also feeling a bit overwhelmed at the time—in addition to being an investigator, I was TAPS's tech manager. That meant I oversaw all the equipment, as well as its setup and breakdown. With the number of wires, cameras, infrared cameras, laser grids, DVR systems, flashlights, and more, it was a huge job. We had a great team and everyone pitched in, but it was my job to ensure that we had everything, check that it was all functioning properly, and then decide where to place it all before overseeing the setup. I'd also help anyone who had issues with the equipment, set up the command center, and confirm that all cameras were a go. Then, at the end of the investigation, I'd have to make sure everything was broken down and safely packed away.

Not only did I have to worry about the equipment but I was also in charge of all the investigators (besides Jason and Grant, as they were on their own). In addition, if there was anyone new on an investigation, I had to see that they were properly trained and doing everything right. The hardest part was that I had to manage all of this *before* I could start to investigate. As I look back even now, the thought of all the work I had to do at Pennhurst is almost enough to make me want to take a nap. In truth, I loved the setup—my only issue with it was having to wait through it all before starting the investigation.

My head swirled over the logistics of how the heck I was going to set this place up, but I was still excited. Pennhurst was your classic abandoned mental hospital, yet with *way* more buildings and land than most others. (It's weird when you realize that abandoned insane asylums are more normal in your daily life than a shopping mall.) Using the owners' reports of incidents they couldn't explain, the team managed to narrow down our game plan to cover a few key buildings and areas throughout the property. These would become the main focus of our investigation . . . though there was one report about an apparition "glowing" that made me reconsider.

• • •

It's a bit on the rarer side, but occasionally we'll hear people describe a full-body apparition or a misty cloud or object as being illuminated. Personally, I've seen flickers and flashes of light, but I've never witnessed a full object emitting light when it shouldn't be able to. So, why do people associate glowing with ghosts and the paranormal?

Since the beginning of modern entertainment, almost every time you see a ghost in a movie, a TV show, or even a cartoon, the spirit "glows," as if they produce some sort of internal or external light source. Patrick Swayze in *Ghost* has a heavenly aura surround him, the animated Casper the Friendly Ghost glows blue, and Slimer from *Ghostbusters* emanates green. In movies, it looks really freaking cool and it helps the manifestations stand out on a dark screen, where you normally wouldn't see them. However, if you stop and really think about it, why would a ghost glow? Although if ghosts are made of energy, couldn't they? Do humans naturally emit light?

Oddly enough, they do. A study has found that humans radiate visible light in extremely small quantities that rise and fall with the day. However, it's a thousand times less intense than the levels the naked eye can see. If the energy that constantly emanates from a living body needs to be a thousand times stronger to even be perceived, then it's a long shot to think that a ghost would possess such an immense amount of energy to produce an actual glow. Bearing that in mind, whenever I hear claims of glowing spirits I typically suspect those claims come from folks who believe what they see in movies a bit too much.

To be fair, I kind of love the idea of a glowing spirit, just like that beautiful scene in *Poltergeist* when a superbright supernatural force comes down the stairs and lights up the room like a mini-sun before it splits off into numerous orbs. But even Dr. William G. Roll, a pioneer in poltergeist research who was considered the definitive expert on the phenomenon (he wrote a book called *The Poltergeist* that came out in 1972, though he never received any credit for inspiring the film), agreed that ghosts would not glow. However, he believed that the film did an amazing job of showcasing how investigators work—the way they set up cameras, establish a command center, and consider everything, just like investigators do today.

Dr. Roll was one of the world's leading parapsychologists and as massive an influence on my career as Ed and Lorraine Warren. I read his books repeatedly when I began studying the craft. I vividly remember one night putting down one of his books to watch *Unsolved Mysteries* with my mother, and Dr. Roll ironically appeared on that very episode. In the segment, which focused on the legendary ghosts aboard the *Queen Mary* cruise ship, there's a re-creation of a worker hearing a small girl laughing by the boat's pool. Checking out the sound, the worker saw the water splashing on its own, then small, wet footprints appearing on the walking path. I know today that it was cheesy stop-motion that created those footprints, but back then the image gave twelve-year-old me chills down my entire body. I was so enthralled by the ghosts on the boat that when Dr. Roll suddenly appeared on my television my jaw dropped. I

A photo I took of Dr. Roll during our time together

was beyond fascinated by his science and research; at that moment, I knew I wanted to be like him when I grew up.

In the early 2000s, before *Ghost Hunters* began and I was teaching classes, Jason Hawes introduced me to people at the famed Rhine Research Center in North Carolina. They eventually asked me to give a speech about the paranormal, specifically ghosts. The Rhine is a facility that tries to bridge the gap between science and spirituality. Unlike common science, where experts won't even have conversations about anything to do with the paranormal, the Rhine's group of like-minded scientists and researchers try to find how both sides can meet in the middle to figure out the unknown. I was honored to be asked to speak there, but when I saw Dr. Roll, the man I grew up admiring, sitting in the audience and interested in what I had to say, I almost fainted.

Somehow, I managed to stammer my way through the presentation. After the event, Dr. Roll—who by this point was in the twilight of his life—slowly walked over, shook my hand, and told me how much he liked my lecture. We quickly built a rapport and he asked how long I was staying in town; I had intended to leave the next day, but I didn't care. I wanted to stick around a while longer. He nodded and invited me to do some research with him. I almost fell over, but I composed myself enough to tell him that I would be honored.

Over the next few days, Dr. Roll and I worked closely on a study to determine how different energies affected readings on various devices. We even made a visit to a local mansion that was known to be haunted, which the institute had arranged for us, and where we spent hours conducting experiments and comparing notes and theories. Dr. Roll was slow to get up from a seated position, but he still had the enthusiasm of a twenty-year-old investigator. He was focusing so intently on an

experiment he had set up, waiting for any out-of-the-ordinary fluctuations that required further examination, which could show him that
some entity could be in the room with us. Even in his late seventies, his
passion was so infectious; he made me wish that I would have half his
drive when I reached his age.

While the research I did with Dr. Roll made me realize it is unlikely
that ghosts would "glow," it doesn't mean I think people are making
false claims about anything they see. A vast majority of the time, clients
aren't lying to us; they're truly convinced that they've seen something.
And we take every claim seriously, regardless of whether or not the client
is experiencing real paranormal activity. What matters most is that *they*
believe in their own experience, and if they do, we try our best to help
them. Disproving the experiences will alleviate their fears and help them
feel comfortable in their surroundings. On the flip side, finding solid
evidence or confirming that what they've seen is real helps validate the
client's experience. At the end of the day, we may investigate the dead,
but what we do is all about the living.

• • •

Because Pennhurst was just a field before any construction of the hospital
occurred, we could clearly pinpoint the time in which spirits originated;
any "period clothing" would be completely plausible, since we knew the
exact dates when the facility was operational. Information like this can
be extremely helpful, especially when examining more intense claims,
such as full-body apparitions dressed in patient gowns (and whether
they glow or not remains up for debate).

Almost every "haunted" location has a standard laundry list of
things that tend to happen on a regular basis. Pennhurst had all of the

standard claims but also some *really* exceptional ones. In addition to accounts of seeing full-body apparitions, several workers asserted that they'd been forcibly pushed, had objects thrown at them, seen creeping shadows scuttle through halls, and heard loud, inexplicable banging sounds or dragging noises one could associate with bodies being pulled down corridors. Claims of such violence aren't common, so when we hear of them we take matters very seriously, as they can be dangerous. A scratch or cut is one thing; a push down the stairs is quite another.

• • •

With everything set up, we began our investigation right after sunset. Now, typically, *if* we experience anything, it's almost never right off the bat. There in Pennhurst, however, just a few minutes after we started, Tango and I had an intense experience.

We were checking out things on the second floor of the Quaker Building when we heard a loud banging noise. Oftentimes, Tango and I will confirm when we both hear something; we know each other so well that we can usually do this with a look and a nod. Then we'll stay still and wait for the sound to happen again so we can pinpoint its location. I'd say about 80 percent of the time what we hear does *not* repeat. Yet as the two of us stood still, staring at each other, there was another *bang*, then another. The noise was startlingly loud, not something in the distance that you'd have to shush your partner in order to make it out. After discussing what it could be, we guessed at the direction it was coming from and, like a pair of stereotypical horror movie victims who walk blindly toward something that common sense would say to avoid, we decided to find out what was making the sound.

As the two of us walked down a long hallway, the pale beams from

Inside the tunnels of Pennhurst
AMITY PHOTOS

our flashlights illuminating the dusty, decaying walls, we heard the noise once more . . . this time a lot closer. After another twenty yards, we felt like we were in the right area. Sure enough, over the center promenade were these large metal shutters that kept patients from breaking the glass and escaping. Grabbing one, I could feel how heavy they were; they were definitely capable of making such a noise as what we'd heard. Tango and I stood quietly and waited for them to move; there was no wind, not even the slightest breeze. I pushed one firmly with a finger. It barely budged. The only way these shutters would move was with a hard push.

Tango walked back to the spot where we first picked up the noise. I pulled at one of the shutters, then quickly slammed it shut. He confirmed that it made the exact same sound we'd heard earlier. There was no denying it . . . the shutters were making the noise. When Tango came back, we tried again to find a way for them to close naturally, but it was *impossible*. They were heavy and rusted, and it took a good effort to move them. *Something* was closing those shutters with force. And just to be certain, we checked the location of everyone on the team; no one was anywhere near the area when the sounds occurred.

This was incredible, but unfortunately, we had no cameras stationed in this area beforehand. While we got audio of the sound on record, we didn't have any video evidence. Wanting to catch the shutter movement in the act, Tango and I set up cameras and waited. The result was the same as when you need to bring your car to a mechanic for making a strange noise—it won't make the sound when you're actually there.

Not catching something we experience is the bane of our existence. I can't tell you how many times I have witnessed amazing things, only to find they were just out of the camera's frame or that the audio wasn't recording yet. Skeptics like to point at this and sarcastically say, "Oh, *of course* the camera wasn't on the right spot," but that's an easy jab. Think about it this way: If you're in a wooded area the size of Pennhurst and you've been asked to capture footage of an elusive animal, do you think you'll get something recorded in the few days that you're there? Even though we didn't catch the cause of that shutter sound on video, I was glad that we at least had an audio recording. This paranormal experience was one neither Tango nor I will ever forget.

• • •

Being a paranormal investigator is an odd profession, to say the least. At one point in the Quaker Building, I found myself sitting in a pitch-black room where people had claimed to have a crowbar launched at them, among other lethal objects that could hurt or kill you. I was talking out loud, almost daring the spirits to throw something at me: *"Come on! If you're here, just do it! Throw something!"* Nothing happened, so eventually I had to move my investigation to another area we were focused on. Looking back now, I know it's crazy to think I was sitting in complete darkness, alone in a haunted, derelict insane asylum, and begging for something not of our world to purposely throw something at me. I desperately wanted to get hit like one of the Three Stooges. What's even odder is that if it *had* happened, I'd be thrilled and giving out high fives to everyone on my way to the hospital.

To most outsiders, being a paranormal investigator can seem terrifying. Every glossy horror movie makes ghosts out to be these demonic entities who are hell-bent on killing the living out of some sort of twisted sense of revenge. In reality, most people in the paranormal community don't fear ghosts. If we did, none of us would be sitting in the dark trying to communicate with them. However, there is a list of things we do fear, and *humans* are on the very top of that list. When you're inside an abandoned building, you never know if there are people without homes residing in it for shelter or drug addicts using it to get high. Running into someone who doesn't want to be found (otherwise, why would they be in an abandoned building?) in the middle of the night can be a dangerous situation. On more than a few occasions, I've run into such scenarios, and it scared the crap out of me.

One time I remember, our team was investigating inside Chicago's Rialto Square Theatre when I heard a strange noise. I went to check it out and followed it all the way to a man shooting up in between his toes. The guy looked at me, finished shooting, tossed the needle aside, and asked if I was a cop. When I said no, he shrugged, put his sock on, and wandered off. Another time, while we were outside Buffalo Central Terminal, the building owner went down to the basement level, before we could follow him. He soon ran back out, his hand mangled and bleeding. Someone had attacked him with a metal bar, simply for walking into his own building. Incidents like these are why the TAPS team follows a general rule to never hunt alone.

In addition to fearing humans, we also have to worry about animals, especially wild ones. I once encountered a mama raccoon that had a nice, warm nest inside a crumbling wall . . . *not* a fun situation. I ran down two halls and three flights of stairs, across a parking lot, and straight into my car to escape her. She wouldn't give up; she chased me, hissing and snapping all the way to the car. Even after I got in (and locked the doors . . . though looking back, I have no clue why, as if she could just open the door on her own), the raccoon walked around the vehicle, acting like some toughie trying to intimidate me. It took almost ten minutes before she finally called it quits and went away. Out of breath and shaking, I was on high alert the rest of the investigation.

Sometimes we also have to contend with dark and unsafe structures. Hardly an investigation goes by where one of us doesn't trip over or cut ourself on the countless hazardous items like furniture, unseen stairs, uneven floors, trash, rocks, and more. There's also been more than one occasion when I thought a floor was going to cave in as I walked across it. Bottom line: Never investigate a building that you don't have permission to access, and always try to check it out in the daylight first for safety issues. Trust me, sometimes ghosts can be the least of your worries.

• • •

Tunnels in old facilities are some of the creepiest places to investigate. They're dark, moldy, and smelly, and they sometimes hold tales of true horror, like how they were used to transport dead bodies so that other patients wouldn't see them. The tunnels in Pennhurst fit all the characteristics of what creepy tunnels should look like and, man, they're massive, connecting numerous buildings over a hundred acres. One could get permanently lost inside them. When you walk through a tunnel that's darker than night and the flashlight beam you're shining down the long emptiness dies off because it hasn't reached the end, your heart sinks a bit and you wonder what could possibly be waiting in the blackness. Of course, with my job, I'm *always* in the dark, but there's just something about the endlessness of a tunnel. A room is one thing; you can light up the corners and see your surroundings in one glance. However, a tunnel that seems to stretch forever, with a maze of offshoots going in countless directions . . . that's my idea of purgatory.

Truth be told, the tunnels at Pennhurst scared me, and not just because they were among the longest and most complicated I'd ever wandered around in. I'm afraid of a lot of things, many of which could be found in tunnels like these—snakes, spiders, and any other creature with more than four legs . . . or none whatsoever. What scared me there the most, though, was coming across human feces.

Tango and I walked through the tunnel one night when our flashlights found a pile of . . . well, crap. It might not have been steaming, but it wasn't dried out or old. That meant someone was probably living there in the tunnel. With thoughts of past experiences and the image of Buffalo Central's bloodied owner flashing in my head, I put myself on full alert. I didn't want to startle anyone into jumping out and attacking us, so I yelled loudly a few times that we were searching the tunnel and meant no one any harm. I didn't hear any scuttling away, and I hoped that anyone there would make themself scarce. Thankfully, they did. We had no run-ins during our time in the tunnel . . . at least none of the living, human variety.

Instead of encountering real flesh-and-blood people, the two of us were met by numerous disembodied voices. Some were faint, some were clearer than others, and some were just off in the distance, like whispers in the wind. Long halls with hard walls make sound echo and bounce, so the voices were almost impossible to pinpoint. You'd turn as you heard a whisper in your left ear, only then to hear it in your right . . . and you would start second-guessing where it came from. We'd hear things like footsteps, kids laughing, and what sounded like someone saying, "*Get out,*" numerous times. Being in pure blackness with ghostly voices and sounds coming at you from every which way . . . it was both maddening and thrilling. At one point, there were so many voices that I started to appreciate what it would be like to go mad, as I had a hard time handling the sounds hitting me from everywhere.

Though some of the voices were clear as a bell for Tango and me, we were able to catch only a few EVPs—one of a little girl whimpering and another of a man mumbling about us "getting out." What's amazing is that I never expected anything to happen in the tunnels, except maybe being creeped out by the wildlife. I mean, no one lived or spent a lot of time in them from what I can tell; they were just used for passage, so why would entities have any connection to them? Whatever the reason

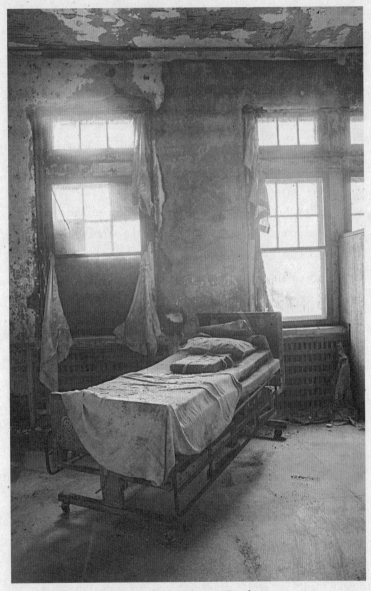

Partitioned patient room in Pennhurst
AMITY PHOTOS

was, they certainly did. Hearing a word whispered by your ear in the darkness of a creepy tunnel, and in an asylum, is one of the most intense, spine-tingling things one can ever experience, and having it happen in Pennhurst's tunnels . . . the memory still gives me goose bumps.

Walking out of the tunnel and into the fresh air, I sucked in a deep breath, feeling like the last survivor to make it to safety in a horror movie; I almost expected something would suddenly grab me from behind and pull me back into the tunnel just as the credits turned black. Fortunately, I lived to tell the tale. I've gone back into that same tunnel a few times since that night and got goose bumps of anticipation every time. I even heard disembodied voices on two other occasions, though they weren't as intense as that first visit.

When the sun came up after that first night of investigating, as the team started breaking down the equipment, I slipped away and ran up the stairs within the Quaker Building, into an old patient's room with a rusty bed inside.

To this day, I have no clue behind this sudden compulsion and where I was going or why I was headed there, but when I got to that room it seemed like the place I wanted to be. The sun was just breaking the horizon, letting a bit of amber light into the room. The two glassless windows slowly started to glow and come to life. Instead of watching the sunrise, I walked over and stood between the windows, then turned around so I could fully see the room. I stared at the bed and thought of the person who was almost certainly forced to stay there all those years ago. My chest got a bit tight and I felt overwhelmed by sadness. After a few moments, I whispered, "I'm sorry you suffered."

Almost instantly, I heard what sounded like a deep sigh, ever so faintly, coming from somewhere in the room. With misty eyes, I walked over to the bed, knelt down, and said "sorry" to all the people who were forced to live their lives in that godforsaken hellhole.

• • •

Pennhurst was, and always is, an amazing experience. We returned to the property to do a live episode of *Ghost Hunters* there. I have been back many times, and it never disappoints. The EVPs I've recorded and scenarios I've encountered inside that mini-city are profound.

I've investigated some places that made me hesitant to say they were haunted, but trust me, Pennhurst is as haunted as a place can be. It's a paranormal investigator's dream locale. I just truly wish it hadn't taken such a dark, disturbing history to make it that way.

This photo was taken in 2019, during my fourth visit to Pennhurst.

YOU'RE NEVER ALONE

STANLEY HOTEL

—

ESTES PARK, CO

OPENED 1909

In 1903, a wealthy inventor named Freelan Oscar Stanley and his wife, Flora, moved to Estes Park, Colorado. He had been prescribed fresh air and sunshine, coupled with a robust diet, to treat his tuberculosis. Though Stanley quickly improved and was taken by the beauty of the landscape, he didn't care for his less-than-upscale accommodations. He decided to buy some land and, a few years later, built a luxury hotel to turn the town into a destination for his wealthy friends. By 1909, the Stanley Hotel had opened, and it was one of the first hotels in the country to offer full electricity. With the land still rugged at the time, Stanley—being co-founder of the famed Stanley Motor Carriage Company—also manufactured his own Mountain Wagons, steam-powered twelve-passenger vehicles made to transport guests through the steep winding road between the train station and his resort.

Eventually having eleven structures constructed on the property, including its very own music hall for concerts and shows, the hotel had become quite a sight to see. Its grand atmosphere, however, was soon tainted by tragedy. In 1911, a thunderstorm knocked out power and all guests were ushered into the lobby so the staff could light the rooms' backup gaslights. Unbeknownst to everyone, a gas leak existed in the hotel's Presidential Suite, room 217, and when a maid named Elizabeth Wilson entered the room with a candle to light the lantern, it resulted in a large explosion. Elizabeth fell through the room's floor and landed in the MacGregor Dining Room, breaking both ankles and incurring dozens of lacerations. The entire west wing of the hotel was destroyed in the explosion.

With Elizabeth in dire need of care and having no family to tend to her, the Stanleys took up the responsibility of helping her heal. Not only did they allow her to recuperate in the hotel but they also paid all her medical bills. At a time when workers' rights were practically nonexistent, this was an extraordinary gesture on the Stanleys' part, and it showed how much they cared for Elizabeth and their other workers. Elizabeth stayed employed at the hotel for another forty years, until her death in the 1950s. With the traumatic event she experienced in room 217 and her lifelong connection to the Stanley Hotel, it is said that she haunts that room to this day. Numerous guests claim that they've had their clothing folded or put away for them while they were out of the room. Furthermore, unmarried couples who stayed in the Presidential Suite assert that they've felt unnatural forces trying to keep them apart from each other in bed.

Of course, it was one of room 217's guests who turned the Stanley into one of the most famous haunted hotels of all time. In 1974, Stephen King, along with his wife and son, checked in at the end of the Stanley's open season, just as the hotel had begun shutting down for the winter (a yearly process that management continued until the early 1980s). The isolation and eerie emptiness of the 140-room hotel closing down for the cold winter months set off fireworks in King's brain. While sleeping in room 217, he woke from a nightmare so vivid that he sat up, lit a cigarette, and, before he could finish it, came up with the "Overlook Hotel" . . . as well as the entire plot to the classic novel The Shining.

King's 1977 bestseller became one of the scariest reads of all time, and resulted in Stanley Kubrick directing one of cinema's greatest horror films. After millions of books sold, two movie adaptations (the latter of which, a TV miniseries, was filmed entirely at the Stanley), a novel and movie sequel that returns to that terrifying hotel (Doctor Sleep), an opera (yes, seriously), and an integral part of Steven Spielberg's film adaptation of Ready Player One, the imaginary legend of the Overlook Hotel has become ingrained in popular culture and endures as the gold standard of ghost stories . . . all because of the true-life hotel and its otherworldly inhabitants that inspired the Master of Horror. And while the hotel might have inspired King, in return his work has made the hotel one of the most famous "haunted" locations in the world. People travel from all over in

Stanley Hotel entrance
JUDY LACHANCE

the hopes of having their own paranormal experience. The hotel even has a separate booking page for the "spirited" rooms like 217, as they're so popular and reserved months in advance. They also hold numerous horror film festivals like BruceFest, featuring The Evil Dead *franchise star Bruce Campbell, as well as séances, ghost hunts, and other events inspired by Stephen King's unforgettable story.*

• • •

Regardless of whether you're a horror movie fan, an avid traveler, a paranormal investigator, or even someone who hates all that stuff, if you know you're heading to the Stanley Hotel, a bit of creepy anticipation worms its way into your spine. When you ride up the long, curvy driveway and see the iconic white building with its shocking red roof, your heart skips a beat or two. After all, this is *the* place that inspired one of the greatest fictional ghost stories ever. Its reputation precedes itself.

Hell, even if you remove the pop culture connections, the Stanley would stand on its own as one of the grandest hotels in America (which seem to be a dying breed; hotels are no longer the focal point of a trip like they were in the early 1900s). With stunning mountains and wild elk roaming the grounds, this Colorado haven is truly a unique and magical place . . . one I would visit even if it didn't have a history of paranormal activity. In fact, I love the Stanley so much that I've been there more than half a dozen times and I can't wait to go back again. Being that it's a forty-hour drive for me, as I don't like to fly, that's saying a lot.

Entering the Stanley's lobby is like being transported back in time. The walls and floors drip with rich, dark wood. A vintage Stanley Steamer car (the vehicle that made Freelan Oscar Stanley rich) resides on full display.

Beautiful flowers, leather furniture, fireplaces, even a piano . . . it's

At the end of the main lobby is the entrance to the billiard room,
where I encountered many paranormal cold spots.
JUDY LACHANCE

easy to feel like you're in another era. You can almost picture people
walking around dressed in big, poofy dress skirts or donning top hats.
Sitting in the lobby and just looking around, you can't help but also
wonder about the thousands of stories this hotel has seen over the years.

Stephen King was right on the money when he wrote in *The Shining*:
"Any big hotels have got scandals. Just like every big hotel has got a
ghost." That isn't exclusive to the Stanley; a lot does happen in hotels,
ranging from happy vacations and business deals to affairs, criminal
transactions, scandals, and more suicides and deaths than one might
think. Hundreds of guests a night, 365 days a year, over a hundred
years in operation . . . we're talking literally millions of guests and an
uncountable number of triumphs, love stories, and tragedies. The next
time you're sitting in a hotel room, think about the innumerable people

who have stayed in that very same space. What could have happened there? One armchair Reddit mathematician estimates that at least one person has died in over 13 percent of all hotel rooms worldwide (thinking about it now, it seems oddly fitting that their calculations landed on that unlucky number). Chances are, you may have unknowingly stayed in one or several rooms right where someone has passed.

My rambling philosophy about hotels notwithstanding, it's safe to assume that the Stanley certainly has more than its share of stories. And where better to start than the famed room 217? (Fellow film buffs may remember that Kubrick changed the room number to 237 in the movie. Stanley Hotel management requested that a fictional room number be depicted, fearing guests would not want to stay in room 217.) The room is iconic; the way it inhabits the dead end of a hallway makes the best Hollywood production designers jealous that they didn't dream it up.

Many people have claimed to see and capture photographic evidence of an apparition on this staircase in the main lobby.
PHOTO COURTESY OF MICHAEL ALOISI

Inside, a massive, richly colored four-poster bed sits front and center as a welcoming beacon of rest. Then there's the bathroom, where the clawfoot tub from that terrifying scene in *The Shining* lies waiting for a brave soul to take a bath; it's a thing of pure terror and beauty.

It can be difficult to separate the book's and movie's fictional moments from the true stories surrounding room 217. It's almost impossible to not think of Stephen King writing up his idea for *The Shining* at the desk in that suite (which, rather fittingly, has since been renamed after him), or of a naked, rotting, laughing woman getting out of the bathtub. However, it's essential that, as investigators, the team members and I focus only on the recorded history, people's real claims, and what we experienced ourselves. Letting stories and hearsay seep into your work can be a downfall; it's an easy trap to fall into for a new investigator. Overcoming this obstacle is especially hard to do at a place like the Stanley, because the fiction is so intertwined with the truth. Plus, it doesn't help that the hotel also has a channel that plays the movie on a twenty-four-hour loop.

Most of the accounts surrounding room 217 focus on employee Elizabeth Wilson. Guests constantly claim that when they returned to their room their clothing would be folded or put away. Though most of the claims are sweet and relate to a helpful maid, actor Jim Carrey once stayed in the room and had a terrifying experience. Upon arriving to film scenes for *Dumb and Dumber* (for that movie, the Stanley was transformed into "the Danbury"), Carrey checked into the Presidential Suite, room 217 . . . only to run out of it an hour later. Rumor has it that whatever he saw scared him so much, he refused to stay in the Stanley and checked into another hotel in town for the rest of the production. Carrey has been asked about what happened numerous times, though to this date he has never gone on record about what he encountered. With the suite having also given Stephen King his notorious nightmare (in which a fire hose chased his then-young son Joe throughout the hotel corridors) and countless others' claims, it is arguably the most notorious hotel room in the world.

But *is* it Elizabeth Wilson who's causing all that activity in the room? The historical evidence and talk certainly suggest that, but I went through the hotel archives and found some conflicting information. A maid named Elizabeth did work at the Stanley, and there was an explosion around 1911. Yet, according to the archives, five different newspapers told five different stories. One reported that the maid's last name was Lambert, while another stated it was Wilson. Some detailed that she had died, others described that she had been injured, and some papers didn't even mention her at all. For every newspaper that wrote about a fire, another said it was just an explosion. These are great examples as to how historical accounts don't always agree.

There was one certainty I could take away from this, however: Not

Inside the infamous room 217
PHOTO COURTESY OF MICHAEL ALOISI

knowing the full history wasn't going to harm the TAPS team's investigation, so long as we kept our questions open-ended and not overly specific. A lot of the time this is the case, as we simply can't find any well-documented history. Before computer backups, history was recorded on paper, which can burn, rot, suffer water damage, or just become lost. I can't tell you how many times we've gone somewhere to conduct research only to be told that the town or location had no historical files because they'd gone missing or were destroyed.

Even when there isn't any written history, there's almost always oral history, stories that have been verbally passed down through generations. If you ever played Telephone in school, you know how distorted information becomes after it leaves the original source, then passes from person to person before it reaches the final recipient. The information is usually so twisted from the original that it's rather comical. Now, apply that to *real* history; imagine what happens over decades, or even centuries, after stories are passed down from generation to generation.

In cases where we don't have a hundred percent of the facts, we're careful not to be too specific when we call out to spirits. If you're constantly attempting to communicate with someone or something that doesn't exist . . . well, you might not see any activity. In this instance, however, we knew that there was *an* Elizabeth working at the Stanley Hotel when there was an explosion, so we could definitely call out that name and ask about the incident.

Now, I'd like to say that I met Elizabeth Wilson, or that I encountered or experienced something else intense and powerful while trying to make contact during one of my several stays in room 217. Sadly, though, I never met her, and I haven't experienced a single event while in that room. Don't get me wrong—being in a place that inspired a classic book as well as an iconic movie, not to mention scared the hell out of one of Hollywood's funniest human beings into never staying there, is pretty exciting. Yet, no matter what I tried, I got nothing. I even left my suitcase unattended and made a pile of messy clothing in the room, hoping that the bag might get moved into the closet or that the clothes would be folded and put away. However, nothing happened . . . and I was left with a self-made mess to clean up on top of my disappointment.

Sometimes it's the luck of the draw; other times, I can't help but wonder if a spirit is conscious enough to pull back when they know they're trying to be coaxed out of hiding. And if you think about it, cleaning staff in the 1910s were trained to be almost invisible, to do their job without disturbing anyone or getting in the way. Maybe Elizabeth Wilson does exactly that—consciously avoids people and only does her job when no one is looking.

• • •

When we first investigated the Stanley we stayed for three full weeks, so our probe never really stopped; we were on location twenty-four seven. Each of the team members took a room with supposed activity in the hopes of having paranormal experiences. It sure worked out well for some of us—Jason had room 401 and encountered so much activity that he contemplated sleeping in the hall. With Jay being one of the most seasoned investigators in the world, his reaction screamed volumes to me. He explained that he'd heard banging coming from his closet so often that it sounded like a party. The same closet door also opened on its own, and when he went to check it out, the water glass on the end table cracked in half and shattered.

During the filming of *Ghost Hunters Academy*, the crew and I stayed in a different building on the property called the Residence, and I had a rude awakening of my own; for no apparent reason, my bed would shake, strongly. At first, I wondered if it was some supernatural force trying to send me a message, but then I took a few moments to catch my breath, sit still, and just listen closely to my immediate surroundings. I soon realized that every time the bed shook, the entire room seemed to move and there was a guttural noise outside. Looking out the window, I saw a sight that left me awestruck. There was a giant elk down below ramming his antlers into the side of the building. He must have been molting and trying to knock them off. Opening my window, I watched with pure amazement as the elk tried in vain for a solid ten minutes before moving on to batter himself against a tree a few yards away. It was wonderful watching nature at work in the moonlight. But what was most important was that I got out of bed to see the cause of the shaking. If I hadn't, I would have thought I was experiencing something radical and terrifying. If anyone stayed in bed in that instance, I could certainly understand how they might think the cause was paranormal in nature.

Overall, the fourth floor seemed to be where the team experienced the most activity, and it's not surprising if you know about the hotel's history. In the early 1900s, wealthy people would stay at the Stanley for extended visits, and the fourth floor was typically reserved for children (to keep them out of the way) and their nannies. Knowing that surely lends credence to the hundreds of claims made of hearing children's laughter and the constant sound of someone running up and down the hallways despite them being completely empty. During a few of my trips to the hotel, Tango and I, along with some friends and fellow investigators, heard similar noises. We also heard doors opening and closing along with the muffled sounds of laughter, as if children were playing a game. Honestly, if I hadn't already known about all the stories of the place being haunted, I'd have been inclined to think that there were just some noisy kids playing outside their room.

A friend of mine, horror legend Kane Hodder, also stayed at the Stanley a while back while he was on tour promoting his biography. When I asked him how he enjoyed his visit, he said it was great, except "the damn kids running around the halls all day drove me nuts." I immediately asked Kane what floor he stayed on, and when he replied that it was the fourth I smiled. When he said it was room 401, I had to hold back a laugh. Sure, there *could* have been kids there, but the Stanley isn't the type of resort where families have their children set loose, especially in the middle of a school week, when he was there. I asked Kane if he ever *saw* the kids; he thought for a moment and said he hadn't. Hearing this from a friend I trusted added to all the other claims I have heard, which he had no clue about. He was just complaining about the noise.

Room 401, where Jason and Kane had each stayed, used to be the nannies' "retreat" room, where they'd relax after a long day of minding rich people's children. Though the kids can be heard all over that floor, a manager told me that guests of room 401 have made the most calls to the front desk with noise complaints concerning the hallway. I would assume back then a nanny sitting or resting would still hear children playing outside the room. This brought up an interesting question: Did we hear the spirits of children, or were they sounds that were imprinted on the location? The chances that a child died in the hotel without it being documented are incredibly low, so why then would we hear them?

One theory can best be explained as *location bonding*. If someone has a very strong connection to a location, perhaps a place where they experienced the happiest memories of their life, their spirit might return

The notorious haunted fourth-floor hallway of the Stanley Hotel
PHOTO COURTESY OF MICHAEL ALOISI

or stay there when they die. Wouldn't you want to rest in a place you love? Could that be why there are loud children's sounds throughout the Stanley Hotel's fourth floor? Perhaps . . . or maybe not. But we *do* know that the sounds are there, and that they are rather consistent.

The floor has another active room—407—where supposedly the only angry spirit of the hotel resides. As the story goes, Lord Dunraven owned the land before Freelan Stanley purchased it and built his hotel. A narcissistic, womanizing criminal who owned a brothel in town, Dunraven was known for often visiting the nannies' quarters and trying to persuade the women into working at his shady establishment. It isn't clear why his spirit would be linked to room 407, but the claims that he favors that space are strong and persistent. Numerous reports describe a man appearing in a window to this room during times when no guests were registered. Guests staying in 407 say they've seen a man who dashes into the closet and vanishes as they walk in the front door. Other guests have stated that they'd awaken during the night to see the figure of a man standing in the corner of the room, only to disappear when they turned on the lights. And if that isn't creepy enough, there are also claims that the lights in 407 sometimes inexplicably flicker, or that items are moved or even violently thrown around the room.

When I hear or read tales such as these, I go back to thinking about the intent and the "why." In this instance, why would an apparition walk into a closet or stand in a corner of a room? If the room underwent a renovation and now had a functional space or hallway in place of the original closet, it might make sense for a residual ghost to try to walk into it. Otherwise, the "why" starts getting fuzzy. A residual haunting would do what it did in life; it would simply repeat actions, so these claims don't necessarily make sense. Mind you, I'm not saying the accounts aren't true—I'm just questioning the actions of what's happening. If I saw a ball rolling uphill, it wouldn't make sense, so I'd want to figure out why and how it was doing that.

As for the lights flickering . . . sorry, but I almost always ignore those claims. Something acting in a way that it shouldn't can be scary, but electrical issues are easily explained 99 percent of the time. A loose wire or one that was chewed on by mice can make your lights act so off-kilter it would make any horror movie director proud. The problem can be easily uncovered by just checking the connections, though pinpointing a problem wire inside the walls or the ceiling can be more challenging. Either way, I always disregard lighting issues unless they're part of a sudden, direct response to questions that are being asked.

Obviously, I can't ignore people's accounts of seeing objects being thrown about. Is that something Lord Dunraven would have done during his life? Throwing things strongly implies anger issues, violence, and an intent to cause harm. Being that he tried to coerce women into becoming prostitutes, Dunraven could have been threatening and violent . . . and he may well still be in the afterlife.

The story of a spooky man haunting a room is terrifying and exciting, but like I said earlier, oral history can be a game of Telephone. The story about Lord Dunraven trying to coax the hotel's nannies into working in his brothel just doesn't make sense, considering he was allegedly doing so *after* he sold the land to Freelan Stanley. According to further research we conducted, Lord Dunraven was run out of Estes Park for trying to swindle the locals, long before the Stanley Hotel was built. In fact, some records show that he left Colorado in the 1880s, more than a decade before construction even began on the hotel. If those records are accurate, he would never have been able to frequent the fourth floor, let alone that one room. I suppose it's still possible that he could be attached to the land, but how and why would he be in one particular room four stories *above* the land, especially when there's also no record of him ever staying at the hotel?

This all goes back to one of the recurring themes in this book: research. There are dozens of websites that tell the tale of Lord Dunraven. Even the Stanley Hotel staff talk openly about him during tours. When a story is eerie, it gets perpetuated and eventually becomes accepted fact. A good story is one thing, but if you're trying to find real evidence, the truth is much more important. When you're told it's Lord Dunraven in room 407, you'll attribute anything you see or hear to him. The reality is, if there's a ghost in that room, it's probably someone else who spent time at the hotel.

Maybe the misidentification is part of the anger the spirit in 407 supposedly has. Imagine trying to reach out from the other side only to be called a different name and be told repeatedly that you were mean and evil in life. After a few decades I can see how that might anger a ghost and make them try harder to get recognized for who they truly are. Maybe the unknown apparition goes to the closet because he hanged himself or was locked in there; we simply just don't know. But if you take away the tale of Lord Dunraven, the "why" of the activity is much more open, as we aren't trying to push the stories told to us upon the location. If someone is trying to reach out to us, don't we deserve to do our best to see who they were, rather than just assume who they were?

All of that being said, unfortunately I've never experienced anything myself throughout my visits to room 407. And yet, as a paranormal investigator, I remain hopeful. It's also important to remind myself that I'm not sure what their interpretation of time and space is. Maybe what is a month to us here on earth is only a moment to them, or maybe it is the opposite. Nobody knows.

• • •

Estes Park sits at a whopping 7,522-foot elevation. Though it's not even the highest level in Colorado, it's significantly higher than those in most states, by far. High altitudes have thinner atmospheres; in the winter, when the air is dry, it becomes an insulator, allowing excess static charge to stick to you until it can move. This means that in the winter the static electricity at the Stanley Hotel is insane. When TAPS was there, I remember it being so strong that if we simply walked down a carpeted hallway and then touched a door handle we could actually *see* the electricity, this tiny blue lightning bolt, jump from the handle to our hand. We made bets about who could generate the biggest static charge—we would drag our feet up and down the halls to build it up, then touch a door handle and get this massive *pop*. It was so crazy, and of course Jay, with the least amount of hair for interference, got the largest of bolts, which actually came down from a pipe in the ceiling . . . so naturally he won.

An interesting thing about static is that humans have subconsciously used it as a tool for as long as we've been around. Everything has a layer of static on it—living things, inanimate objects, walls, all of it. As we move through the environment, our static layer interacts with all the atoms in Earth's magnetic field, even if we aren't aware of it. The static layer surrounding us is in constant fluctuation, which subconsciously transmits information to our consciousness, which could help it make decisions.

In science, this is known as "primal gaze detection." It's a throwback to when our ancestors were out trying to kill animals for food or when they had to hide from danger. Their subconscious ability would help them detect any predators sneaking up behind them. It's a genetic biological evolutionary trait that we all still have and use to this day. If you've ever "felt" that someone was in a room before you saw them, the movement of static is subconsciously telling you that someone is there. This information can be pretty handy when it comes to investigating the paranormal—if you're truly alone in a room and detect a presence, it could be that the static was disturbed in some manner. With the extreme dryness in Colorado, any activity that's present could possibly be enhanced by these static charges.

Though not directly related to static, the dryness in the environment there also causes a lot of temperature changes. It was cold outside most of the times I've investigated, but the hotel itself was well heated. However, like any old establishment, there are a lot of drafts and non-insulated windows that cause unwanted breezes. It's easy to pinpoint whether something is a cold spot or just a breeze. While investigating, we experienced a lot of temperature changes, but the Stanley's billiard room, during a live Halloween special we filmed at the hotel, had a cold spot that was intense. It was right above me and I could only feel it when I reached up. It was so well defined that I could literally put my hand halfway in and feel the difference in temperature; my hand would be cold, while my arm was warm. What was fascinating was that it felt like I put my hand into a statically charged freezer, almost like I was inserting my arm into a substance. It was unbelievable and to this day one of the most intense cold spots I had ever experienced. I'd feel a few more around the hotel, but nothing was as strong as that one. It was inexplicable and utterly thrilling for someone in my line of work.

• • •

Even though I've investigated the Stanley Hotel three times on television and several times without camera crews, I still feel like there's so much more I can experience there, with all of its hidden surprises waiting to be uncovered. Not only does the Stanley have one of the most legendary fictional ghost stories tied to it, but it's also a genuine American treasure. Filled with captivating history and ongoing paranormal activity, it is one of my favorite places in the world.

CHASED BY SPIRITS

TRANS-ALLEGHENY LUNATIC ASYLUM
—
WESTON, WV

OPENED IN 1864

During its 130 years in operation, the Trans-Allegheny Lunatic Asylum
(later renamed the West Virginia Hospital for the Insane, then the Weston
State Hospital for its last eighty years of service) housed thousands of
"insane" patients. Of course, back then the term was a more hurtful label
that included the mentally challenged and mentally ill, with "deviants"
like drug addicts, alcoholics, and criminals. Intended to accommodate up
to 250 patients when it first opened in 1864, the hospital rapidly became
overpopulated—by the 1950s, more than 2,400 resided in Trans-Allegheny,
the conditions of which had also greatly deteriorated by that point.

    In an effort to reduce the severe overcrowding that plagued Trans-
Allegheny and other asylums, state officials instituted the West Virginia
Lobotomy Project. This arcane and controversial procedure involved
doctors either cutting holes into a patient's skull or hammering an ice pick
through an eye and severing connections to the brain's prefrontal cortex.
In theory, the procedures were supposed to cure patients so they would
no longer need to be housed. In truth, "Operation Ice Pick" (as it was

coined in newspapers) did nothing but torture and permanently damage thousands of patients, and ensure that many of them could never return to or function in society.

Dr. Walter Freeman II was the founding father of the lobotomy practice, using Trans-Allegheny as his testing grounds. Instead of researching cases to see who would be a good fit, he would simply ask a nurse to bring him "a patient"; he would then perform the gruesome surgery under the context of "curing" them. In one particular week, he hit a record of 228 lobotomies in Trans-Allegheny. If that weren't horrific enough, Dr. Freeman was a neurologist, with no surgical experience. While he used the facility as his testing grounds, Freeman eventually performed over four thousand lobotomies across twenty-three states.

Like most mental hospitals of the time, Trans-Allegheny encompassed massive amounts of land in Weston—numerous buildings sat on more than twenty-six acres—and was portrayed to the public as a self-sufficient refuge for its "deranged" inhabitants. Instead, it was a hellhole that existed solely to lock away the people society didn't know how or want to deal with. An alcoholic or someone with a learning disability might have been thrown in there for their entire life, forced to work and live in unsanitary quarters filled well past capacity. In 1949, a series of reports published by the Charleston Gazette greatly detailed Trans-Allegheny's deplorable conditions, citing insufficient sanitation, not enough furniture, inadequate heating, and patients being forced to sleep on cold, dirty floors for months at a time.

The walls at Trans-Allegheny hold countless terrifying, sad, dark, and bizarre tales that can be hard to stomach. In one particularly grisly account, two patients wrapped a bedsheet around a mute person's neck, then threw the sheet over a bedpost and pulled him up and down while taking turns beating him. When their victim didn't die, the duo placed his head under a metal bedframe, then jumped on the frame repeatedly until one of its legs crushed the man's skull. The staff, who at times were outnumbered 248 to 1, were also consistent victims of violence. One poor nurse went missing, only to be found two months later deceased and rotting in an unused stairwell. Then there was a patient who walked up to his roommate one evening and forced both of his thumbs into the man's eyes, popping them like tiny water balloons. The patient then washed his hands and went to dinner as if nothing had happened. When guards found the eyeless roommate on the floor, they approached his attacker, who was heartily eating his meal, and demanded to know what he had done. He just smiled and replied, "Have you tried the meatloaf tonight? It's rather good."

Even though the adverse living conditions at Trans-Allegheny had become a matter of public record, incredibly the hospital remained open until 1994, and it closed only because of the sweeping changes that had been made to patient treatment by that time. No one knows the exact number of patients who lived out their lives within its walls, though it's often said that so many of these tortured souls have never left.

• • •

One would think that if you've been to one abandoned insane asylum, you've been to them all . . . in other words, and especially for my line of work, that they would lose their morbid and scary appeal. But I'll never get enough of them. I've been to dozens of asylums, institutes, hospitals, and the like—some of them multiple times—and it's the thrill of pulling up and seeing massive, sprawling buildings, Gothic architecture, and spooky, crumbling facades. Being a die-hard horror fan helps; I love everything that most folks consider creepy. Yet even if I weren't, there's just something beautiful about the stillness of a long-forgotten building and the stories it holds.

What saddens me, though, is that these buildings are almost *completely* forgotten, and they're disappearing rather quickly to make room for more megastores, condominiums, and luxury homes. If it wasn't for paranormal enthusiasts' love and passion, the few that remain would likely be gone as well. Many of these structures have endured thanks to the efforts of paranormal organizations that banded together and contributed money to keep the buildings from the wrecking ball. Many others continue to survive by hosting tours and haunted house events. Saving historic buildings is a wonderful by-product of our field.

Trans-Allegheny is a famous Kirkbride-style building that still stands, thankfully. In the 1800s, Thomas Story Kirkbride designed a specific architecture that he believed would best suit the mental health of patients

Front entrance of Trans-Allegheny Lunatic Asylum
JASON NELSON

housed within insane asylums. His design utilized a "batwing" floor plan formation, where there was a center hub with winglike offshoots, and the buildings focused on natural lighting and airflow. His theory, along with that of a lot of doctors at the time, was that fresh, open air and light would help calm or even heal unruly patients. These structures were so popular that over seventy institutes around the country used the "Kirkbride Plan," including the Danvers State Hospital, which once resided outside Boston. (A quick aside: Danvers is believed to be the inspiration for the Arkham Sanitarium in H. P. Lovecraft's classic short story "The Thing on the Doorstep." In turn, that story's asylum is believed to be the inspiration for Arkham Asylum, which resides in the Batman universe, which is known worldwide. When I found this out, I couldn't help but picture a rogues' gallery of villains as I walked around Trans's crumbling halls. In a way, Kirkbride and his asylums live on within every Batman comic, movie, cartoon, and video game.)

A patient hallway where sightings of apparitions have been reported
JASON NELSON

Around thirty of these Kirkbride-style structures still stand today, with only about a dozen deemed to be in good condition; the rest are at risk of being demolished or falling apart on their own. As someone who loves history and architecture, I get excited every time I get to visit one of these buildings, because I know there might be a day when they no longer exist.

• • •

I get chills every time I drive up the path and see the two-hundred-foot white clock tower at the center of Trans-Allegheny. The pale, decaying behemoth stands there, its hands still moving to show us the passage of time, while all the buildings below remain frozen in the past. When you look down from the tower, you really appreciate the entire structure's sheer immensity. The building stretches out like a shed husk of snakeskin, dried, cracking, and almost never-ending at over thirteen hundred feet long. Almost a thousand dark windows glare back at you when you try to take it all in. I also find it staggering that this monstrous edifice was made entirely out of hand-cut sandstone. Literally, every inch of the building was carved by hand, with chisels. It's the largest hand-cut structure in all of North America. Just the very sight of Trans-Allegheny is overwhelming . . . and I love it.

Though we don't usually have time to do as much research as I'd like for our investigations (beyond the essentials), I made time to read a bunch of old patients' records after TAPS was called in to investigate Trans-Allegheny. With my love for the macabre and the past, these files were fascinating to read . . . from the wording and the way they were written to the archaic techniques they explained, these documents blew my mind. Even though a guide had told us about the eye-gouging

The last time I visited the Trans-Allegheny Lunatic Asylum, 2016

incident beforehand, when I read the document I had to put down the paper and take a moment to remind myself that these stories were *real*, not fabricated tales from my favorite genre movies.

Some of the hardest files to read focused on the lobotomies. As someone who's suffered one too many nasal swabs that went a bit too far up my nose, I can't begin to fathom the horror of someone using a friggin' *ice pick* up there or in my eye socket. And so many of these patients were *conscious* through all of it.

Back then, the lobotomy was thought to be some cutting-edge procedure that could cure patients of pretty much any mental illness— depression, anger issues, alcoholism . . . even someone who just rebelled

Medical ward
JASON NELSON

against society could allegedly be "fixed" by poking holes into their brain. Of course, all of this was done without *any* solid science behind it or results to prove it worked. In the early fifties, during a single week at Trans-Allegheny, 228 lobotomies were performed—more than 32 a day. . . .

If you've ever seen *One Flew Over the Cuckoo's Nest*, you pretty much know that the end result of a lobotomy wasn't a successful one. Very real outcomes showed that some patients died, some lapsed into a persistive vegetative state, and most developed severe personality disorders that were worse than their original conditions. One doctor likened it to making patients almost childlike, to the point where some would have to relearn basic tasks and functions, like speaking or going to the bathroom by themselves. Only a handful of "success stories" were ever documented, and who knows if those were completely true or accurate.

It's beyond terrifying to think that science embraced lobotomies throughout the 1940s and 1950s. In the United States alone, over forty thousand of them were performed in the hopes of curing every perceived type of mental illness. Hell, despite not even having any proof that they worked, the procedure was performed all the way up until the 1970s . . . and some countries did so up until the 1980s. When I was a kid, people were *still* having holes drilled into their brain, with "experts" working under some deranged notion that doing this would magically cure their patients. *That* is insanity, my friends. That is *real* horror.

While reading the files, I also became enamored with checking out Trans-Allegheny's Forensics Building, the most notorious and intimidating structure on the grounds. Created and used to house the "criminally insane" (yes, a real-life term once used that has since become another Batman comics reference), this large, ominous edifice looks like it might have more in common with Chernobyl's grounds than those of an asylum. It was added onto Trans-Allegheny in the 1950s, and it completely lacks any architectural beauty. Sporting sharp lines, boxy sections, and window bars, the Forensics Building feels quite out of place among the grounds' other hand-sculpted structures.

The building's insides aren't any better. Institutionalized tile covers all surfaces. Large, open rooms, dripping in white, scream "mental hospital" so loudly that it almost makes you desperate to throw something through a window and escape. Old, delicate curtains hang in front of welded wrought-iron bars, as if designers thought that hanging patterned fabric might add a "homey" touch to the place. In the corners of these large rooms sit cages that the more violent patients were forced into, to "help" these individuals feel included with the daily masses. When I saw the cages in these rooms . . . the whole thing felt surreal to me. If you were dropped into this building and told nothing beforehand, it wouldn't take more than a few glances to figure out that you were inside a place built for the criminally insane.

When we first entered the Forensics Building, Tango and I both wore breathing masks out of a concern that asbestos might still be within the walls. It has become a more common practice for us to wear masks in these older buildings, but that first time, having something on my nose and mouth while trying to focus in the dark was pretty distracting. As the two of us walked around, our shoes crunching anywhere we stepped on the debris-covered floor, both of our heads suddenly snapped to the left as we heard the incredibly loud and clear sounds of a woman's laughter.

Our mouths dropped in unison, and our masks skewed as we nodded in agreement that both of us had heard the same thing. The building had contained mainly men, though records showed that a few women had also been placed there over the years, as well as possibly a few female employees (most of Trans-Allegheny's buildings were separated by gender). Being that the vast majority of patients weren't female, the laughter Tango and I heard was definitely intriguing, as it narrowed down who it could have been. Even more astounding was its volume and clarity. Usually, when investigators hear a disembodied voice, it's mumbled and sounds far in the distance; half the time you're left guessing or debating over what you actually heard. This was unquestionably a laugh—no need for guesswork or a debate.

Tango and I tried encouraging the laughing voice to repeat itself. When we couldn't get it to engage with us, we set out to see if we could disprove or re-create the sound. I can't stress how important disproving is to the craft. There have been so many occasions when I've done an open investigation where we invited the public to check out a location with us and the second there was a sound of any magnitude, people jumped and immediately attributed it to the spirit world without a second thought that it could have been created by something else. I'd say that with a bit of work, 80 to 90 percent of the time you can find a logical explanation for a sound. It's the *10 to 20 percent* that we're truly after. If we just accept every sound or movement as being paranormal in origin, we're doing a great disservice to our field and clients. We need to find that small percentage and document it as best we can.

With all of this in mind, Tango and I took turns trying to re-create the sound in other rooms and outside. We straight-out laughed, yelled, and made tons of noise; nothing even came close to what we had heard. There was no longer any question that the laughter came from the room we'd been in. With no female TAPS members in the same building or anyone nearby on the outside, we were convinced that the sound was paranormal in origin.

Hearing a true disembodied voice is so bizarre. It's an extraordinary and rare occurrence that sends a chill of excitement down my spine. The thought that something outside of our living world is right next to you in the same room, and trying to communicate with you or repeat actions it did in its past, opens a deep and phenomenal thought process. Does it completely mean that an area is haunted? While it is unreal evidence of *something*, I wouldn't say that a place is haunted based on a voice. It could be the result of other things, like energy, a playback of something stuck on a loop, or even heightened EMFs. There's strong evidence that when you're in a raised EMF you can experience a heightening of synapses firing in your brain. Dr. William G. Roll, the man who coined the term *psychokinesis*, once showed me how magnetic fields can truly manipulate our thought processes. Could hearing that laugh have done something similar to Tango and me? Would it have caused both of us to hear the same sounds? Probably not, and we'll likely never learn what it really was. Nevertheless, any time I hear something that clear and loud, I treasure the experience.

When Tango went outside and yelled, laughed, and made other noises so I could listen to what they sounded like from the inside, I distinctly heard footsteps come up to me, pause, then quickly move away. They were so clear I thought that someone from the team was playing a trick on me or coming to check on us. When Tango returned and as soon I started telling him about the footsteps, he suddenly heard them too. And they kept happening—*step, step, step*—right by us, then away from us again. A few times it sounded like someone was running fast, parallel to our location and toward one of the building entrances. In a way, it felt almost like a childish game where people kept approaching us, one after another, to see who we were, then walking away. As it kept happening, at some point we decided to follow the sounds along to wherever they were headed.

Chasing disembodied footsteps was quite thrilling. Tango and I pursued them throughout the building, all the way down into a closed-off tunnel, where they finally stopped. There was no one around. Nothing. It was a career highlight for two paranormal investigators, an experience that, to this day, neither of us can really explain or disprove.

• • •

One of Trans-Allegheny's best-known resident ghosts is a child named Lily. The facts behind the haunting of Lily are unclear, but many of the stories say that she was born to a patient, lived in Trans-Allegheny, then died there from pneumonia at age nine. This poor child spent her short existence within this asylum's walls, without ever leaving the grounds. If that story is anywhere close to true, then it's heartbreaking on levels that I can't bear to even think about. However, there are zero facts and a lot of holes to this local legend—the main one being that a child wouldn't have been allowed to stay in the facility and would have been moved to an orphanage. Granted, there *is* a small chance that a pregnant woman could have been committed, or that a patient got pregnant on the grounds, but there are no records we uncovered to show that. Despite the unclear reasonings, there are numerous claims surrounding this child spirit . . . so many that frequent visitors and the owners dedicated an entire room on the fourth floor in honor of Lily.

In this barren, derelict area with fading green walls and white chipped girders, the floor and windowsills are filled with children's toys left by past investigators who attempted to interact with Lily's spirit. When you enter an empty room in an abandoned insane asylum that has bars on the windows and you see dusty dolls, half-inflated balls, rubber duckies, playing cards, and jacks on the floor, you half expect something out of the horror movies I love to pop out and say hello. This space would be much more in line with a themed haunted house than an old hospital. Alas, this is part of the job, so we gleefully investigated it like any other room.

The claims I had previously heard about Lily ranged from standard (toys being moved, footsteps, and laughing—shades of our earlier experiences there) to the extreme. Some sources insisted that they played with the ghost, rolling a ball back and forth with her for over forty minutes, or that they watched her open and eat a box of Cracker Jacks. I wish I could experience something like that, but for me, Slimer from *Ghostbusters* is the *only* spirit I have ever seen eating food. Ball rolling, on the other hand, I could see happening. However, most of the time I will not think a ball moving is paranormal related, as there are so many other factors involved. If it moved on demand or in a way that's impossible on its own, that is different. In a paranormal documentary I co-directed called *The House in Between*, we captured footage of a baseball that had been completely motionless suddenly moving on its own. And I don't mean an inch or two; it actually rolled forward and down a flight of stairs. This wouldn't be that fascinating, but it went from being perfectly still on a carpet (which lessens its chance of moving) to being propelled forward over a wooden lip. We tried to re-create the scenario, but when we couldn't we brought in scientists and structural engineers to examine what happened. Even then, we couldn't get any concrete answers. Therefore, I can easily see how a spirit could propel a ball forward to get it rolling, though I'm not sure they could do so for an extended amount of time (and if it happened for more than thirty seconds, let alone forty minutes, why the heck didn't anyone film it?!).

Anyway, I was a bit excited and eager to go into Lily's creepy playroom. It was on the smaller side, so Tango and I took turns going in so we wouldn't overwhelm any spirits. I went in first and instantly loved the spooky atmosphere that the room gave off. Investigating a child spirit can always be a bit tricky—how do you talk to them? Will they trust you? What if they're shy like a lot of children are? Are they even intelligent beings or just a residual haunting? I decided to speak to the ghost as if it were really a child. I offered toys and asked questions. I played with the items already in there myself. I even tried to engage in a round of hide-and-seek, wondering if that might encourage the spirit to play along. Unfortunately, at the end of the day, neither Tango nor I had any experiences whatsoever in that room.

That doesn't mean I thought there was no paranormal activity inside the room; I'm only saying that *I* didn't experience anything myself. Plus, if you think about it, little girls tend to be more comfortable with women. If Lily was alive in the early 1900s, then a man covered in colorful, off-putting tattoos might look rather intimidating, regardless of whether he was hiding in the corner of the room like some goofy version of *The Blair Witch Project*.

● ● ●

The evening after I tried playing hide-and-seek with a spirit, a surreal incident with fans made me realize that my life had changed. By this point, *Ghost Hunters* had been on television for a few years and it was a big hit. I was getting used to being recognized in public and getting my picture taken with fans here and there. It was weird, but I met a lot of great people that way. However, during my first time at Trans-Allegheny, the reality of being on television became abruptly apparent.

When we film an episode for the show, we typically try to keep everything low-key and not make any posts or announcements that we're in a town or at a location; after all, we want to focus on the investigation. Unfortunately, someone told the locals that we were at Trans-Allegheny and the word spread like wildfire. By the second night of our investigation, we had hundreds of people outside the gates taking pictures, yelling at us for autographs, and just trying to catch a glimpse of us. Part of me really couldn't understand what was happening. At first, I thought the hordes at the gate were a protest of some sort, or possibly the start of a zombie apocalypse. When I found out they were there for *us*, though, my mind had a hard time comprehending it, especially when the fans stayed day and night.

The day after trying to contact Lily, Tango and I went to eat at a Chinese restaurant, thinking we would have a nice meal alone without the crew. Within ten minutes, there were over forty people in the small space, and *none* of them were there for the food. There was even a line out the door and people looking in the windows trying to take pictures of us. We quickly finished our meal and paid as dozens of eyes watched us. We did our best to be polite and just sneak out, when a local news van pulled up and a young female reporter jumped out for an impromptu interview. Before I knew it, I had a microphone in my face—and still had rice stuck on my cheek—as well as dozens of hands coming at me with cameras and pens. I instantly thought I was in a movie where a big trial had just ended, with me as the newly freed man coming down the courthouse steps.

We were there so long answering questions, getting our photos taken, and signing autographs that one of our producers actually showed up looking for us and pulled us away from the crowd. When we finally made it to our car and drove off, Tango and I were silent for some time, not really knowing what the hell to make of the incident. I don't know what Tango was thinking, but in my head I couldn't believe that I used to keep my passion between me and fellow investigators. Now I was being swarmed by strangers for having that same passion. Life can be strange at times.

...

Though we always take our work seriously, when you're in a location alone for hours, sometimes night after night, you do have to have a little fun . . . and Tango and I are notorious for causing trouble with each other. At one point, after a long stretch of nothing happening, we went looking around an old room. I took a peek in a pile of old equipment and found a bedpan. Old items like that are common in buildings like this, as a lot of them just were shut down with everything left exactly how it was. However, what I found inside the bedpan wasn't ordinary—it was a petrified pile of feces.

Now, Tango and I constantly make bets. Holding this bedpan in my hand, I knew a wager would have to be made. I offered him fifty bucks to take a deep whiff of the crusty pile. Always up for a spontaneous wager, he instantly said, "You're on," and walked over to the pan I was holding. As he began leaning over to take a deep sniff, I thrust the mummified poop toward my best friend's face. Afterward, I felt a bit bad about it, but Tango laughed his ass off, plus I gave him the fifty bucks. Besides, I knew he would get me back sooner or later, and probably with something much worse.

• • •

Experiences truly rack up at Trans-Allegheny—beyond what I've revealed in these pages, I've had dozens of other occurrences there, so I always know I'm in for a memorable and thrilling time whenever I see that clock tower in the distance. I've gone to Trans-Allegheny so often over the years, in fact, that I almost feel like I've become a part of the local Weston community. Every time I show up, one of the workers on the grounds bakes us so many goodies it's hard for me to not gorge myself. Then there are the locals I got to know so well that we go out to eat and drink whenever I visit. Tango and I have had a blast taking quad bikes out in the woods nearby (though he and I once almost had heart attacks after his then-girlfriend flipped her vehicle over and went down the side of a hill). I've visited so many places in town that I feel like I know them all. One time I didn't make it back to my hotel until the sun was coming up and the front desk manager was brewing coffee.

My point is, I've had some fun, crazy, embarrassing, and heart-warming times in that town that I would have never experienced if it wasn't for what I do combined with a decrepit lunatic asylum. It makes me appreciate the fact that while my career revolves around the dead, the best times in life revolve around the living.

IT'S NOT ALWAYS
TRAUMA AND TRAGEDY

ALEXANDRIA ZOO

—

ALEXANDRIA, LA
OPENED 1926

What started off in 1926 as a row of cages that showcased discarded pets in Bringhurst Park now consists of five hundred sprawling acres and more than that number in animals. The first few decades were meager, with typical exhibits and only a few exotic creatures, but it still became a place frequented by locals and visiting outsiders. It wasn't until the early 1970s, when Robert Leslie Whitt took on the role of director, that the zoo turned into the full-fledged menagerie it is today. Whitt—or Les, as most people knew him—passed on in his late fifties, but his tireless efforts breathed new life into what was a small, cute mini-attraction, transforming it into a renowned zoo that is now the number one family destination in central Louisiana.

Although many hauntings and activities are associated with past pain and suffering, the paranormal activity that surrounds Alexandria Zoo seems to be from passion and love. Whitt's connection is so closely tied to the zoo that most think he has never left. Occasionally a ghostly vestige of

Les can be seen working and tending to the wildlife, his voice can be heard in the whispers of the wind, and at times animals inside the zoo seem to respond to a person when there's no one there. The reports and hauntings at this zoo might only be about one man, but they are strong, significant, and meaningful . . . and a powerful reminder that not all hauntings need to be dark and fearful.

. . .

I'm taking a few minutes here to step away from all the mental institutes and places that have seen nothing but tragedy to examine a location that's filled with good memories . . . one that may also be haunted by a kind soul who's simply looking out for the animals in residence. All too often, we focus on ghosts as if they're terrifying, evil creatures not of our world. Every Hollywood movie treats them as such—dark, demonic, and nasty. Even when it's a "nice" ghost, they're usually fighting off evil ones to protect their loved ones. Ghosts are hardly ever humanized when, in most cases, that's exactly what they were: *humans.* They may have passed, but somehow they remain or are stuck behind, either imprinted on their mortal environment or choosing to return to our world.

When you're checking out a place where hundreds, or even thousands, have died in horrible ways, individualizing an investigation is often impossible; many times you just end up walking around using all of your tools and techniques and hoping that something gives you a sign that it's there. If it does, then you can eagerly follow up and try to figure out what or whom you're dealing with. During these large-scale investigations, you're more inclined to study the location as a whole rather than try to contact individual spirits. Some places tend to have stories, but they tie specifically to ghosts they name; in some cases, they're just assumptions that have no historical connections.

At Alexandria Zoo, it's the complete opposite. It's rather clear to the locals that there's one spirit haunting the grounds, and they know why he's there—he just couldn't leave behind the animals and the park he loved so much.

• • •

Being a huge animal lover (well, *most* animals anyway; there are some that truly scare me), I was rather thrilled as I neared Alexandria Zoo. I was excited to have the opportunity to walk around a zoo late at night. We had been to other large outdoor places like theme parks, but I personally had never investigated a zoo before, so while we had a bit of experience in large spaces, we were all still curious as to how things would play out. I knew a lot of the animals would be sleeping, but I couldn't wait to see what the surroundings would be like at such a late hour and with no one else around. What noises would we hear, which animals would we see moving around . . . and, most importantly, would we experience anything paranormal?

My excitement suddenly turned into surprise—police were blocking the main roads to the zoo. My heart sank as I thought about the possibilities: Was there an accident? Did one of our crew get hurt? Did an animal escape? Why on earth were the roads closed? When the officer standing in the middle of the road looked toward my windshield, he came up to the side of the car and gave a big smile. "Dispatch, I got a Ghost Hunter at the south entrance," he squawked into his radio. I was so confused, sitting there with a dumb grin on my face, not knowing if I was in trouble or if someone was about to tell me bad news. "Mr. Gonsalves, we're going to have an escort come bring you to the entrance immediately," the officer said to me as if I were some high-up brass. It felt surreal to me to get this level of attention, but I went along with it. With the show growing in popularity, we were getting used to things changing, but this was a new one.

Following our police escort, I rolled into the zoo and jumped out of my car, still curious as to what was going on. When I saw one of our producers and asked him about it, he casually explained, "Oh, the police chief is a big fan of the show, and he wants to make sure everything goes well while we're here." Throughout that entire weekend, the team and I had a constant police presence; the chief even came over and regularly checked on us. At first, I thought it was overkill, but I soon realized that it was pure southern charm. There was a big TV show in town, so the local authorities wanted to make sure it went smoothly. Which it did . . . mostly.

As the sun set, we were all a bit anxious to start investigating. Jay and I were walking down a long pathway by various enclosures when we heard a light fluttering sound. It was unique, and hard to place its origin point as it was such a soft noise. We turned on our flashlights and discovered a sleeping giant anteater and a dark cage for an African pygmy goat. After a while, we stopped before a large tree and gave up on finding the source of the sound.

Figuring out where to go next, Jay asked if I could go back to the van and get a new battery for the thermal camera. Not thinking anything of it (I was the tech manager at the time, after all), I walked under the tree, toward the parking lot, while Jay moved in the other direction. Just as I passed beneath some dark branches that rustled heavily, I heard a loud slamming noise behind me. Not only did the cacophony startle me, but it also stirred a massive flock of birds that had been sleeping in the tree above (the source of the soft fluttering sounds).

The tidal wave of caws that came from the trees was terrifying. I stood there, looking up at the tree like an extra in *The Birds*, holding my flashlight as if it would protect me, when *it* started to happen.

PLOP.

What was that?

PLOP, PLOP.

Wait a second. . . . I started to realize what was happening but still was unable to vocalize or move.

PLOP, PLOP, PLOP, PLOP . . .

It was like some scene out of a kid's movie, in which the unsuspecting target walks past a building and suddenly gets pummeled by water balloon after water balloon. Only *I* was the kid in this scene, and the water balloons were actually watery white-and-green globs of bird poo raining down on me from just about every angle.

After quickly shining the light on my jacket to see the mess, I screamed and ran. I could hear the *PLOP*s all around me. It was as if the birds were trying to tell me to leave their territory; why else would they all crap at the same time? By the time I got to safety, I was completely covered in gooey spots. I had been wearing a black jacket, so I looked like a dalmatian. It was so bad we had to stop filming so I could properly clean up, which took almost half an hour.

I knew from the second this all started, from their laughing, that Jay and Tango had set me up. These evil geniuses knew that if the birds were startled they'd all freak out and start crapping, so my teammates devised a plan in which Jay would ask about the thermal, giving Dave time to position himself, then have Tango bang a trash-can lid off in the distance as soon as Jay made it to safety. Their plan went off without a hitch, and I was left the victim of a "crapscare."

The birds weren't the only animal-related mishap during our investigation. Since we had to investigate all night and the zoo's staff had to open the facility in the morning, they went home for the evening and entrusted us with the keys . . . *all* the keys. Unlike most locations we've explored, Alexandria Zoo wasn't some abandoned building; it was a place with hundreds of gates and cages that needed to be secured so that animals couldn't get out. So, every time TAPS team members finished examining an area, we'd lock it up and ensure it was closed just right. We seemed to have the system down pretty well . . . until we discovered we didn't.

I took a quick nap following our first night of investigations, then headed back to the zoo to meet up with Jay and talk to a local historian. As I walked up to Alexandria's main gate, carrying my bag and a big cup of iced coffee, I was shocked to see what seemed like pure chaos inside the grounds. I slipped through security and walked right into a pale pink flamingo. I wasn't scared of it; I was more startled by what I was witnessing. One staff member ran past me to chase a similar freed pink bird, while another staffer quickly walked by with their arms outstretched, trying to coerce a lemur to head back to its enclosure.

There was a full-scale animal jailbreak in process, and I worried that it was our fault. Thankfully, it seemed to be only the exotic birds and lemurs, though there were so many people racing around, it was hard to tell how many things were loose. If it were the lions from the African exhibit, I don't think everyone would have been as calm.

I set down my bag and coffee, ran to the closest staff member I could find, and asked what I could do. The employee, who seemed understandably frazzled, blurted, "Shoo anything that should be in an enclosure into one!" I put my arms out and walked back toward the big, beautiful flamingo, hoping it would listen to my commands. Amazingly, it did, and for the next two hours all staff hands and I ushered birds into gates and closed-off sections. Once order was restored, I expected to be met by a furious zoo director who'd insist that we leave at once. Instead, there were a lot of laughs and an overly kind crew who said it was "the most fun we've had in a while, probably for the birds too." I never figured out how the animals got out or who on our team might have been responsible, though it is always a possibility that our investigating stirred up a spirit enough to cause the chaos. But personally, I think the birds that crapped on me were in on it.

•••

Once the day's hijinks had subsided, the team got serious and went back to work for our second night of investigating. Regardless of the steamy southern humidity sticking to our skin, I was outdoors at a zoo and thrilled to be there. Some animals dozed quietly, others were loud as hell, and a few of them watched us with a lazy curiosity. It was hard not letting myself be distracted by them; I wanted to walk over and baby-talk to each creature I saw, but I did my best to save that for the daylight hours.

It's not often that one gets to walk around a zoo at night with just a flashlight, so I treasured every moment of doing this at Alexandria Zoo. Of course, it wasn't without some unique challenges. There are hundreds of animals that we don't normally encounter, making dozens of sounds that we would never hear during a normal investigation. This led us to chase a lot of false noises. Some we could instantly figure out, like when we discovered a capybara was shoving a metal food bowl across its pen. But there were others—most notably, dragging, huffing sounds that were away from all the cages—that kept us guessing. In the end, we just had to focus mainly on visual experiences and distinctly human voices, as there was just too much noise pollution.

At one point, our client Bill, who was a friend of the park's late director, joined us and shared stories about Les Whitt. We asked him to come along, as maybe Les would be more likely to interact with his friend. Tango and I were in the process of trying to communicate with Les, talking to the open air near some enclosures past the zoo's train depot, which was close to the entrance and by the spider monkey and tapir exhibits. Bill mentioned how Les loved to jump-scare people, so we tried to get Les to do that to us by asking him out loud to scare us. At first nothing happened, but then Bill felt something cold on his arm. We were trying to pinpoint it when, without warning, the silence was broken by piercing screeches. Several spider monkeys, who'd been sitting and observing us quietly in their cages seconds earlier, began freaking out. Their shrills caused the three of us to jump in unison, and we found ourselves laughing over it a few moments later. Bill mused that this might have been a joke orchestrated by Les, since he would have thought it was funny to have a dozen monkeys frighten us all at once. It wasn't provable, but I guess it is plausible.

A small part of me also wonders if what happened to Jay and me later that night might have been another of Les's pranks, since I'm still not entirely sure how it occurred. We were passing through a series of interconnected gates behind some cages (where Bill would have worked and other zoo staffers could access more restricted areas) when we suddenly found ourselves three feet away from a porcupine. For a second, we thought it was cute . . . until it dawned on both of us that the little guy wasn't behind a fence or in a cage and a lot of his quills were starting to stand upright. We couldn't figure how he got out of his enclosure (knowing it couldn't have been our fault again), and then we saw we were standing on dirt. Jay and I had somehow walked *into* his exhibit, and he was being joined by several prickly companions that started emerging from the shadows.

Before we learned firsthand what a pincushion feels like, Jay and I ran backwards out of the enclosure. We had been so focused on our investigation that we had no clue where we were accidentally wandering. Lesson learned: *Don't* open random fence doors when you're in a zoo and in the dark.

Paranormal jokes and mishaps aside, that evening in the zoo also provided some interesting food for thought. I can't remember how exactly we got on the subject, but while we were walking the grounds, Jay and I began talking about animal spirits. Jay thinks it's possible and that he might have even encountered one. Theoretically, it makes sense—if humans can become spirits, why can't animals? However, up to this point, I've never seen much compelling evidence that supports it. I've done well over a thousand investigations, in almost every state, and while I have caught an animal EVP (the sound of a horse and carriage), nothing would make me think I had encountered the actual apparition of an animal. I think a residual type of haunting, where an animal had imprinted on the environment, is a much stronger possibility than it being part of an intelligent haunting. Even then, I've never experienced either. That said, my cat means more to me than most humans I know, so I'd absolutely love the possibility of her sticking around to visit me after she's gone.

• • •

Though my memories of Alexandria Zoo's ambience and being around the animals still feel like a warm hug, at the time I didn't think I had personally gathered much during our investigation. It wasn't until afterward, while examining the evidence, that my initial thoughts were shattered. First, on a recording from the gift shop, we caught a male voice on audio that sounded like it responded with "*Yeah*" whenever we asked a question. It was followed closely by another word that we couldn't make out. However, when we played the audio for Bill, he recognized immediately that the voice was saying *two* words, and he knew what they were: "*Lee Ann*." When I listened back, I could hear it as well. Bill explained that Lee Ann was Les's widow. The connection to that evidence was both stunning and moving . . . a lovesick husband calling out from beyond to the wife he'd lost.

As we were going over the audio and processing what we had just learned, I started to hear sobbing behind the camera. Excusing myself, I got up and walked over to a woman who had been standing off to the side, trying to stay out of the way. I asked her what was wrong—still clearly emotional, she managed to give me a big smile and utter, "Thank you." Turns out it was *Lee Ann Whitt herself* and she believed that she'd just heard her beloved husband's voice once more.

Lee Ann was a local politician who declined to appear on *Ghost Hunters*. My thinking was the small-town politicians didn't feel it would be a good look to be on a paranormal show. Bill had known she was there for the reveal, but he did his best to honor her wishes of not being involved in the production, so he didn't point her out to any of us. And I'm glad he didn't, because her reaction was one of the most unexpected and genuine things that I have ever seen. I gave her a hug and told her everything would be all right. She responded that nothing was wrong; she simply hadn't heard her husband's voice in fifteen years and now she got to hear it again, calling her name. Love like that is so rare and wonderful, potentially breaking the restraints of life and death. Being a part of that moment was fulfilling on a level so deep that I'm not sure I could ever properly explain it.

As amazing as that audio was, it wasn't even the best evidence we collected. One of the infrared cameras we'd set up in the zoo's gift shop caught a person walking in the distance, between some displays. It seemed innocent enough . . . except this footage was recorded *after* hours, when the gift shop was closed and no one was in there. Upon further review, we also determined that the camera did in fact capture a full-body apparition. In the video, we could see the legs and waist, plus a faint outline of the top of a body.

It's stunning evidence, the kind that we live for, and it got even better. Not only is it extremely rare to capture footage like this but we also knew *exactly* who it was. When we showed the video to Bill, his eyes welled up and turned red. "Steve," he said, choked up and barely able to speak, "I know when I am looking at a friend and when I am looking at a stranger. And *that* there is my friend." Bill said that the outline of the figure had Les's posture and exact mannerisms while walking. He then shook his head in disbelief and started chuckling to himself. "I knew Les wouldn't let go of the zoo until his African exhibit and enclosures could be built and finished," he told us. "It was his dream." When I looked up and saw Lee Ann in the background, smiling and nodding at what she'd also seen, there was no doubt in my mind that we had caught Les on camera.

It seemed that Les still truly cared about the zoo and just couldn't leave it behind. Because he was in the middle of overseeing a major expansion of the African-themed exhibits, maybe he really wanted to see it come to fruition. When he was alive, the gift shop was his office, so perhaps he was doing work there. Could it have been Les who made the spider monkeys shriek? We couldn't be certain of those things, though we did conclude our investigation with one irrefutable fact: that Les Whitt was a kind and loving person. It's interesting how all our case studies and experiences point to the fact that you're the same in life as you are in death, whether caring or cruel. Personalities seem to transcend time and space, as well as life and death, and Robert Leslie Whitt was evidence of that.

Collecting real, solid, *tangible* evidence that leaves little to no dispute regarding its origin is incredibly rare in this business. To identify this apparition as Les, elevating him to a ghost, is something that isn't possible most times. I've watched dozens of "professionals" attribute any evidence they find to a specific name's ghost, but they almost never have any proof. And yet here we were, with evidence that Les's friend and wife both confirmed was a ghost of their loved one. This truly was one of the most emotional and meaningful finds of my career.

A case like this, with all its insane evidence and emotional ties, fills me up with joy and pride that I get to do this for a living. In addition to finding true evidence that the field can use in the future, we helped some people learn that a lost loved one's spirit was still checking on them and the location that he'd adored. Not only is Alexandria Zoo a wonderful place to visit, but it's also home to one of the sweetest, kindest spirits I've ever encountered. If you ever visit, keep a close eye on the animals. See if any of them suddenly start acting like someone is near them. And if they do, be sure to give Les Whitt a nod and tell him that Steve says "hello" . . . and "thank you."

HISTORY REPEATS ITSELF

USS *NORTH CAROLINA*

—

WILMINGTON, NC

LAUNCHED 1940

DECOMMISSIONED 1947

Constructed just prior to World War II, the USS North Carolina is a massive battleship that stands nine levels high and, in its prime, was considered one of the greatest weapons on water.

With nine 16-inch, .45-caliber guns placed in three turrets, the North Carolina was the war's most decorated battleship—it participated in every major naval offensive in the Pacific, during which it earned fifteen battle stars (one for each conflict it fought), destroyed twenty-four enemy aircraft, and successfully carried out nine shore bombardments.

The ship survived numerous near misses and one direct torpedo hit in 1942, thanks to the heroic efforts of its nearly twenty-four hundred crew members . . . though ten men died and almost seventy were severely injured during the underwater attack.

In 1947, the USS North Carolina was decommissioned. For the next fourteen years, the vessel sat in a New Jersey dockyard as a reserve ship. Though it was scheduled to be scrapped in the early 1960s, a statewide

USS *North Carolina* mid-voyage in 1946
NAVAL HISTORY AND HERITAGE COMMAND

USS *North Carolina* dry-docked in Wilmington, North Carolina
CHAD MORIN

campaign to save the ship brought it home to Wilmington, North Carolina. There it became a museum ship, dedicated as the state's memorial to honor the eleven thousand North Carolina natives who died in the war.

It wasn't long after the ship earned its dedication from the state when people started reporting that peculiar things were happening on board. To this day, throughout the massive steel corridors and rooms, unexplained noises are heard by guests and workers. Distant shouts and screams have echoed around the vessel, while door slams and other metallic clangs allegedly resound through the corridors. Flickering lights tease those who walk through the mess hall. Unseen hands touching shoulders and mysterious whispers rushing by visitors' ears are commonly reported occurrences. And then there's perhaps the most frightening claim of all: Full-body apparitions can be seen looking out the portholes and walking the deck. Though it might no longer be in service, it's possible that a ghost crew may be manning the USS North Carolina.

• • •

What came before us is what shapes us today and what dictates our future. When it comes to the paranormal, without our history there would be no detectors of ghosts. After high school, when we're no longer forced to sit through dry history lessons, we tend to forget the importance of our past as our present takes up our daily lives. We live in a time when we have such immense and instantaneous access to our history, but if we don't seek it out it just fades away from our consciousness.

For me as a paranormal investigator, examining history is a vital part of my job. Sadly, I've found certain novice and even seasoned investigators often do little to no research. Usually, they just want to contact a spirit or get a great piece of evidence. How the ghost came to be, why they're at a location, where they came from . . . all these details become afterthoughts. It's understandable; I was the same way when I started out. Over the years, though, I've learned that the more you know about a location, about what happened there, and about the people who lived in or inhabited the dwelling, the better your chances are of gathering solid evidence and experiences, which is usually the ultimate goal.

Before I visited the USS *North Carolina*, I enjoyed history and used it when I thought it was necessary for investigating . . . but I didn't think it was vital. My time exploring the old battleship changed me, though—my interest in history went from mild, trivia-level to a full-blown love and passion. I'm not sure if it was the splendor of the vessel or the stories it told, but ever since I left that floating behemoth I've taken the history of every location much more seriously. It made me realize just how important it is that we investigators don't only rely on a biannual museum visit or the occasional tune-in to the History Channel. We need to utilize and research history to hone our craft and aid us with our work. And I like to believe that ever since I adopted this philosophy I've become a much better investigator.

Even knowing our own field's history can be of great benefit to an investigator's success. *Ghost Hunters* created a massive boom in the industry by bringing paranormal research to the mainstream (which still blows my mind), but we were nowhere near the first people to do what we do. Of course, I already mentioned Ed and Lorraine Warren, who were the field's proverbial rock stars for years. But they were long preceded by Harry Price, who in 1936 published a book called *Confessions of a Ghost Hunter*. Then there's the Society for Psychical Research, a nonprofit organization whose essential work has included studying, investigating, and writing about the paranormal for nearly 150 years—twenty years before anyone even had cars, they were hunting ghosts and writing books about it! So yes, the field has grown dramatically over the past few decades, but there's a *long* list of investigators who came before us, and I know that there were many more before the paranormal pioneers I've mentioned here. We're just the next generation with fancier toys and updated techniques.

Why does knowing this history matter? Because there's no point in reinventing the wheel if it isn't broken. By studying our predecessors' research and examining how they did their work, we can advance their findings. We all need to discover and determine what works best for us, but we can learn from our forerunners' mistakes and take inspiration from their triumphs. Speaking for myself, it's important that I honor those who came before me and make myself a good steward of their legacy, so I can be a proper ambassador of our craft. Being featured on television, I take that task seriously, as I want our field to be respected and presented properly. If you investigate the paranormal, I hope you do the same, showing respect to locations and to anyone you work with. Ours is a craft that still has more than its fair share of skeptics, and we need to demonstrate to the world how serious we are.

I take a fifty-fifty approach toward research before I start an investigation. If it's a historic location with a lot of information tied to its past, I research what I can beforehand so I have a better idea of what to possibly expect. When I visit a residence, I prefer to hear about its history from the owners before I fact-check everything through third parties (plus, unless there was a murder or other crime committed at the house, it can be difficult to find specific information that's relevant to a residential home).

When I heard we were going to investigate the USS *North Carolina*, I was intrigued despite not knowing much about the site, or battleships in general. I only remembered my parents taking the family to see one when I was a kid and my being impressed by its size and craftmanship. So, I looked up whatever I could find on the internet—since this was almost twenty years ago, such online information wasn't yet at its best—and I supplemented that by going to the local bookstore and library to confirm facts, as not all websites can be reliable. Using these sources, I managed to take a deeper dive into some of the battles the ship had been in, and I was hooked. The history of the *North Carolina* was fascinating. This was much easier to do once the team got on-site; the closer you are to such a landmark, the more history you can uncover at the local level.

• • •

When we first arrived and I saw the ship in the distance, its immensity sank in. I couldn't help but imagine the massive cannons on top of this steel behemoth shooting off during real battles. Being in the middle of the ocean, hundreds of miles from land, side by side with other battleships, gunfire and torpedoes firing everywhere . . . it had to be frightening for the young sailors on board. Standing on any ship in the ocean gives me anxiety as it is—I can't comprehend the fear of being shot at or wondering if these might be my last moments. The thought made me extremely grateful for all the people who are in the military for their service, and especially for those who were drafted back then.

Within minutes of talking to those already on location, I learned *not* to describe the USS *North Carolina* as a "boat." When the word first slipped from my mouth, you would have thought I had cursed out someone's mother. Open cringes, and their faces scrunched up at the very mention of the B-word. A staff member of the North Carolina Military Historical Society was there and heard my mistake, so he put a hand on my shoulder and gently explained, "A ship can carry a boat, but a boat can't carry a ship." I had never heard this, and though I was confused for a second, I quickly got the message. The word didn't leave my mouth for the rest of the investigation, and I still keep this incident in mind when I'm talking about different vessels.

I was eager to start exploring, but because I oversaw the tech for TAPS at that time, I was also extremely concerned about the logistics of setup. Having to run wires throughout the former warship was going to cause a lot of issues; if I wanted to run any from the fifth deck to the bottom deck, I'd have to zigzag through the halls and down ladders. Plus, I couldn't just set wires on the floor where they could be tripped over, nor could I hang them for fear that anyone might walk into them.

Then there were the doors. Every door inside a ship means a massive step over a foot high to keep water from entering and flooding different compartments. Because the doors close and interlock to become water-tight, I was terrified that someone might shut one and accidentally cut the wires to our surveillance system, destroying hours of work and potential evidence collected in the process. Communicating through walkie-talkies was also going to be a challenge; just about everything inside the USS *North Carolina* was made of steel, so wireless signals would have a hard time transmitting through it.

Without question, this was going to be one of the most difficult set-ups of my career with TAPS. I couldn't wait to start investigating, but I dreaded the very thought of doing all the prep work in an environment that was anything but accommodating.

• • •

Danny Bradshaw was the caretaker of the USS *North Carolina*, a lovable man with a thick southern accent and the strong, unyielding scent of a ship's engine room. He showed us all of the vessel's hot spots, then shared with us his own onboard paranormal experiences. He claimed to have had so many run-ins with ghosts on the *North Carolina* that he would sleep with his room lights on and lock his door, even though he was the only one there.

According to Danny, he had also seen a full-body apparition on three occasions, including one time with his friend. They'd been talking outside the ship when they both saw a man pull back the curtain in Danny's bedroom window and look outside. The man's face stayed in the window for nearly ten seconds before disappearing. Because Danny always locked his room with a padlock, he knew it was impossible for someone to be in there. Yet when the two of them raced back into the *North Carolina* to check the room, they found that it was still locked and no one was inside. Between this incident and dozens of inexplicable noises he'd heard and sights he'd seen, Danny had had more experiences than most investigators I know.

• • •

Once I finished learning about the *North Carolina* hot spots, it was time to set up. As I expected, it was chaos. Wires snagged, we didn't have enough wire to reach certain areas, and we repeatedly got lost within the warship. We always set up during the day so we can see things, but time doesn't really matter aboard a ship. Since the vast majority of indoor areas had no windows, you couldn't tell if it was day or night anyway. Thankfully, there were lights, but even then, some areas were so dim it was very hard to see.

The worst part, though, had to be the low pipes and small doorways. I had tried to account for every potential stumbling block during

USS *North Carolina* artillery ammunition room
CHAD MORIN

setup, but this was one that literally had gone over my head. The night before, while we were at a pub where we stopped for dinner, an old naval officer advised us to wear caps during our time on the ship. He explained that naval personnel wore caps because the headgear would make contact with a pipe or doorframe a split second before a sailor's skull, giving them a chance to react and avoid unnecessary injury.

Unfortunately, even though we listened to his advice, everyone on the crew hit our heads, including me. I thought I'd be fine because I always wear a hat anyway. Boy, was I wrong—I was focused on getting ready and banged my head half a dozen times during setup alone. In one particular incident, I smacked my head into a doorway so hard that

I saw stars and had to close my eyes and steady myself. Thank God I had listened and wore a hat. It got so bad that I started to walk in slow motion anywhere I went aboard the *North Carolina*, just so I wouldn't hit my noggin again.

Those old sailors knew what they were talking about, and they were a lot of fun to hang with that night before. I remember one salty old man grabbing and pulling my forearm toward him. The guy had just bought me a drink, so I did my best to not jerk back while he carefully examined my tattoo sleeve. He nodded, then let me go, rolling up his own shirtsleeve to show me a hairy arm covered in old, faded ink. His tattoos clearly weren't done by a professional; they were blurry and almost indistinguishable due to their decades of age. Yet that didn't stop him from showing me each one and explaining the different locations where he acquired them—the naked lady in Guam, the anchor in Alaska, the crossed guns in London, and so on. The art may have been crude, but the stories behind them were brilliant and beautiful. The old man smiled with pride as he finished talking about his tattoos, and then asked about mine.

If you see any episodes of the show, you can immediately tell that I have a *lot* of tattoos. When people ask about them, all I can say is that they're hard to summarize, so usually I just show a few on my arms. I have a full sleeve dedicated to the greatest holiday of all, Halloween, featuring jack-o'-lanterns, candy corn, a black cat, a witch, candy apples, a kid with a goblin mask carrying a trick-or-treat bag, autumn leaves, and more. Since the man was pretty old, I thought those would be the easiest to show him; I mean, everyone knows Halloween, right? But then he saw one of my Jack Skellington tattoos and blurted out that his grandkid made him watch *The Nightmare Before Christmas* over and over again one year. That caught me off guard, and it made me want to buy him a round, as I have numerous tattoos based on that classic animated movie.

Seeing as he was more observant than I expected, I started to show the man the rest of my ink. They range from movies like *Day of the Dead, Pumpkinhead, The Evil Dead, The Exorcist,* and *Re-Animator* to things like a haunted house, Bela Lugosi, and some of my favorite bands. Every one I showed him had the guy's approval and appreciation. When he asked what my parents thought about all of them, I couldn't stop myself from laughing. My mom and dad were concerned about "careers and regrets," yet they were always tolerant of my tattoo obsession. They understood how much having ink meant to me.

I was nineteen when I got my first tattoo (Boba Fett), but I'm not really sure when my fascination with them started. They've just looked badass to me ever since I was young. I also get that not everyone is a fan of tattoos. When I became a police officer, they certainly weren't as popular as they are today—in fact, I was asked to wear long sleeves and cover them up, even in the summer months. My superiors were worried that old-timers in the community might not respect a cop with tattoos. I understood their concerns so I did what they asked, as it didn't matter to me whether my tattoos were on display or not. However, whenever civilians *did* see them, I never got anything but compliments and comments about how cool it was to see a cop with ink.

Years later, when *Ghost Hunters* started, I was shocked to find out that the producers *loved* my tattoos. Even in the early 2000s, you didn't see that many "tatted" people on television. Yet they thought it was my signature look, and even told another cast member not to get any more ink because "those are Steve's thing." I thought the comment was ridiculous, but I didn't understand then that, even in reality television, shows try to have "characters." In our producers' minds I was our show's "lovable tattooed guy," and it's still quite odd to me how we were seen as characters when none of us on the show ever did anything but be ourselves.

• • •

After everything had been set up and shortly before we started our investigation, I slipped down into the bowels of the USS *North Carolina*. To my knowledge, I was the only person down there; no one was nearby and there were no cameras following me. I found a small, flat steel space that looked like it was covering some sort of moving part of the ship and sat down. I needed my flashlight to see anything; we already had the lights off throughout the ship—I mean there was *zero* light.

I let the darkness envelop me, put my hands on my lap, and settled myself with a few deep breaths. Then I silently paid my respects to the brave souls who died aboard this vessel and gave their lives in service to our country.

USS *North Carolina* artillery cannons
CHAD MORIN

I'm not sure what prompted me to do that—I'm guessing it was the overwhelming sense of history behind the *North Carolina*—but it felt right to me. It was one of the first times I had sought a quiet place to take a moment of silence in a location I was investigating. Since then, it's something I try to do whenever I visit a place that I know has seen tragedy. I don't get to do it every time, but it's become more important to me over the years. It helps me mentally, and I think it's important to show respect to the location and to those who lost their lives.

Not knowing how much time had passed, I realized that no one had chimed in on my walkie-talkie. Normally, the team relies on them to communicate with one another, but I hadn't heard a word from anyone. I knew the investigation should have started by that point, so I turned on my light, grabbed the walkie, and began talking into . . . nothing. I adjusted the device's knobs—still nothing. It wasn't working. Looking around the steel hull that surrounded me everywhere, I remembered that the transmissions simply couldn't pass through the ship's body, just as I'd figured. The thought of not having that lifeline while I was alone on the lower decks, of not being able to call for backup or assistance if I got lost, made me a bit uneasy.

After a few twists and turns I eventually found the team, and once I shook off the disorienting feeling of being lost it was time to start investigating. Though Tango is my trusty partner for most of the investigations I recount in this book, the USS *North Carolina* investigation occurred just before he had joined the team. So, I spent most of my time aboard with either Andy Andrews or Dustin Pari.

Almost from the very start, the ambient sounds on the *North Carolina* messed with us. The echoing hallways made it very difficult to tell what was where or even identify what certain sounds were. However, more than once I definitely heard boots scuffling, metal clangs resonating, and hatches opening and closing. There were also a few times I heard running footsteps, as if one of the ship's crew members had been rushing to an emergency. We're always careful to make sure our team members work far apart from one another to avoid causing sounds like this, so I was convinced that what I kept hearing wasn't Andy, Dustin, or anyone else from the team. However, the fact that sounds could echo off the metal and travel long distances through the silence made it difficult to distinguish which noises might have been natural from those that might have been paranormal.

•••

Speaking for myself, the greatest part of our night aboard the USS *North Carolina* was that the naval commanders and the historical society let us have access to *any* part of the ship we wanted. Only a small percentage of the vessel is used for tours, so we got to enter some areas that hadn't been open to the public in over sixty years. I remember thinking how really cool it was to hear that; it made me feel like one of the Goonies, exploring places that no one had seen in generations.

At one point, after climbing down ladder after ladder and going through hatch after hatch, we made our way to the bottom, which I later found out was called the orlop deck. It was one of the floors that hadn't been entered in over six decades. I had to use my shoulder and push with all my might to crack open the door and get inside, like Indiana Jones discovering a long-lost tomb. Instead of treasures, though, this area revealed several inches of rusty, greasy water that we reluctantly sloshed our way through. The oily, metallic smell stung my nose and made me appreciate all of the hard mechanical work the crew must have done to keep this vessel afloat. It also made me understand why Danny, the caretaker, always had that particular odor . . . only on him, it was pleasing. Down here on the orlop deck, the stench was overpowering.

The darkness made my eyes ache, and knowing we were under the waterline, cut off from the rest of the world by eight decks of solid steel directly above us, made me feel claustrophobic. The slime filling up my shoes and soaking my socks was not only uncomfortable but it also sped up my heart rate, as I truly felt like an explorer. I had high hopes of experiencing something magical on the orlop deck . . . but sadly, other than constant echoes and dripping noises, there wasn't much to discover.

• • •

While we were filming our investigation aboard the USS *North Carolina*, we were surprised to find out that Wilmington, the city we were shooting in, was a hotbed for TV shows. *One Tree Hill* was filming down the street, and *Dawson's Creek* was in production right across the way. It was weird to think that millions of people in over 150 countries could watch not one but *three* shows that were filmed within a mile of one another at the same time. As I was still new to the medium, this thought blew my mind.

At one point we saw a crew off in the distance, so we shined one of our work lights over at them. Seconds later, they shined their lights toward us, so we kept it up and flashed ours in return. Back and forth it went. We thought it was a fun game until a production assistant raced his car into the parking lot, skidded to a stop in front of the *North Carolina* like some action hero, and frantically ran out toward us. He waved his arms in our direction, and after we waved back he started to yell up to us. We came to find out that our lights were messing up their shots and he was sent over to ask us to please stop—whoops.

• • •

The second time I went down to investigate the old battleship, Danny gave me a copy of his book, *Ghosts on the Battleship North Carolina*, which detailed all his paranormal experiences aboard the vessel. It was very kind of him, but what touched me more was that he also set aside some old documents he'd found for me. They were some original papers about Pearl Harbor that he thought I would like to own. At first, I turned them down and said they deserved to be in a museum, but Danny assured me that the historical society gave him permission to offer them up for my personal library. I gave him a big hug, taking in a big whiff of his "natural" oily scent, and thanked him dearly. Danny truly loved the USS *North Carolina* and its history—he saw how much the ship meant to me as well, and that was why he wanted me to have the documents. I had them framed, and to this day they're a treasured item.

I visited the USS *North Carolina* more than four times, a few even for public events and with *Ghost Hunters Academy*, and during those visits I didn't get to experience much—with the *Academy* show I was teaching the investigators, and with public events there is usually so much going on that I don't get enough quality time alone for investigating. The one thing I did make sure of every time I visited was to poke my head into Danny's office to sit and chat with him. Sadly, Danny passed away a while back. I haven't returned to the *North Carolina* since, but I truly hope that whoever took his place has the same passion and love for that old steel-gray behemoth.

I also wonder sometimes if Danny chose to stay on the ship after he died. He loved it so much that I can't imagine that he wouldn't want to spend his afterlife there and give some new investigators something to talk about. My hope is to get back there soon, if only to see if he's still taking care of the old beast.

IT HAPPENS RIGHT IN
FRONT OF YOU

SLOSS FURNACES
—
BIRMINGHAM, AL
BUILT 1881

If you ever want to know what it feels like to walk through the set of a terrifying horror movie, then there's no better place than the old iron mill Sloss Furnaces. This turn-of-the-century factory looks like Freddy Krueger's dream (nightmare?) home, an endless maze filled with furnaces, tubes, pipes, and decaying metals that can make even the toughest of people tremble.

Built in the late 1800s as an iron-producing plant, Sloss's large, intense blast furnaces would hit temperatures up to 2,300 degrees to burn air into raw elements and smelt them into iron. Working inside the factory, with its excruciating heat and dangers beyond comprehension, was more of a punishment than a job. Unfortunately, at that time these dangerous work conditions were suffered by people who had no choice but to be there.

Using "free labor" made Sloss Furnaces a fortune. Following the American Civil War, newly freed Black men were arrested on trumped-up charges like "vagrancy" and imprisoned. Under a system called peonage—also known as debt slavery—companies like Sloss would purchase these convicts

STEVE GONSALVES

Sloss Furnaces
LIBRARY OF CONGRESS

and make them work off their debts to society for the alleged crimes they'd committed. In addition to being forced to work in these harmful, even deadly environments day and night with no pay, many workers lived on the factory premises, within one of four dozen cottages spread throughout Sloss's fifty-acre property. Unfortunately, most of them never left Sloss after their false arrests, since the system was hopelessly rigged against them. Often unable to work off their debt, they remained as slave workers in the factory until they were incapacitated or died. This inhumane system remained in place for decades, until Alabama finally outlawed it in 1911. By that point, the pain and suffering tied to Sloss had become immeasurable.

During all its years of production, Sloss's blast furnaces had to be fed coal around the clock, twenty-four hours a day. If they weren't, they would lose the intensity needed to smelt the materials. This demand worsened already horrendous conditions, in which workers had to suffer constant ear-damaging noise and temperatures that ran well over 120 degrees (and

156

*as high as 150 degrees during the summer), all without breaks. Once using
the enslaved for free labor was no longer legal, only the poorest and most
desperate of workers would take on this aptly named "graveyard shift," as
it was akin to living in hell. Dozens routinely perished, while others suffered
burns, heat exhaustion, heart attacks, and other debilitating injuries. More
than a half-dozen workers even lost their sight in an on-site explosion. The
furnaces were hot, angry, and unforgiving.*

*Incredibly, Sloss Furnaces stayed in operation for almost a hundred years,
until the demand for iron lowered, costs skyrocketed, state and federal laws
forced humane working environments, and pollution grew too high. There's
no way to know how many lives were lost or permanently damaged from
working within the horrific environment at the plant. Regardless, it seems
that some of the workers who died on the grounds are still there to this day—
reports of slamming metal sounds, screams, apparitions, and being pushed
by unseen hands are all commonplace occurrences on the derelict grounds.*

Sloss Furnaces slag pots, circa 1906
LIBRARY OF CONGRESS PUBLIC DOMAIN ARCHIVE

The most terrifying accounts are the stories of a sadistic foreman named James Wormwood, who was called "Slag" by the factory's crew. Known for being cruel and uncaring, he was intent on impressing his bosses, ramping up productivity, and pushing workers beyond their limits. Slag would shove, slap, scream at, and hit workers with any object he had close by. Anyone who dared challenge or disobey him would be placed in the harshest sections of the facility, without any water breaks, and forced to work until they collapsed. As night shift supervisor, Slag was responsible for the deaths of forty-seven men, ten times more than any other Sloss manager. His own life would also end abruptly in 1906 when, after becoming dizzy from inhaling fumes, he fell off the highest furnace, called Big Alice, and landed directly in a vat of hot molten iron. Slag's body instantly burned and melted as he screamed and reached for help from the men he abused; they rendered no aid, content to watch him incinerate.

At least, that's the story the workers told. There are others who have insisted that Slag, being a supervisor, never climbed the furnace towers. They hold the theory that the workers finally had enough of his cruel ways and threw him into the vat, making it look like an accident. It's also believed that Slag still roams the Sloss property, pushing people and demanding they work. Shortly after the foreman's demise, reports of hauntings at Sloss Furnaces started surfacing. Around the 1920s, one watchman was shoved and told to get back to work by an unseen force. In the forties, three supervisors went missing—they were found hours later, unconscious and locked in a boiler room. All three stated that the last thing they recalled was a badly burned man shouting at them to "push some steel!" In the 1970s, another watchman said he came face-to-face with an "evil presence" that pushed him up some stairs and then beat him. These eerie stories of Slag—or something that's attributed to him—remain a constant mystery.

Along with the countless tortured and lost souls in this place, the callous controller's evil presence is considered among the most prevalent at Sloss Furnaces.

• • •

Sloss Furnaces had always been on my list of legendary locations that I wanted to investigate, so I was thrilled to learn that TAPS was finally going to get to check out the place. But when I also found out that the iconic rock god Meat Loaf wanted to join us—for the second time, no less—I let out an audible whoop of excitement.

Music has been a cornerstone of my life. I was a massive metalhead while growing up in the late eighties and early nineties, and I still am today. Even back then, I could trace most of my favorite bands' over-the-top theatrics to them watching Meat Loaf perform. The man himself had said that he was an actor and performer first, and then a musician. He saw himself as a character emoting his songs whenever he was onstage. You can see his love for performing and singing really shine when he performs as Eddie in *The Rocky Picture Horror Show*; for me, he pretty much steals the movie.

I can't tell you how much I love playing the drums. My dad, who's an amazing musician himself, has always nurtured my love for music. He would teach me about rudiments, playing the right parts for the right music, timing, the importance of being well-rounded, and more. As much as I was into metal, Dad also made sure my ears were never too far away from jazz, funk, classical, and big band. He was always buying me drum kits and encouraging me; he still does, in fact. When I turned a spare bedroom in my house into a drumming studio, Dad gave me advice and helped me set it up.

Over the years, I've split any free time I have between ghost hunting and music. I've played in bands, mostly metal, in shows all over the East Coast for decades. But I've also jammed with funk and folk groups, and I've found the most musical success playing with a blues-rock band. I couldn't believe that I could have a kick-ass time up onstage playing the drums and getting paid to do it. It's just like with investigating the paranormal . . . it still astounds me that I make a living doing what I love. My schedule now has me too busy for a band commitment, but I still enjoy just sitting in my room at home and going to town on my kits.

I've also always loved going to shows and concerts. The music, the atmosphere, the crowd going nuts, feeling the drumbeat thumping in your chest . . . exhilarating. And when you're seeing in person someone you've listened to over and over again . . . nothing beats it. Yet even if you make it toward the front row, the performers are always at a distance, just like celebrities and other idols. Even if for some reason you manage to get backstage and meet them for a brief moment, it's just that . . . a momentary encounter with a rock god. With my bands, I was fortunate enough to open for some big acts and to meet so many rock gods, but I never imagined that someone I looked up to would want to work with *me*, and more important, I never thought I would become great friends with one like I did with Meat Loaf.

People say that you shouldn't meet your idols, as they can never live up to your expectations. That couldn't be further from the truth with Meat Loaf, who had the opportunity to join us during Season Five of *Ghost Hunters*. We were filming an episode at a massive home on a private island in New York and he was our guest. As a fan of the show, he was so excited that he showed up the day before shooting and sought us out. We were in the hotel parking lot where the crew had a small base camp set up when he arrived with the biggest smile on his face, shaking everyone's hand one by one. When he saw me, we locked eyes, and his face lit up with excitement. Within seconds, this rock legend who had never met me rushed over, but suddenly the smile turned to a look of horror as he pointed to my shoulder and screamed, "Dude, you have a spider on you!" Of course, I jumped and looked at my jacket, only to find him laughing and seconds later giving me a big hug. Before any pleasantries, he asked about my cats. I didn't recall at the time, but I guess I had mentioned my kitties on the show before and he remembered—*Meat Loaf* of all people truly wanted to know how Sassy Lashes (for some reason he liked her the most) was doing. He was so interested that we had an entire conversation about cats right then and there. Seeing his big grin as I showed him cat pictures on the phone, I realized whom I was talking to. He wasn't some rock star hanging around with us—he was just Meat, as he told us to call him, just like his real friends and family did. He was an instant friend.

I also quickly discovered how much of an avid viewer Meat was of our show. Not only had he watched every episode, but he'd seen each one several times. During our talks, he'd have a better memory of things I did on a particular episode than I did. It was so weird but also exciting that someone I had always looked up to was so into what we were doing. At the time, Meat had wanted to do his own investigations and was really into the paranormal. He was pretty obsessed with it and was the one who reached out to us not necessarily to be on *Ghost Hunters* but just because he wanted to talk to us about cases and pick our brains regarding certain topics. Those initial conversations led to him joining us on the show when we investigated the Isle of Pines in New York.

The work Meat did during our investigation of the island was kind of unexpected, as he was there to dig in, not just to have fun; I think he may have done more research on the location than we did, and he showed up right as we did, ready to get going. I also remember that while all of us were having a thirty-minute lunch break one night (even if it's midnight, we call it a lunch break), I was sitting in the van enjoying a sandwich when Meat came knocking on the door and told us to hurry up and not waste time eating. He truly couldn't wait to get back out there—it reminded me of when I was a kid and friends would eagerly knock at the door, wanting us to get back to whatever game we were playing. His enthusiasm was infectious, and I was really looking forward to seeing him in Alabama and hunting with him again.

• • •

The day that we pulled up and saw the twisted metal maze of Sloss Furnaces, I instantly ignored the nightmare in front of us and looked for Meat Loaf. He jumped out of a van across the lot and ran over to us with a childlike enthusiasm, giving us hugs and going on and on about how excited he was for the hunt. His pure joy gave us all a shot of adrenaline that was more than we normally had before starting an investigation.

The happy reunion didn't last too long for me, as there was work to do. I felt a chill as I started walking around the Sloss Furnaces grounds. The place looked like it was created for some big-budget *Hellraiser* movie in which we got to see where Pinhead slept at night: Boilers everywhere, rusted vats, chains swinging and hanging. Derelict train tracks that led to dead ends. Tall, steely smoke towers. Creepy walkways between machines that ended in blackness. Tunnels that looked endless. And the unique part of all this . . . half of it was *outside*. Some large structures had no side walls, while others only had roofs. Sloss's structures weren't falling apart; they were deliberately incomplete, as they needed the airflow to prevent the excessive factory heat from rising to deadly levels (even though oftentimes it still would).

The property is now a national landmark, but the owners did a fantastic job keeping the facility close to what it was when it was up and running. During the day, it's open to the public for tours, and it even attracts numerous educational field trips. At night, you might think the plant would be open for ghost hunts; instead, they rent the place out for weddings and parties. When I first heard this in the factory, I literally stopped in my tracks and looked around me. I could maybe see a macabre-themed wedding, but a normal one? This place could double as the backdrop for a horror movie, and yet there are seven different areas regularly booked for events.

After I saw some pictures of weddings that were held there, my brain finally grasped the striking beauty that could be created through the balance of an antique steel background with a grand ball decked out in lights and flowers. It really was an inventive, unique way to bring in funds to the preservation. Still, my stomach knotted a bit at the thought of wedding guests dancing to "Y.M.C.A." next to the boiler that had burned a man alive.

• • •

Once the sun had set and the lights had gone out, I felt a bit more keyed up than I normally do during an investigation. There was something about standing next to a giant machine while also feeling the night air tickling your skin. The sounds the wind made dancing through and around the millions of pounds of steel were eerie but also beautiful. Part of me wanted to find a quiet area where I could sit down and look at the grounds in pure silence, but we had a job to do.

It wasn't long after starting that Tango and I found ourselves near a ladle car on some train tracks. This transport was a massive steel bucket that sat on wheels and ran along the tracks. It would be filled with molten materials and transported to other parts of the facility, where its contents would be dumped wherever they were needed. I was excited to investigate this spot—there'd been numerous claims of a figure seen walking and dragging a shovel along these very tracks. Others maintained that they'd heard the sound of scrap metal being dragged. Personally, I thought some of these accounts sounded a bit too inspired by horror movies—a worker would carry a shovel, not drag and dent it, thereby making it harder to use. Yet the claims had been so frequent that the police were called out to the site several times to check on the reports of this mysterious figure. Amazingly, though they never found anyone, several of the officers did hear the same sounds and even went on the record about it.

After a few minutes of nothing happening, I decided to use a technique we call familiarization. It's quite simple: Basically, you call out or talk about things that would be "familiar" to the alleged spirit. If your suspected ghost was a nurse, you could talk about caring for a patient. If you think he was a worker who died while building the structure you're standing in, you could talk about the construction. You can also do role-playing, reenact situations, wear certain items the ghost might recognize, and bring in items. Of course, familiarization only works if you know not only the location's history but also, more important, the history of the person whom you're trying to contact. If you start talking about the space race in the 1960s, but the spirit was a farmer from the 1800s, this technique might not do you any good. However, if you're in a place like Sloss, which was open for a set amount of time and did only one thing during that period, then familiarization is the perfect technique to use.

Standing near the tracks, I started things off by yelling, "We need help over here! Someone just spilled some—" And before I could finish, Tango and I heard what sounded like a person running on the gravel. The noise was so loud and clear—it was as if someone had been standing not far from us, then started to race toward our location when I gasped. They were definitely not animal-scurrying sounds.

As we shined our flashlights around, I saw something straight in front of us. It moved around a bit, then retreated right back into the blackness. It was an almost-brown color and shaped like a human . . . about the same height as me, but featureless and definitely not a shadow. While I explained to Tango what I had seen, I saw it again, about forty yards away. Racing toward the area, I looked around. There was nothing there but a solid cement alcove. If a person or an animal had entered, they would have been stuck there with no way of sneaking out.

An experience like this always gets the adrenaline pumping. It's astounding to see something perfectly with your own eyes. Yet, like always, if the camera doesn't catch it, it's only a personal experience and not evidence that can be shared. Thankfully, the audio did pick up the gravel sounds of whatever was running, but even that doesn't help us prove much. From a personal standpoint, the encounter was intense. Was it a ghost . . . or something else?

Moving shadows and black masses come into play a lot in the paranormal world. In fact, you're more likely to see those than a full-body apparition. This is known as a "shadow phenomenon," and in my experience (both personally and from reported accounts) it's much more common than other anomalies. Could the shadow be a form that spirits take or possibly a different thing entirely? When it comes to shadow phenomena, the theories vary wildly.

Shadows can only be created when a light source is blocked, and

This is where I saw shadowy figures walking.

they can only be cast "on" something. These are not really shadows in that sense—they are free-floating dark masses that move on their own. Sometimes they can look like a black blob or cloud, and other times they take the shape of a human or part of a person. They can be rather common, though I also think that when you're sitting in extremely low lighting a legitimate shadow can play tricks with your mind. Your brain has a hard time interpreting things in complete darkness, resulting in more claims than actual experiences. In one respect, that's the first theory—we can't visually record a shadow phenomenon because we might simply be experiencing an ocular illusion caused by our eyes straining to see, and our mind rapidly trying to figure out what's in front of us.

Take a hot summer day, for instance: When you look off in the distance, heat waves can twist and distort images. If you stare into the dark long enough, your eyes start to perceive things out of context, bending and shifting whatever light might be available.

Floaters in your eyes can also create chaos in the brain. When a floater is seen in bright light, you recognize what it is and blink it away. In the dark, you have no sense of depth, so the small globule floating around in your eye could look like a black mass in the distance if there is a contrasting light source. If you think that's what you're seeing, blink your eyes to try to clear them, but whatever you do, don't rub your eyes, or you'll create phosphenes, or flashes of light, that take a long time to go away. You don't want this when you're trying to see things in the dark, as it will truly mess with your vision and what you think you see. After you blink, if what you saw is no longer there, then it's very possible that you saw a floater and not something related to the paranormal.

Sometimes these optical illusions can be accompanied by delusions. And no, I'm *not* saying that some investigators are delusional in any way; however, delusions *can* be commonplace in the dark. The effects of sensory deprivation are well documented, especially when a person is in the dark for over an hour, with their eyes open. One study showed that prolonged darkness can make a person lie, cheat, feel confused with normal tasks, and even see things. If you're in the dark too long, it's always better to have some light source so that you won't suffer any ill effects while on an investigation.

Sleep deprivation can also cause hallucinations, some of them terrifyingly real. If you worked a day job on a Friday, then committed to an investigation and are still awake at 4:00 AM in a dark room, you just can't fully trust your senses or mind. According to medical journals, over 80 percent of people experience visual hallucinations when they are sleep-deprived. This is due in part to the fact that they can suffer from "micro naps" while fully conscious. During these split-second naps, they actually fall into a dream state while being fully awake, having no clue they had just slept for a brief moment.

Now, if you aren't sleep-deprived and you haven't rubbed your eyes when you see a shadowy figure move . . . then what you're witnessing could very well be paranormal. One idea about these figures is that they're "normal" spirits seen in a state before or after being fully formed. Investigators on the more spiritual side tend to think that "shadow people" are evil, possibly demonic forces. Personally, I've never experienced anything malicious whenever I've encountered one, so I don't put much faith in assuming they're inherently evil.

Lastly, if you want to get really deep into scientific theory, most physicists believe in other dimensions and that there are likely to be light and sound waves in those places. Whether or not they have intelligence, no one knows—could shadow phenomena be interdimensional? Could they be wisps from other worlds trying to come through, which quickly disappear into themselves like a collapsing wormhole? Or maybe there's another scientific explanation for these shadows that we just haven't figured out yet? There are so many possibilities to consider . . . though I know deep down that whatever I saw at Sloss Furnaces didn't obey any of our scientific rules.

• • •

The next night, Tango, Meat Loaf, and I found ourselves in the metal bowels of the facility, wandering through the endless maze of rusty ocher-colored pipes. What was odd about Sloss was not being able to just say, "I'll be in X building"—things there are not that clear. With parts opening to the outside and other areas having roofs with no walls and endless sections with snarls of tanks, it's easy to get turned around. The three of us found ourselves walking through the same areas numerous times without realizing it. We were walking back down one particular cement-and-iron-encased hall we'd just passed through minutes earlier when we suddenly smelled the overpowering stench of mothballs. It was like entering an overzealous grandmother's cedar closet at the peak of a humid summer. The smell was so strong it burned into our noses, and the three of us were positive that we hadn't smelled anything like it in the general area. When we took about ten more steps forward, the stench was suddenly gone.

Normally, when you pass by something so pungent, the smell fades as you move farther away from it. This odor, however, had *completely* disappeared, like it was never even there. Understandably intrigued, Meat, Tango, and I doubled back to where the scent had been strongest, but we could no longer detect even the slightest hint of it. If there had been mothballs or chemicals anywhere in the area, we definitely would have smelled them again. There's no such thing as "shutting off" a scent, but that night we seemed to experience precisely that.

A few minutes later, Meat was using an EMF meter around the facility's trestle/tunnel area; he started loudly asking questions to establish a rapport with a presence we thought was around our vicinity. Earlier that evening, he and other TAPS members had some success identifying a possible spirit's name as Paul, and when Meat asked if that was our ghost's name, the gauge lit up with excitement. Seeing this, Meat asked "Paul" if mothballs were used around that part of the facility. Again, the device danced and flashed like a giddy child.

Between experiencing the smell and seeing the meter react to a possible presence, Meat was rather thrilled. I was intrigued by the meter, but the smell is what truly enthralled me. I've experienced phantom smells numerous times, but never one that just "shut off" like the Sloss mothball stench. That experience was so profound it made me look into constructing a device that could "sniff" the air and read any chemicals or odors so we could document similar phantom scents. I knew such devices existed for things like gas and air quality, but I had no clue that the FBI and CIA actually employ a gadget that does something similar to what I'd love to have. Of course, it's used for detecting bombs, drugs, and other hazardous items, but it would also work for our purposes. I've wanted to try out that device, but it's way too difficult to get your hands on one; they cost more than a luxury car. Maybe one day the air-sniffing device of my dreams will become standard practice for paranormal investigations . . . but unfortunately, not just yet.

In the meantime, Meat Loaf, Tango, and I made our way to Sloss's blowing engine room, the oldest building on the property. This large structure held beastly caged machines that instantly made me think of "The Mangler," Stephen King's short story from *Night Shift*, about a demonically possessed industrial laundry machine that kept killing its workers. Monstrous metal gears like those in Sloss are an ominous sight, especially the giant steel "flywheel" gears that were easily twice my height. Row after row, there were half a dozen of these preposterous wheels, each strapped to massive crank rods that disappeared into dark holes in the ceiling. They used to provide air for combustion in the furnaces and would spin at ninety miles an hour. I couldn't imagine the cacophony of noise they must have produced when they were all roaring along at terrifying speeds. The thought made me understand why they now had cages around them, but back in the day, before safety in the workplace was a concern, they used to be completely exposed, hungrily spinning and practically waiting for a worker's errant sleeve to come too close. Sloss's owners only put the cages around these apparatuses in the 1950s, after one too many workers met a horrific end.

Once the three of us were finished marveling at the engines' size and power, we climbed up a few ladders to go deeper into the machines . . . though not too high, as I can't handle climbing more than one story up. Out of nowhere, we heard a loud, sharp noise that sounded like a cold, robotic bark. After some investigating, we found a large piece of steel that, when pushed, would hit a metal girder and produce the *exact* sound we'd heard. We tested the steel's weight, and it was well over thirty pounds. There was no way that some random gust of wind could have pushed the steel and made it hit the girder. No matter what else we did beyond moving the steel, we could not re-create the sound.

• • •

I tell you, there was no shortage of memorable experiences or excitement during TAPS's investigation at Sloss Furnaces. In addition to what happened to Meat Loaf, Tango, and me, Jay Hawes and Grant Wilson reported seeing full-body apparitions. Grant claimed he was actually pushed while checking out the tunnels, and Jay heard a voice say to him, "*Hey, look.*" Meat also spotted a figure in the tunnel that disturbed our laser grid. It's amazing that all seven of us investigators had at least one experience at the plant; that is *not* a common occurrence. Plus, we found even more evidence when we analyzed all of the footage. The gravel scuffle I'd heard was caught on audio, and we also picked up a child's voice saying something akin to "*Daddy*," which seemed incredibly out of place. Maybe it was a child who had lived in one of the property's cabins? There's no telling. To me, though, the best piece of evidence our cameras caught, completely by accident, was an apparition that looked like a worker sitting on the floor. It was just for a split second, but it's a clear and powerful image—the ghostly figure of a man taking a break.

After the experiences we had there, I can confidently say that, without a doubt, I believe Sloss Furnaces is haunted, and I would go back anytime to do another investigation. I just wish I could do it again with Meat Loaf. The man was so dear to me, and I'm grateful that I got to see him in December 2021, just a month before his untimely passing, when he joined us at a haunted farmhouse in Tennessee for one more investigation on *Ghost Hunters*.

Having had years to hone his investigation chops, Meat Loaf had come up with a new technique that he showed Tango and me during our final investigation together. Basically, he would open up to the spirits by telling them about himself. This is something we rarely do in our own investigations. We might mention one or two minor personal points, but we almost always focus on asking the spirits questions about themselves. Meat's thoughts were simple: If a perfect stranger just ran up, stuck a camera in your face, and asked you question after question, you'd most likely shut down and get the hell away from this crazy person. Therefore, he believed that if you could make a spirit feel comfortable and safe by simply talking about yourself and opening up to them, maybe they would react in kind and open up to you.

I remember watching him sit there at the farmhouse, hoping to make contact with the spirits and talking out loud about himself . . . why he was there and what he was hoping for. He looked so happy and confident, and you know what? It *worked*. Meat Loaf gathered a lot of evidence on that case, and most of it by using his new technique. I was so impressed by what he did that I plan to start doing it myself, just to see if it will work for me. Maybe I'll even call it the "Meat Loaf Method." It's a very deserving name, because the technique is about being kind and truly caring, which is exactly the kind of person Meat was.

During filming breaks, Meat took the time to teach me how to play the pump organ, which is sort of like a church organ. Even when I was clumsily fumbling with the keys and pedals, he was nothing but encouraging and excited when I hit the right notes. Seeing that from him, I couldn't help but smile.

Hearing that he passed so shortly after we'd worked together was absolutely gutting to me. Not only did the world lose a genius performer,

The last day I saw Meat Loaf; showing me
how to play the pump organ

but his family lost a loving father and husband, and I lost a good friend. I'm beyond grateful that I'll always have my memories with him.

Before that episode aired, I received the sweetest text from Meat Loaf's daughter. It said she was happy that her dad's last appearance was on our show, because he was truly himself around us. Instead of watching a performer onstage, an actor in the spotlight, or a celebrity giving an interview, people were seeing Meat as himself, doing what he loved with friends. She went on about how much he loved ghost hunting and being with all of us in TAPS. When I read her comment, I cried—it meant everything to me. I'm devastated that he's gone, but I also know that Meat has finally discovered the afterlife he was always so eager to find.

The first time I met Meat Loaf; note his
fly-fishing shirt, a sport he loved

SEEING IS BELIEVING

WAVERLY HILLS SANATORIUM

—

LOUISVILLE, KY

BUILT IN 1910

The tunnel was pitch-black, its stench unbearable. Body after rotted body was dragged across the cold, stained cement, day and night, for years. Sometimes they would sit in piles, clogging the cramped space because the workers couldn't burn them fast enough. These bodies had names, lives, and families; within the tunnel, though, they were just kindling for a fire that was set to destroy their disease-riddled corpses.

During the worst years of the tuberculosis (TB) epidemic in the twentieth century, tens of thousands died within the walls of Waverly Hills Sanatorium. The mortality rate was so high that the facility's staff tried to keep morale up by having the bodies disappear through a hidden tunnel and loaded up for the incinerator. This 525-foot journey was the last trip these victims took on a long, morbid journey to being burned or buried.

Waverly Hills opened in 1910 as a two-floor hospital that could accommodate up to fifty TB patients. Over the next several years, to keep up with the surging "white plague" that ravaged the United States, the sanatorium was forced into rapid expansion. By the peak of the outbreak, the building

175

Tina Mattingly, the co-owner of
Waverly Hills, and me

had lengthened to a sprawling 185,000 square feet and housed thousands
of patients. Unfortunately, it still wasn't enough to quell the epidemic's
enormous death toll—more than sixty thousand people died during the
sanatorium's fifty-year existence. How many of those souls stayed behind
in the crumbling clinic is anyone's guess, though many people seem to agree
that it's the most haunted place in America.

By the early 1940s, after a new antibiotic was found to treat tuberculosis, the demand for the hospital slowly declined until it was no longer
needed. After closing its doors in 1961, it was converted into a nursing
home the next year, which operated until widespread reports of patient
neglect and abuse forced its permanent closure in 1982. Numerous plans
were proposed for Waverly Hills—at one point it was going to become a
prison, then a worship center. When those plans fell through, the building
fell into disrepair and sat abandoned for nearly two decades. Then, in
2001, Tina and Charlie Mattingly bought the building with the hopes of

preserving Waverly Hills' history and creating a place for paranormal en-
thusiasts to congregate. In the years that followed, the Mattinglys opened
the sanatorium for ghost hunts, tours, events, and a haunted house during
Halloween, with most proceeds going toward keeping the vast property in
shape. While preservation has been at the forefront of its restoration, it is
the active spirits who keep visitors coming back to Waverly Hills.

• • •

After driving up its long, winding wooded road, you feel like your mind
and body have somehow been prepared for the ominous ambience that
practically oozes out of Waverly Hills. The massive, intimidating structure
looks like it should have an unmoving dark cloud hovering over it, yet
at the same time, it also has a stunning, majestic allure.

Built five stories high, slightly curved, and running the length of two
football fields, Waverly Hills stands like a nightmare frozen in time—every
window is gone, smashed out by either vandals or Mother Nature over

Waverly Hills front
JASON NELSON

the decades, and a rustling, howling wind now whips through its carcass. The window frames, without any glass to keep the outside elements at bay, look like sunken-in eye sockets. Even if you didn't know the hospital's gruesome history, it would be almost impossible to suppress any goose bumps upon viewing the structure. Knowing that countless people suffered and died within those walls makes the place even more terrifying.

• • •

As a paranormal investigator, I find that Waverly Hills is the one place that comes up in discussions more than any other location. Of course, I wanted to investigate it for years, but I didn't get an opportunity until we got called in for an episode of *Ghost Hunters*. When I learned of our plans to explore it, I was beyond ecstatic to experience a place with such an amazing history. I felt like I'd just won the lottery—I wanted to scream for joy and run around, but I did my best to keep my composure in front of the others. I usually try to set my expectations low before seeing any of the places we investigate, but with Waverly Hills I couldn't help but be so excited. Little did I know that the location would surpass anything I could anticipate.

When I first took in the building back in 2005, my heart fluttered; it was as if I were staring at the biggest, most beautiful bowl of mint chocolate chip ice cream that I'd ever seen and it was all mine. I swallowed cartoonishly hard—like that giant *gulp* Shaggy does whenever the Mystery Machine pulls up to an abandoned structure—as I stood and surveyed the expanse of the building. The size of the location and the legend that preceded it were pretty daunting. It would take weeks to thoroughly investigate the entire place, but we only had a few nights. Lost in my thoughts, I didn't move until someone on the team nudged my shoulder and I heard, "Sorry, man." I was so enthralled I didn't even know who had bumped into me.

After getting over the excitement and awe of Waverly Hills, we met up with owner Tina Mattingly; she talked about the property with Jason, Grant, and me, then gave us a quick tour of its most active locations so we could decide where to set up. As we walked through the halls, I touched some of the paint that was flaking off the faded, slightly mildewed walls, wondering what had transpired in this place over the last hundred years. (I then also started wondering how much asbestos and lead paint the structure contained, which made me quickly wipe my hands on my pants.) This place had contained thousands of suffering and dying patients . . . dozens per day, on many occasions. What were their stories?

The realization of how much loss had occurred within these walls really seeped in once we reached the notorious "Death Tunnel" (also known to some as the "Body Chute"). For any investigator approaching

Fourth-floor patient hallway
JASON NELSON

this tunnel for the first time, it was the age-old question: Would the experience live up to the hype, or would it be a bitter disappointment?

I remember looking down the tunnel's long, dark emptiness and being surprised at how smooth the walls were. For some reason, I was expecting them to be jagged and raw, like what you might see inside a cave; instead, the passage looked like an aqueduct that secretly led to a hidden chamber. There were small patches of wear and a bit of graffiti, but it wasn't the overly ominous portal that I'd been expecting. At least, not until I tried looking down it and saw nothing but blackness—that's when the chills started creeping in.

As Tina told us stories about how busy the tunnel used to be and how corpses were snuck through it, my anticipation started to build like a pressure cooker. My thoughts turned from creeped out to sympathetic as I heard these tragic tales of horror. Sometimes when we investigate, we forget that the "activity" we're hoping to get is from a human who was once a living being. Someone with a loving family, with ambitions and goals, who loved and lost—just like all of us. The thought of over sixty thousand people dying here, most of them alone and tormented, was almost too much to consider. Thinking about the pain these patients must have endured as they expired from such a debilitating disease, I could understand how pieces of them might have stayed behind. I forced myself to brush these thoughts aside, and replaced my dread with the ever-present thrill that I'd soon get to investigate the dark tunnel.

As the sun set and turned the horizon into a brilliant fuchsia-orange, I snuck off to an empty room on the second floor. While the rest of the building had vague scents, this room had a musty, metallic smell that quickly filled my nose. It wasn't unpleasant; if anything, it was in some ways intoxicating. It was like the building had somehow manufactured its own distinct scent, if only to demonstrate its age and pain for these "sudden intruders" (meaning Tango and me). The paint on the walls was chipping off in heavy chunks, as if some giant monster had barreled its way through and dragged its massive claws across the deteriorating plaster, sending paint flying off in large clumps. In the center of the room, I noticed an outline on the floor that appeared to be where a hospital bed once sat. I hovered over the spot and considered how many people must have died right in this area—it was a heartbreaking thought. It also made me realize the horrible Catch-22 we face as investigators: The more pain and suffering a location has seen, the greater the chance there is for paranormal activity. It's macabre, but at locations like Waverly Hills, where so much anguish occurred, the odds of having an experience are tremendously amplified.

•••

If you've ever been to the Magic Kingdom within Walt Disney World, then you're familiar with the excitement that bubbles up inside you as you approach the gates. Maybe that feeling sits with you days before you even get there. The night before, you have trouble sleeping. Then, when the moment finally arrives and you start walking Main Street, USA, your mind swirls with thoughts about where to go and what to do first (though I always race right for the Haunted Mansion before anything else).

Waverly Hills Sanatorium is the Disney World of locations to investigate the unexplained. For those who know me, Disney World is my happy place; I go there at least two or three times a year. So, for me to compare Waverly Hills to my favorite place, you know it has *something*.

Setting up equipment around a location is an activity I usually enjoy,

Entrance to room 502, where legend says a nurse's life ended

but at Waverly Hills it was torture—I just couldn't wait to start investigating. I felt like a kid who'd been told they had to eat breakfast before they could open their Christmas presents. By the time I finished up, the sun had gone down—Tango and I looked at each other, smiled, took deep breaths, and got to work.

Normally, I'm pretty calm when I embark on a new hunt, but that night I could feel my pulse racing more than usual. And even though it was rather cool inside Waverly Hills, sweat lightly beaded my forehead as Tango and I made our way upstairs to the building's top floor to start investigating. Along the way, we discussed a grisly story that we'd heard about that area. During the peak of the TB outbreak in the early 1920s, when the mortality rate of the disease was still at around 80 percent, one of the nurses got pregnant out of wedlock with a doctor. Distraught and scandalized, she hung herself. Some people said she had contracted the disease and didn't want the child to suffer; others believed the doctor had coerced the nurse into suicide or, worse, murdered her. Regardless of how it happened, it's suspected that she haunts the sanatorium's rooftop, below which her body was found swinging from the ceiling.

The top floor looked much like any other part of Waverly Hills—crumbling, smashed-out windows, and empty rooms filled with a creep factor that would make even the toughest of people shiver. The floor was more open than others within the sanatorium . . . it appeared to have been a recreation area at some point. Tango and I took opposite sides of the main room and had started looking around when, out of the corner of my eye, I saw someone walking next to me. It made me jump slightly, but then I figured that it had just been my reflection in the glass of a window. I noted it to Tango across the room, and he stopped dead in his tracks.

"Steve," he said, "there's *no glass* on the windows."

Until Tango said that, I had momentarily forgotten that the windows were blown out throughout the facility. My heart thudded inside my chest. I looked around to see if I could figure out what I had just experienced. I also retraced my steps to that spot and walked the path again, but this time I noticed nothing. I had just seen an apparition walking right next to me.

I'm not a big sports person, but I imagine the emotions that raced through my body right then are akin to those experienced on scoring the winning touchdown on the last play of a football game. It filled me with pure joy and adrenaline—one of the very reasons *why* I avidly investigate the paranormal. There's nothing like the rush of knowing you might find something that will help definitively prove the existence of supernatural presences. In a way, it provides a dose of fear that would make most people run away and scream in terror; it compels me to do the exact opposite, however, and run *toward* the phenomenon.

Hoping we could capture some intriguing footage, Tango and I set

One of the hallways where we were hearing
doors opening and closing
JASON NELSON

up a thermal-imaging camera and focused it on the area where I'd seen the figure walking next to me. We let it record on its own for a few hours while we investigated the rest of the floor and Waverly Hills proper. A thermal-imaging camera detects fluctuations in temperature using infrared radiation technology; when a thermal anomaly goes by the lens, the camera reads it and displays a visual image of it for you. When we did our analysis of the footage the next day, we caught odd thermal hits going by the camera at different times. To be clear, this didn't *prove* the existence of anything paranormal, but it certainly added some credence to what I'd experienced that night.

Occasionally, during all the days we investigated, Tango and I would hear whispers and voices throughout various locations. Most of the time they were unintelligible, little wisps of breath. Occasionally, though, it seemed as if someone was standing right next to us, speaking.

There was also a jolting bang that we'd hear at times. It was a loud, metallic slamming noise, like someone angrily shutting a door. We'd hear the sound often in the faraway distance and sometimes immediately next to us. We can easily disprove the possibility of a presence by checking a door and seeing if it can be pushed closed with one finger. If it slams shut with just a light touch and there's a window in the room (remember, none of the sanatorium's rooms had glass in the windows, which allowed for constant breezes), then it's not only possible but also very likely that the wind had pushed it closed. However, depending on the amount of force needed to close the door, we might have been able to rule out the wind being a factor.

Some of the doors in Waverly Hills were almost impossible to move, but there were a few that were rather loose and theoretically could be slammed shut by the wind. For an investigator, this is always a tough situation to figure out. Technically, for a door to slam closed, there would have to be a good, strong breeze. Plus, if that was the case, then several doors should have done the same or at least moved. There was very little wind blowing outside that night, so could it have been that? Possibly yes . . . but from my perspective, it probably wasn't.

• • •

All the activity that Tango and I had experienced up to that point put us on full alert while we finally made our way down to the Death Tunnel. We paid close attention to every little thing as we entered, even with fireworks of anticipation exploded in my head. The dank, dark, cement-lined passageway was eerily similar to a sewer, only with smoother walls and no dark water (and definitely no sign of a few young, anthropomorphic turtles with a penchant for martial arts).

As I shined my light around the tunnel's curved walls, the hairs on my neck started standing up. A subtle breeze tickled my skin and rolled in waves down my torso, sparking a gurgling deep in my stomach that was more excitement than nerves. Looking at Tango, I could tell he was feeling the same way.

The long chamber made even my gentle footsteps echo ominously. We stopped about forty yards in and looked around, trying to imagine ourselves as the workers who had to push countless bodies down this long pathway. Taking a deep breath, I turned off my flashlight, crossed my arms, and looked in the direction of the rough brick wall. Tango followed suit. The blackness was immediate and dense, as thick as a heavy fog. It should have felt unnerving, but it was rather calming to be surrounded by darkness and still air in a tunnel that was notorious for ferrying the dead. I turned on my audio recorder, and for over an hour Tango and I asked questions of the overwhelming darkness, sympathizing and trying to build a rapport in the hopes of gleaning answers from the beyond.

After a while, the oppressiveness of the Death Tunnel really started to feel daunting. When we finally turned our flashlights back on, the brightness stung my eyes. The image of dead bodies inside my mind—not to mention the innumerable insects likely crawling about that I couldn't see—instinctively made my insides tighten. Ultimately, Tango and I didn't experience much activity inside the tunnel; since it was primarily a transportation hub for dead bodies and no one had actually died inside

Waverly Hills's infamous death tunnel
JASON NELSON

it (that we knew of, anyway), we concluded that not many people would be attached to that location. Even so, I'll go on the record here as saying this subterranean passageway was probably one of the creepiest places I have ever investigated.

...

After emerging from the tunnel that first night, Tango and I eventually made our way to the morgue (under our own power, thankfully). Though bodies have passed through just about every inch of Waverly Hills, the morgue was the building's official space for the gathering of the dead.

As one might expect, any morgue, whether new and clean or old and decrepit, instantly evokes thoughts of spooky stories and horror movies. So, as we walked down the hall toward the morgue's entrance doors, I could feel my heart speed up a bit. While I'm always amped during an investigation, it's moments like these—seeing the proverbial scariest areas of a location—that switch my gears into full adventure mode. I feel like an explorer about to search an ancient cave . . . or, if you're a film buff like me, like one of the Goonies about to see One-Eyed Willy's ship for the first time.

I focused my flashlight toward a sign on the door. It was aged and fading but still readable: *Morgue: Authorized Personnel Only*. Once I was inside, the room wasn't really what I expected—instead of being full of stainless steel cabinets, everything was painted white. The walls, the gurneys, and even the body fridges were covered in what appeared to be peeling paint. Instantly, I found myself gravitating toward the body lockers, a small stack of three white metal compartments that sat alone against the wall. It struck me as incredibly odd for a place associated with more than sixty thousand deaths to have such a small handful of these lockers.

As I placed my hand on the cold door handle to one locker, terrifying bedtime tales from my youth started resurfacing in my mind. I had to shake them off with a long, hard blink and remind myself that this was a real place, with real stories. When I wrenched the door open, a burst of dry, stale air wafted into my nose, and a strange impulse suddenly overtook me: I wanted to know what it was like to be one of the corpses in Waverly Hills's morgue. I also decided that this would be a great place to try an EVP session. Sure, you might be more likely to receive a paranormal response where a person actually died, but the facility's

Me and Jason in front of the Waverly Hills
morgue drawers with a fan inside

morgue locker would have been the last spot where most bodies were stored before being cremated, so it was worth a shot to try this technique. Besides, I didn't know if I'd ever have a chance to be in one again!

My hands trembled as I pulled the body tray out of the locker; it creaked with an awful dry scraping of metal on metal. I tested the tray to make sure it was sturdy, then lay down on it, setting my camera and recorder on my chest and holding on to my flashlight. Tango already understood what I was doing, so I didn't even have to ask him to push me inside—a second after my head hit the dusty surface, he asked, "Ready?" I nodded and said, "Pull me out in an hour."

The eviscerating metal sound filled my ears, and I held my breath as if I were plunging underwater. I saw the top of the box pass my eyes and the crusty alloy roof slowly inch by, a mere finger's length above my nose. Once I was all the way inside, I felt comfortable enough to breathe again; the air was stale and smelled like someone put rusty metal and a moldy sock into a blender. The box was hollow and deep sounding despite being shallow, though I could hear Tango mumbling something about me being crazy. The door behind my head creaked shut and the blackness consumed me. Trying to ignore the rusty dust that was tickling my nostrils, I began thinking about how most of us will end up inside a box one day . . . and how many bodies in particular had been placed inside this one. It was a simultaneously horrific yet electrifying revelation. It brought on a flood of thinking about the fragility of life, but I pushed it all away and concentrated on the job at hand.

Photo from 2007 during our live episode investigation setup

While inside, I did my best to do a mini-investigation by asking questions and recording to see if I could catch any EVPs, which I didn't. There was also a camera on me to see if something happened, but in such a small space we didn't expect anything amazing to occur and not much did. I heard some voices here and there, but with the twisted filter of ancient steel there was no way for me to know if I was just hearing the sounds of people outside the drawer. After about a half hour, the air inside the box started to get dry and thick. I was hoping this experience would last longer, but I really wanted to get out, even if the full hour hadn't gone by. I told myself that I must have been nuts for thinking I could make it that long. Instead of yelling, I lightly knocked on the side wall as a signal to Tango that I'd had enough. I was relieved to hear a metal *thud*, as if someone was tugging at the door . . . but then it thudded a bit harder and I heard the mumbling of frustration. Tango couldn't get the door open.

Is he kidding? I thought, half trying to convince myself that Tango was probably pulling my chain and not the door handle. It didn't work—my relief instantly turned to panic. I tried sitting up but hit my forehead against the old, rusty ceiling. I fumbled for my flashlight, but it fell off to the side and I couldn't retrieve it from under the body tray. Sweat dripped heavily from my forehead as I began seriously regretting my impulsive idea . . . until a *whoosh* of fresh air ran up my torso as the door finally flung open. Seconds later, I exited the cramped space, feeling alive, free, and incredibly grateful. I started to laugh, no longer caring if Tango had been messing with me or if I'd really been temporarily stuck.

As I calmed down, I realized how visceral my experience had been. I was inside a body locker in the morgue of the world's most haunted building, in the middle of the night. That might be someone else's nightmare, but for me, it was a life goal achieved. Despite what happened, I had the biggest smile plastered on my face as we went back to our investigation.

• • •

Overall, our investigation of Waverly Hills Sanatorium was an unforgettable experience. It was so great, in fact, that TAPS returned there in 2007 to do a live Halloween episode of *Ghost Hunters*, which was quite surreal. Viewers knew ahead of time that we were going back, so when we arrived there were already hundreds of people lined up down the road, chanting for all of us. Seeing all the tents and chairs in the vicinity . . . it was like a tailgating party for the Super Bowl. Before we went live, the crowd was chanting for us so loudly that a few of us drove a golf cart down to their area to say hello and kindly ask them to quiet down so we could properly investigate without outside contamination. I felt a bit bad about having to do that—seeing them cheer us on reminded me of that great scene near the end of *Ghostbusters*, when the team walks out of the Shandor Building as heroes and all the New Yorkers gathered around them go wild—on a much smaller scale of course. But the meet and greet worked, as the crowd eventually dispersed.

The situation was also more stressful than a normal investigation—filming a live event is rather different from our usual investigations. Normally, we film for hours on end and over the course of multiple nights and the production company edits all that footage into a tight, forty-two-minute episode. Doing the show at Waverly Hills in real time meant having to set up cameras with live feeds before the event and hope everything worked out according to plan. For the show, we had the always amazing Josh Gates host the evening. Watching him run around the place all night and keep what's typically a quiet and intimate process interesting for live viewers was a kick. He bounced around like a Ping-Pong ball, ricocheting his way through the halls, constantly updating anyone watching at home, and racing to hot spots over and over. Josh is truly a wonder; I love working with him.

The live show was a daunting task, but it worked out great. Viewers really felt like they were a part of our team, getting to watch live feeds and comment online. There was also a "panic button" on the website that they could hit to alert us if they saw something. I was a bit skeptical that we'd experience anything with the sort of setup we had, so I was very surprised that I had my own intense paranormal interaction. At one point, while walking through a hallway, I felt something slapping across my legs, then pulling at my pants. I looked down to see what it was, but there was nothing there. I used my flashlight to search the hallway for signs of anything that could have been hitting my legs.

This is the hallway where I felt something slapping against my legs.
JASON NELSON

Again, there wasn't a single thing around that could have possibly done it. I walked the same path several times, but I couldn't re-create the sensation.

It was one of the more interesting paranormal experiences that I've ever had, but looking back, I wonder if it was some sort of environmental anomaly rather than a ghost. My thought process behind this, and other experiences like it, falls into the "why" category: If it was some sort of intelligent being or something trying to communicate, why would it slap and spin around my leg, and why only for a few seconds? What would be the intent behind that interaction? When something out of the ordinary happens, it's important to consider the intent, and in this instance it just didn't make sense. Therefore, I lean toward chalking up this encounter to an environmental experience that can't be properly explained: maybe some sort of indoor microburst (if that's even possible) . . . I honestly don't know. In the end, what I experienced was definitely paranormal— I'm just not sure it was a ghost.

It's also important to keep in mind that the word *paranormal* is *all too often* associated with ghosts. Society has become too accustomed to using that word to mean a spirit or haunting, but the actual definition via *Merriam-Webster* is: *not scientifically explainable*. That definition is extremely broad and covers a *lot* of things, including ghosts. However, it simply means that something happened and we can't yet explain it. Just remember: When the term *paranormal* is used to describe something, it doesn't necessarily mean *ghost*.

• • •

Over the years, I've gone back to Waverly Hills Sanatorium more than ten times. I've even investigated the place completely on my own. Being alone there at four in the morning . . . *that's* a whole other story, which could fill another book entirely. Between having so many other places to investigate and Waverly Hills being a fifteen-hour drive for me, the fact that I keep wanting to make that trip and head back there means that it's more than special to me—in fact, it may be my most favorite place of all.

I also love that I don't have to worry about Waverly Hills being torn down anytime soon, unlike so many other locations that are at risk today. The sanatorium is now on the U.S. National Register of Historic Places, and there are efforts underway to preserve its history. If it isn't hands down *the* most haunted place in America, it's pretty damn close, so I'm thrilled that it will remain there for generations of paranormal investigators to come.

PEOPLE CAN BE SCARIER
THAN GHOSTS

JOHN SOWDEN HOUSE
—
LOS ANGELES, CA
BUILT 1926

In 1926, famed architect Lloyd Wright (son of the more famous Frank Lloyd Wright) custom-built a six-thousand-square-foot, neo-Mayan-themed home for wealthy photographer and painter John Sowden. Wright's imagination, along with Sowden's unusual requests, resulted in one of the most unique homes in America. The front of this residence, aptly nicknamed the "Jaws House," features flat concrete walls and a creepy yet elegant structure that gives the impression of a large stone mouth gaping open, ready to devour any guests. Upon visitors' entering the cave-like entrance, a tomb-inspired staircase brings them up to the main hall—a rectangular, open layout that drips of an elegance and eccentricity that was coveted during the early Hollywood era.

Sowden had wanted a unique and stunning setting to entertain his filmmaking friends. Instead, its harsh, drastically odd design drew widespread criticism and ultimately motivated him to sell the house after only a few years of living there. (Ironically, many years later, the Sowden House is recognized as one of Lloyd's most important works.) Ownership of the residence changed hands several times until 1945, when it was purchased by George Hodel, a well-to-do LA physician . . . and a sadistic, murderous monster.

On the morning of January 15, 1947, the body of Elizabeth Short was found lying in Leimert Park, cut in half, drained of blood, and mutilated in horrific ways. Because her body could not be easily identified at the time, Short's black-dyed hair and clothing earned her posthumous notoriety as the Hollywood murder victim known only as the "Black Dahlia." Though the crime remained unsolved, police looked at numerous persons of interest . . . including their eventual main suspect, Dr. George Hodel.

Dr. Hodel had drawn the LAPD's attention several times throughout the 1940s—he was a person of interest in the 1945 death of his secretary, Ruth Spaulding, and he was interviewed by police about the "Green Twig Murder" of Louise Springer in 1949. (The latter accusation wouldn't become public record until nearly seventy years later.) However, it was Hodel's 1949 arrest and trial for the alleged rape and impregnation of his own teenage daughter, Tamar, that made him a prime suspect in Elizabeth Short's murder. During the trial, Tamar claimed that her father was the Black Dahlia killer, and police suspected that Short's body had been bisected by someone with a surgical skill set.

Dr. Hodel was acquitted of his incestual abuse (and ending his daughter's pregnancy with an abortion procedure) due to insufficient evidence; however, the trial prompted the district attorney and an LAPD task force to monitor the Sowden House in the hopes of recording evidence of his guilt for his other crimes. Though he was never charged with any homicides, the doctor was recorded on one tape as saying, "Supposin' I did kill the Black Dahlia. They can't prove it now. They can't talk to my secretary anymore because she's dead. They thought there was something fishy. Anyway, now they may have figured it out. Killed her. Maybe I did kill my secretary."

Years after the doctor's death, his son, retired LA homicide detective Steve Hodel, set out to write a book that proved his father's innocence. However, after Steve found so much evidence to the contrary, his best-selling book, Black Dahlia Avenger: The True Story, provided detailed evidence that pointed to Dr. Hodel having tortured and murdered Elizabeth Short in the master bath of the Sowden House. Steve also claims to this day that his father had killed numerous people inside the residence, then buried the bodies either in the basement or the yard. Furthermore, Steve has also connected his father—who had relocated several times, both around and outside the United States—to being the "Lipstick Killer" of Chicago, the "Jigsaw Murderer" of Manila, and the legendary "Zodiac Killer" of San Francisco . . . all locations that the doctor lived in around the same time their respective slayings occurred. A handwriting analysis even matched the Zodiac's letters to those of Dr. Hodel.

If Steve Hodel's findings and claims are accurate, then George Hodel was allegedly one of the most deranged serial killers this world has ever seen . . . and he used the John Sowden House as his perverted playground for years. There's little wonder as to why the home is widely purported to be haunted, with numerous sightings of black masses, sounds of bodies being dragged, and a mysterious apparition of a woman looking terrified for her life.

• • •

As mentioned in the introduction to this book, the movie to which I most attribute my fascination with ghosts and investigating is *The Entity*, having been based on a true story. Knowing that the paranormal events inspiring the movie happened in Los Angeles, every time I travel there I can't help but think of the story that started it all for me. I had been to Los Angeles a few times before this case and loved it—it *is* the film capital of the world, after all.

Several years before being called out to investigate the John Sowden House, the TAPS team and I headed to the City of Angels to check out the property where the Charles Manson murders took place. The original Sharon Tate home had been demolished by this point and the address changed to remove the stigma of the horrific crimes committed there, yet the new owners insisted that the house was haunted. It was a dark and heavy investigation, and just a terribly unsettling experience to be where those atrocities occurred.

Thankfully, we took on a much lighter investigative case nearby that same week . . . at Jim Henson Studios. If you're a child of the 1970s to the 1990s, or even just the nineties, Jim Henson played a major role in your life. Whether it was *Sesame Street*, *The Muppets*, *Fraggle Rock*, *The Dark Crystal*, *Labyrinth*, or one of many other films or TV shows, Henson's creative wizardry was a constant for multiple generations. He and his team brought his inanimate creations to life in such brilliant ways that it's impossible not to feel nostalgia just hearing the name Henson. Having the opportunity to tour the studio that made my childhood so wonderful had the inner kid in me beaming with joy.

Long before it became the Jim Henson Company Lot, the studio was owned by comedy icon Charlie Chaplin. Around 1917, he purchased the property—which consisted primarily of a farm of orange and lemon trees—and transformed it into the legendary Chaplin Studios, which produced some of cinema's most revered silent films, including *The Kid*,

The Gold Rush, and *City Lights*. It might sound overly sentimental, but the idea of standing in a place that made films that changed the world is something I take very seriously. Whenever I visit such a historic location, I like to stand still and imagine the greatness (or tragedy) that occurred in that very spot. So, I couldn't wait to be among these film legends, all while picturing Chaplin dancing around with that giant balloon globe from *The Great Dictator*.

I was excited when we arrived at the studio, which is normal before a hunt, but this was more akin to going to a theme park than an investigation. When I saw the Jim Henson Studios sign and a beautiful statue of Kermit the Frog dressed as Charlie Chaplin next to the gates, my gut rolled with anticipation, just like walking through the gates at Disney. As we drove through the lot, I saw various paintings and signs of Chaplin on doors and walls, along with plaques stating what movie was filmed on which stage. It was like traveling through a film history documentary.

We got out of the van and entered a courtyard where I saw Charlie Chaplin's actual footprints in cement. It must have been close to a hundred years later, but I couldn't believe how perfectly preserved they were. Then we were introduced to Brian Henson, Jim's son and the chairman of the studio. He was so gracious and kind—we chatted for a bit and he walked us to the sound stage before saying his good-byes and letting one of his workers give us a tour. There was memorabilia everywhere I turned—cases of Emmys and other awards, photos, and props on proud display . . . it was mind-boggling. I saw puppets from *Fraggle Rock*, *The Muppets*, *The Witches*, and one of my ultimate obsessions growing up, *Labyrinth*. I watched that movie almost weekly for years, so seeing actual puppets from it was like encountering a celebrity I thought I'd never meet.

Before Brian left us, he noted, "Our house is yours. Have fun in here. Go wherever you want; do whatever you want—just don't break anything." I couldn't believe he was giving us complete and utter access to absolutely anything we wanted as part of our investigation, but then came one last request: "The original Skeksis from *The Dark Crystal* are in the costume department under a protective tarp. Please don't touch them." Brian had mentioned that they were in a bit of disrepair and his team was getting ready to restore them. But as soon as I heard him mention *The Dark Crystal*, childhood memories of sitting on the carpet and watching the film over and over again flooded my mind . . . so I just couldn't resist taking a look.

Tango and I snuck away from the rest of the team, and I found a giant tarp and instantly knew it contained the creepy robed birds I loved from that movie. I knew I wasn't supposed to touch it, and technically I didn't, but I *did* lift up the tarp to see a terrifying, vulture-like face staring at me. Here I was, in Hollywood, staring at the Skeksis from *The Dark Crystal*. I couldn't believe that my love of ghosts had taken me down such a crazy path to this moment. But before I could soak in that moment, the guide's cautionary words echoed in my head. He was so kind and it was his only request, so I had to be respectful of his wishes. I ignored my urges to touch and take pictures, and I lowered the tarp.

The paranormal claims at the studio did not center around Chaplin, Henson, or any of the major stars who had history with the lot, though they did seem to be centered around the early days of Hollywood. There were stories of a man in a top hat and suit being seen on the roof, a woman in a frilly dress who would disappear by walking through a door, a man with a handlebar mustache who had been seen strolling across the sound stage, and voices and whispers being heard on the catwalks high above the studio floor. Given that it's an active film and TV studio, where actors are in costume on a daily basis, I had to take the claims of people in period costumes with a grain of salt, as they could have easily been extras in the wrong place. Regardless, we took our investigation seriously as always.

I only heard a few phantom footsteps myself, but Jay and Grant caught an amazing heat signature on the thermal camera around the sound-stage area. The image clearly looked like a woman. When they tried to re-create the image, they had to move a set of stairs over to the area, as the heat signature appeared more than five feet off the floor. Being that this matched the most common claims in that building, this was some great evidence. Just thinking about all this again and writing it here . . . I have to say, out of all the places that I've investigated, the Jim Henson Studio was probably one of the most interesting places of my career.

• • •

Of course, our reason for being LA bound this time was nothing to sing about; we were going to investigate the residence that was connected to the notorious Black Dahlia murder. I've always been fascinated by true crime, and this gruesome case has perplexed the world for decades and spawned dozens of books, numerous movies, and countless TV specials. The idea of walking around what was most likely the scene of the crime gave me chills that wouldn't go away. What if we could find something new, or make contact with Elizabeth Short herself—or her killer?

• • •

I spent the next five days driving across the country, keeping a laser focus on the road and wishing that the trip to Los Angeles would go faster. Thankfully, I had three true crime audiobooks to keep me company.

Audiobooks are one of the greatest perks of driving. I love reading physical books, but when you're in a car with miles of road and hours ahead of you, there's nothing else to do but sit and listen. In fact, I sometimes find myself looking forward to driving so I can keep listening to whatever book I'm obsessed with at any given time. These days, I have access to an entire library of titles with the touch of a button on my phone. I get to check out dozens of books a year that I never would have if I didn't drive. Granted, the open road has so much to offer, but I will always associate driving with audiobooks and podcasts.

When we all finally arrived and saw the giant Hollywood sign up on Mount Lee, I smiled as my lifelong childhood associations with film and television flooded into my head. I don't get out to California much, so I wanted to take full advantage of my time there. Tango and I drove out a few days early so we could rest up from the trip and do the whole tourist thing. But the one thing we did that knocked my socks off the most was visiting the Magic Castle.

If you aren't familiar with this legendary place, it's a members-only club for professional magicians run by the Academy of Magical Arts. Part museum, part dinner-and-a-show, the Magic Castle hosts legendary magicians past and present at this prestigious club. To perform there as an illusionist is one of the greatest honors of the trade. Many of them will try out new tricks inside the dinner theater; they know that if their act goes over well with a house full of magicians, it will work with a wider audience. Because of the Magic Castle's exclusivity, you can't get in without an invite from an active member. Fortunately, one of our producers *was* a member and he got invites for me, Tango, and a few other lucky people on our crew. Donning crushed-velvet suit jackets (such attire being required), we all walked into the century-old institute and enjoyed an unforgettable evening. And as memorable as it was for me, it was even more special for Tango, since he's a card-carrying magician himself and had always wanted to visit the castle.

• • •

After I fulfilled my Hollywood wish list, it was time to get serious and head to the John Sowden House. There would be no childhood nostalgia while investigating this case . . . just pure, unadulterated horror. To be perfectly honest, looking at this massive home from the outside made me scratch my head. There was beautiful, lush vegetation along the stairs, but as I viewed the structure itself, it didn't even look like a house. Two sides of it resembled the back of a department store— smooth, flat walls with zero windows, design elements, or even color. It was as if someone had forgotten to finish parts of the building. In the middle was a bizarre structure that reminded me of the Skeksis that I'd recently seen in the Jim Henson facilities. A series of windows sat where the "mouth" would be, and a door was almost hidden from view under the "jawline."

Inside the home was a different story. It was one of the most unique and beautiful places I had ever seen, even if it did have an ominous feel to it. Mayan-themed stone carvings and warm-climate plants throughout, though gorgeous to look at, made it similar to an antique resort hotel you'd find on some lone tropical island, complete with an indoor koi pond. High vaulted ceilings and floor-to-ceiling windows made most of the rooms feel enormous. In fact, one of the bedrooms was so large it had a swing about fifteen feet in the air, but how anyone got up there I couldn't tell you.

A courtyard within the center of the Sowden House made me almost

believe I was in another country. It had the unique feature of providing almost every room in the structure with direct access to the area.
Originally, the courtyard had been a lush lawn that was intended as a
performance space. Years later, by the time we saw it, it had been turned
into an artsy pool and sitting area. The idea of every room opening to
one central place, as if it was necessary for them to provide instant access to this spot, made me a little curious. It instantly reminded me of

A 1940 street view of the entrance
LIBRARY OF CONGRESS

a cult compound, where all members had easy access to the altar they worshipped.

I certainly appreciated the architecture, but something about the home made me uncomfortable, and it wasn't just for the obvious reasons that had brought us there. The place gave off a vibe like it had been designed by Patrick Bateman from *American Psycho*—clean-cut elegance with a cruel darkness hidden deep inside. It's hard for me to believe there was nothing sinister about its design. Whether it was the stories that were attached to the house, the cold, unwelcoming aesthetic, or something else that I couldn't put my finger on, it truly felt . . . *off*.

I was very excited about meeting Steve Hodel, having heard about his book *Black Dahlia Avenger: The True Story*. Steve had such intimate knowledge about the case, and he was more than kind enough answering the thousand questions I had about his father, as well as the heinous actions inside the Sowden House. From the evidence Steve collected, he believed that his dad killed Elizabeth Short in the master bathtub and up to nine women in the basement. Though nothing was ever proven inside a court of law, Steve's stories were chilling and sobering to hear. That such a rich, posh home, built for lavish parties and to entertain the elite, could have been a house of torture is truly a dichotomy that only Hollywood could create.

• • •

The claims of paranormal activity within the Sowden House were on the milder side for a place that might have witnessed such unspeakable horrors. Previous tenants claimed to hear strange voices and dragging sounds in the hallways; one owner got so used to the noises that he'd just say, "*Oh, it's George again. Go to bed.*" Among several reported sightings

Courtyard view of the studio entrance
LIBRARY OF CONGRESS

Interior hallway leading from the kitchen to the
master bedroom
LIBRARY OF CONGRESS

of female apparitions within the basement, there was one in which the spirit allegedly appeared only from the waist up, as if she'd been cut in half. Another account spoke of a dark figure that stood over their sleeping children's beds; being that George Hodel was arrested for sexually assaulting his own daughter, I found this claim especially upsetting.

From almost the very start of our investigation inside the residence, I heard footsteps close behind me, several times. At one point, I could hear what sounded like something being quickly pulled off a table, even though I was in the hallway and not near a table. I wanted to call out whenever I heard these noises but was unsure how to talk to the spirits in this house. I debated whether to reach out to the female victims or to attempt speaking directly to George Hodel. Normally, I try to be kind and welcoming to spirits. However, I saw this as a rare situation in which I would also need to be stern and provoke the spirit a little. I started with the victims, and I did my best to be gentle and open; honestly, though, based on how these poor souls perished, I don't think there was anything I could say that would be positive.

Bearing that in mind, I turned my attention to George and quickly became comfortable using a more aggressive tone. It isn't the kind of thing that I'd do often; it's disrespectful overall, and you never truly know who you're communicating with. The theory is that George Hodel had drained Elizabeth of her blood in the tub of the master bathroom, so I sat in the area and focused my time there, hoping he might have some sort of sick emotional connection with the space. We managed to collect some EVPs, though none of them came from George. I suspect that was because it was the victims who were stuck here in the house, not him.

We got three more great albeit unsettling EVPs later that night. One sounded like a child saying, "*It's George*," as if attempting to reveal the killer's identity, while another said, "*Did you even know my name?*" The third EVP was hard to discern, but it sounded like a woman struggling. Truthfully, it was awful to listen to, especially because it made me think that the poor woman who suffered might be repeatedly reliving the experience of her murder. I could only hope that it was a residual haunting, so she wouldn't have to suffer those tortures more.

EVPs can sometimes leave us, as investigators, struggling to connect what we think we hear with the actual case. But it is important to remember that not all EVPs are connected to the deaths in a location. However, the three EVPs in this instance were so direct that it's hard to deny their implications. George Hodel was a suspected serial killer; was one of his victims trying to reach out and tell us that he was her murderer? The second EVP was agonizing to listen to. Was it Elizabeth Short, asking her killer if he even knew her name before he took her life? Or could it have been one of many other suspected victims asking the same thing? While we'll likely never know, a part of me prefers to think it was the Black Dahlia desperately trying to finally speak out to the world.

• • •

Since it's believed that George Hodel killed some of his victims in the basement, we decided to bring in a cadaver dog to sniff around and perhaps uncover any evidence of remains. These dogs are amazing—they can smell bacteria that feasts on human blood and decomposition as deep as forty feet underground with a 95 percent accuracy. They can also locate bodies that have been buried for decades. Because they only react to human remains, there's zero chance that they could have false "hits" from an animal carcass. Admittedly, we were skeptical of the dog picking up on anything after so much time had passed. But the basement had a dirt floor, which made the chances of discovery much greater than if the floor had been cemented over (and on a personal sidenote, I found it odd that a multimillion-dollar home would have a dirt basement rather than one that was finished).

In talking to Steve Hodel before the investigation, I learned he was convinced of his research and firmly believed that his father had committed homicide in that basement. So, when Buster the cadaver dog ran down there and signaled almost instantly that he'd found something, I couldn't help but chuckle slightly at knowing how right Steve was. In various places in the basement, Buster pointed out numerous spots where he detected human remains. Impressed with how well he performed, we went out and let him sniff around the yard. In the very back of the property, the dog came up with a few more hits, this time under some plume flowers (which, according to what we were told, are associated with decaying material).

Based on Buster's discoveries, soil samples were taken from the basement and backyard and sent off to be analyzed. Months after our investigation, the results for the yard samples came back. They were analyzed by Dr. Arpad Vass, a forensic anthropologist who worked on the Casey Anthony case. His report stated: "Chemical analysis of the irrigation box soil showed numerous markers for a decompositional event. These markers were human specific and indicate that human remains were, or are, present in the vicinity of where the soil was collected. Data analysis suggests human remains may have been present at location in excess of forty years." I can't say I was shocked, though I was excited that we'd get to share these results in the episode we shot; after all, this was a major development in one of the greatest unsolved murders of all time. We notified Steve Hodel and the homeowners of our findings, and I believed they would keep us in the loop about what they found when they dug up the basement and yard. To my surprise, not only were we never called back, but all our findings were cut completely from the episode.

Not long after the investigation, news articles began popping up around the world, from the *Los Angeles Times* to the UK's *Daily Mail*, detailing the cadaver dog's findings. Being that I didn't stay in touch with Steve, I'm not sure if he used the investigation we conducted or if he expanded on his own search based on our discoveries . . . because no reports mentioned our investigation at all. We didn't need credit for the findings—it was just very odd that something we did became a worldwide news story, yet there wasn't even a passing mention about us.

I think what shocks me more is that our own show didn't capitalize on any of this and that our results were intentionally left out of the episode's final edit. There had to be a very specific reason why we weren't taking credit for something that earned major headlines—I just wish I knew what it was. What's even stranger is that, at least to my knowledge, no one ever dug up the basement or any of the other spots that Buster hit to look for any remains. Regardless of everyone else's actions, I feel very confident that something sinister happened in that basement, and I'm proud we found the evidence to support that theory.

• • •

When an investigator is dealing with ghosts, we're also dealing with death. That's the job. But when the details surrounding those deaths are so sickening and painful, it can be very hard to cope sometimes. This particular investigation was one of the few in my life that was so dark and heavy that it made me want to shower the moment I left the location. Even then, I felt that darkness cling to me for weeks following the investigation. I'm not sure if it was something about the house that attached itself to me like a tick or just the mental weight of the experience there. Whatever it was sure as hell affected me deeply, just like Steve Hodel's story. He started out writing his first book to prove his father's innocence, only to reveal that his parent might have been much darker and more evil than anyone ever realized. While I always like to trust people, it goes to show you that as much as you think you know someone, there could be a whole other side of them you don't know anything about.

The John Sowden House is one of the most unique and intriguing locations I have ever visited. Even with its uncomfortable vibes and terrifying past, it truly was an unforgettable experience to investigate a place that's synonymous with Hollywood's dark history.

A LAYERED HAUNTING
IN BIGLERVILLE

WITCHING TREE, PRIVATE RESIDENCE
—

BIGLERVILLE, PA

EARLY 1800s

Just before the American Civil War, an elderly Irishwoman in Biglerville—a rural village outside Gettysburg—couldn't afford to pay the loans on her property. When her home was forcibly taken, she cursed the land and the residents of the small Pennsylvania village. The following day, livestock around the area started to grow sick. Soon after, cows, chickens, and pigs died one by one. The well, the town's main source of water, began drying up. It was all too much of a coincidence; the townspeople decided that the old woman must have been a witch and they needed to take action in order to save their land. Grabbing pitchforks, torches, and any other weapons they could carry, the townsfolk organized into an angry mob and eventually found their suspected "monster" hiding in a small attic room above a pub.

Fearing for her life, the woman frantically insisted that she had only fabricated the curse out of anger. The unruly mob refused to listen; dragging her downstairs and to a field outside, they took turns beating the defenseless woman with shovels, sticks, rocks, and canes. She continued begging and pleading her innocence until finally succumbing to her injuries. When the mob's fervor died down, they realized what they had done. As they looked at the woman's broken body, one person suggested that the only way to contain a witch's spirit was to bury her and plant a tree on top of the grave. As long as the tree survived, the thinking went, the spirit could not escape to harm them. A collective agreement was made. By sunrise, a new sapling had been snugly planted into the fresh dirt that now also served as a gravesite.

The tree was strong and still growing in 1868 when Henry Lower, who owned the house a mere hundred yards away, was buried alive at the bottom of a ditch he'd been digging. It was deemed an accident, although how such a tragic event could have occurred to someone who had dug hundreds of ditches is a mystery. Around 1930, the new owner of the home, Ellis Collins, was found dead in a field a few miles away. A reputed heavy drinker with a bitter attitude, Collins was the victim of alcohol poisoning, though it was not accidental. A group of men had been seen earlier that day forcing him to drink as they tried to make him fill out a blank check. Had Ellis become another victim of the cursed land?

More than 150 years after the tree was planted, a woman named Glenda Farquhar bought the house on the property. The very first day she moved into her new home, she came down the stairs and saw a man with bibbed overalls and a cap standing by the door. Thinking it was a neighbor, Glenda paused to say hello, only for the man to vanish into thin air. Not long after, she saw an elderly woman with her hair in a bun, standing in the kitchen, wearing an apron, and holding a basket. After making eye contact, the woman turned and walked away, disappearing from the residence. Similar bizarre experiences continued happening in the home, but Glenda, fearing she'd be deemed insane, kept them to herself—even after her new husband, Steve Banasick, moved in. It wasn't long before one evening Steve saw the same woman with a basket standing on the porch, with snow blowing around. When he told Glenda about his experience, she finally opened up to him that she had seen the same person. The first time Steve saw the male apparition, he was peeling an apple at the kitchen table. After the room suddenly went cold, he heard a man's voice behind him say, "That's woman's work." Steve spun around and saw an old man standing there and staring at him. Startled, Steve jumped and lost control of the knife he was using; it skidded across the apple and stabbed into his hand. The old man then said, "It's getting crowded in here," and vanished before his eyes.

After Steve related this encounter to Glenda, she revealed that whenever she performed hard labor on the farm an old man would appear, tell her to "act like a lady," and then disappear. After contacting a local paranormal investigator to help them, the newlyweds discovered the legend of the witch and the tree that was on their property. The tree had died, split, and dried out many years earlier, leaving Glenda and Steve to fear that if the legend was indeed true, then the old woman's spirit was free to exact her revenge.

· · ·

Up until now, every location I've referred to in this book has been of a larger scale—asylums, closed factories, prisons, Hollywood mansions, even a restaurant/bar. So why, you might ask, did I put a residential farmhouse in Biglerville, Pennsylvania, on my list of favorite places? Perhaps the best way I can answer that is with a question of my own: "Why *wouldn't* I?" The legend of a witch, curses, multiple strange deaths on the property, and full-body apparitions, along with an unraveling mystery and a sense of *something* being there, as well as the opportunity to help people (which isn't always the case in big locations) . . . this place deserves to be on the list. Add the intense, renowned battles that occurred just down the street at Gettysburg, plus the rich background of the abolitionist movement's Underground Railroad in the area, and you have a location that's over-flowing with history . . . and ripe with paranormal activity.

We were called to investigate Biglerville, which ended up being on our show *Ghost Nation*, which featured just Jay, Tango, and myself. *Ghost Nation* is more intimate than *Ghost Hunters*; we focus on helping people with their paranormal issues more than the locations and activities. Though I investigate because I love the thrill of adventure and solving mysteries, my goal has always been to find the answers to my own questions. Close behind that, however, is my sincere desire to aid those in need. Living in a house that has frequent paranormal activity can tear a family apart. If I can use my knowledge to help out *and* collect evidence at the same time, it's a win-win for everyone involved. That was certainly my hope for the newlyweds in Biglerville; the activity in their home was creating a rift in their relationship, and they simply didn't know what to do.

• • •

I've grown accustomed to winding roads that suddenly open up to reveal some long-gone architect's grand structure. This drive, however, brought Jay, Tango, and me through a rural town of rolling hills, farmland, and quaint homes. We pulled into Glenda's driveway, which seemed just like the hundreds of others we had passed along the way. Taking in the property, we saw there was a main house built around the start of the 1900s, a good-sized barn, and a summer house, all of which Glenda and Steve claimed to have had paranormal experiences within. The house itself looked perfectly normal—certainly not haunted, ominous, or evil in any way (Hollywood would not have approved). The grounds were spread out and flat, like any farm . . . except for the striking dead tree out in the middle of the field, behind the house.

In meeting with Glenda and Steve, I could tell how rattled they'd been by the activity in their home. They talked about the constant disruption with us, along with Patty, a local paranormal investigator who'd contacted us about this case. After planning out the investigation, we set up our equipment and settled in for a full week of research and investigation.

Our primary focus was the house, as the couple claimed that they'd both seen full-body apparitions of an old man and woman on numerous occasions there. Glenda and Steve agreed to stay in a hotel for the week, which gave us free rein over the property, and we decided to start with the main dwelling.

The tree that the "witch" was allegedly buried beneath

In one of the claims, the old man walked through the dining room and right into the wall, where a window was located. Like always, we asked ourselves the "why" question—specifically, why would the spirit walk right into a wall? Our research uncovered that there used to be a door where the window was now located. So, it made perfect sense that the mystery man would walk to that spot if that's where he used to exit the room while he was alive.

Typically, if a ghost repeats an action they did back when they were living, without reacting to the current time and space, they're considered a "residual haunting." The old man's repetitive behavior made me suspect that's what we were looking at here . . . except Glenda and Steve each noted that both apparitions had spoken with them. And not just words said out loud without context . . . both entities looked right into their eyes and addressed them. That would indicate an "intelligent haunting" or, even better, a "layered haunting," a combination of either residual and intelligent hauntings or haunts from different eras of time. It's unknown variables like these that always make investigations invigorating. Were both types of hauntings really involved? What would we find?

To help get us some answers, we set up our new sonar scanner in the kitchen. The device works like those that boaters use for finding fish underwater—it produces sound waves, much like a bat's echolocation. Basically, it reads and maps a room and picks up any disturbances, giving us a visual interpretation of what's happening in that area. We let the scanner do its work while we asked questions aloud around the kitchen, trying to build a rapport with whatever was there in the hopes of capturing an EVP, a disembodied voice, or even better, one of the apparitions. We didn't have much luck with either the scanner or our questions; however, one of our cameras in the kitchen focused on the dining room entrance, and it caught a shadowlike figure moving across the dining room. The figure was faint but as clear as day, and its shape looked just like a person. The video evidence was rather unnerving, but for me as a paranormal investigator, it set off internal fireworks of excitement.

Next, we made our way to the summer house, which was pretty much a large, unassuming storage shed with windows. The activity inside was nonexistent, though Tango and I discovered what looked like an entrance to a tunnel beneath the structure. With stories about the Underground Railroad fresh in our heads, we wondered if this had been one of the passages used to help the enslaved escape to free states. It didn't look safe, so we decided to wait until daylight before doing anything with our discovery. Of course, watching Tango peer down the tunnel opening with his flashlight, I couldn't resist giving him a quick scare. I snuck up behind him, grabbed him tight, and screamed, *"Don't fall!"* Tango hollered at the top of his lungs and clutched his chest, then spent the next two minutes trying to catch his breath. The two of us had a good laugh about it . . . but I knew he was silently plotting a swift payback.

The following day, we looked around the property to see if we could find anything like our tunnel in the summer house. Just off the road, we noticed some construction work that had been left covered up. When we inquired about it, we learned that the gas company had been doing some digging, but they found part of an old tunnel underground and stopped work until it could be examined. Based on both discoveries, we decided to call in an infrastructure engineer who specialized in historical properties to look at the crawl space and tunnel.

The engineer was quickly able to determine that the tunnel under the summer house was indeed just an old crawl space that was most likely a root cellar for storing canned goods. Tunnels for the Underground Railroad would connect to other homes, whereas the one we'd discovered had no entrance or exit. He was also able to establish that the structures by the road weren't Underground Railroad tunnels either but more likely long-forgotten drainage channels that once connected to a nearby factory. This was mostly confirmed, as they led right toward a nearby stream, which probably served as a dumping area. I found this revelation fascinating—we never know the history that could lie under our feet—but we decided not to investigate them any further since there were no claims of paranormal activity surrounding them. That doesn't mean it isn't haunted; it just means we needed to focus our time on where the family was having their experiences.

. . .

With our tunnel situation resolved, Jay, Tango, and I went out to the barn to investigate the claims of hearing footsteps in the upper area, seeing items mysteriously move, and picking up sounds of children playing. Jay had noted footsteps in the barn the night before, so I was excited about what I myself might experience there. As soon as the three of us entered the barn, we heard several odd noises, including one that sounded like rocks being thrown. As we stood still listening, a loud *bang* came without warning, like someone hitting a metal cabinet with a baseball bat. We searched everywhere around the floor but couldn't determine what had caused the sound. That noise didn't reoccur, but we kept hearing what sounded like rocks hitting things upstairs. I decided to head up to the barn attic alone, either to find the source or to see if I could re-create the noise for Jay and Tango below.

The barn attic looked like your typical horror movie set—old items strewn about, some covered in dusty sheets, others broken and laced with spiderwebs. It was creepy to say the least . . . so I was right in my element. I brought a rock with me so I could launch it at the ceiling to see if any birds or bats were hanging around up there. Nothing stirred when the rock clashed against the tin, and I saw no visible signs of animal activity up there. Just to be certain, I also pulled out the thermal camera and scanned the room, since it would pick up a signature of any wildlife. There wasn't a trace of heat anywhere. The attic was animal-free, so I completely ruled out that the noises were coming from a natural source.

Even after I scanned, that sound kept occurring, over and over. Since we couldn't find the source, Jay, Tango, and I figured the phantom noise had been our only experience in the barn that night. However, following the investigation, when we went through the evidence, we found an EVP on our recorder . . . that of a child. While I was heading upstairs to the barn attic, the recorder caught a young voice whispering, clear as day, "Where'd he go?" It's a rather chilling EVP that seems to confirm Glenda's and Steve's claims that they'd heard sounds of children playing in the barn. But who were they, and why were they attached to this place? There was no mention of children in any of the initial research we conducted, but this discovery prompted us to set out and do some more digging into the matter.

• • •

Tango had done the heavy lifting on research for this investigation, so he went into town to find out whatever he could. He didn't uncover anything involving children, though he was able to confirm that the stories told about the property were, in fact, true. A man named Henry Lower had indeed perished on the grounds, crushed to death under mounds of dirt while digging a hole. Tango also learned that years later, Lower's wife,

Hannah, had also passed away on the property, from natural causes. This information was all fascinating, since most of Glenda's and Steve's claims revolved around seeing an older man and woman. The name Henry was also intriguing, as Patty, the local investigator, had earlier caught an EVP that mentioned that specific name. Could it be possible that Henry and Hannah had never left the home they loved?

What proved even more mind-blowing was that Tango learned the story about a real person accused of being a witch was true, and that she'd been blamed for the deaths of the town's livestock. Whether or not she ended up under that tree on the property, we did not know.

Outside of the Salem Witch Trials, there aren't many documented cases or much historical literature that directly calls out such a figure. Yet here in Biglerville, we managed to find an old newspaper article that actually claimed a witch named Suzy H. had put a curse on the property. This revelation floored me; I couldn't tell you how many times I've heard a spooky story or lore about an evil entity on some parcel of land—*every* town has a story like that—but there's never a lick of any real evidence or history. Yet here in Biglerville's library was actual documentation about the claims pertaining to Glenda and Steve's property. This discovery made the possibilities of the land being cursed and a body buried under the tree much more plausible.

Curses and magic aren't necessarily things I personally subscribe to; however, I've learned over the years that if someone truly believes in something, their belief becomes a fact to *them* and no one can convince them otherwise. It's the placebo effect—if you're given a harmless sugar pill but told it's medication, your body may feel better because your mind has been conditioned into helping you feel better. If you truly believe in a curse, then your mind might blame that curse for anything bad that happens. This can also set off a chain reaction of others believing what you tell them, because it happened to you. It's amazing to think how insanely powerful and how susceptible the human mind can be.

Still . . . a witch? It was hard for me to think that the activity on the farm had anything to do with the supposed curse. Other than the one farming accident that took the life of Henry Lower, nothing appeared truly out of the ordinary here. More important, none of the activity seemed to have any vengeful or evil intent. Most of the accounts were of apparitions of an old, cranky couple . . . scary and unsettling, perhaps, but harmless. Nevertheless, even though the haunting seemed to be more grounded in reality—a couple who loved their home and didn't want to leave—we still had an obligation to look into the allegations of the witch.

• • •

To help us with our "witch hunt" and literally get to the bottom of what was under that tree on Glenda and Steve's property, we called in a crew with professional cadaver dogs. We were really pleased when we used super-sniffing K-9s like Buster for our investigation of the John Sowden House in Los Angeles, and I was looking forward to watching them work here. Dogs' noses are little miracles—with up to *300 million* olfactory receptors (as opposed to the mere 6 million humans have), their sense of smell is unlike anything we can imagine.

When the crew first showed up, Jay and I asked them to have the cadaver dogs search the entire property. We intentionally left out the detail that we were mainly interested in the tree, as we didn't want to influence their search or what they found in any way. One at a time, they let each dog run around and smell every inch of the grounds. As I watched the first dog dart around and sniff everything, he reminded me of the old Looney Tunes canine characters, with their butts high in the air and their noses pressed to the ground as they searched for an offending odor.

Being my skeptical self, I really wasn't expecting the dogs to find anything on the property. Yet that pessimistic thought had no sooner run through my head when the first dog made a hit . . . right by the tree. After closely sniffing the roots repeatedly, the dog sat down right beside the base of the tree, indicating that he had found the scent of bacteria that feasts on human remains. My jaw almost hit the ground in shock, but that was just the first dog. When the crew sent the second cadaver canine out to run around, I felt my stomach knot up. Acre after acre, the dog found nothing . . . until he got to the tree. Just like his companion, the dog smelled everything numerous times, then finally lay down to signal he had found something around the area. This time I think my jaw *did* hit the ground. When they let the third dog out, I didn't have to worry about picking up my chin, because I knew exactly where he was going to stop. And, sure enough, he did.

Having three confirmed hits made us pretty confident that human remains were under the tree. With the dogs' 95 percent accuracy rate and all three hitting independent of one another, this was the closest to a definitive answer we could get. We had also used cadaver dogs while working on my documentary film *The House in Between*, and I'd had a great conversation with their trainers. They explained that what the dogs actually smell is a certain bacterium that forms on decay that is present only on human remains. The bacteria can stay on those remains for hundreds of years, if not longer. It can also travel through tree and plant roots and make its way up into the canopies and leaves. Hearing all this really made me think about how amazing life is.

The cadaver dogs' discovery, though, put us in a tricky situation. Ethically, we had to notify the police. However, if they came out, they could possibly shut down our entire investigation and seize Glenda and Steve's property for weeks, perhaps even months. It was distressing to think about having everything shut down just as we found something that could help our clients, but it was the right thing to do. After consulting with the homeowners, we called the police and explained the situation.

In addition to being a former police officer myself, Steve was also a retired cop. We knew our call might be handled with skepticism, but we still expected the local branch of the state police to show *some* professionalism. Instead, they were snide and treated us like *we* did something horribly wrong. We had to argue and explain to them what was going on, but they remained dismissive and rude. They ordered us to stay away from the area and for our film crew to shut off the cameras and to keep back when they showed up. Upon their arrival, we did as they instructed and stayed out of their way. But making us feel like criminals when *we* had called them . . . I understand that they could have thought it was some sort of prank or even a trap, but they didn't need to treat us in such a manner.

Sometime later, a few more officers showed up, and thankfully, one of them happened to be a fan. He told the rest of the officers that we were legitimate and not part of some sensationalized reality TV scam. That made the situation a whole lot better, even though the police explained that a forensic team had to come out and investigate the area. If they found any evidence of a crime or what they considered fresh remains, they would have to shut us down completely and the place would become an active crime scene. However, if the forensic team discovered evidence of remains that were over forty years old, they would be considered historical remains, which would thereby allow the landowners to decide what to do with them.

Admittedly, I found this fact to be a little shocking, so I later did my own research. Turns out that yes, if you find human remains on your property and they're deemed not to be part of a crime, it is up to you as to what you do with them. This was fascinating, and it meant that if the police found no evidence of foul play, Glenda and Steve would have to make the final decision regarding what to do with any bones we found. Talk about a heavy weight on one's shoulders.

. . .

The next thirty-six hours were a waiting game as we held off filming until the forensic crew showed up and did its thing, which involved investigating, taking pictures, and sampling dirt. As I watched the examiners from a distance, I felt a bit of kinship. We were all investigators, both groups trying to find the dead; the difference was that one side looked for physical remains while the other looked for the spirit. It took a while, but they finally determined that the ground and tree hadn't been disturbed in some time, meaning it wasn't an active crime scene. With that, the forensic team simply packed up and left, leaving us with the decision of what to do next. Knowing there had to be *something* under the tree to make the cadaver dogs signal hits, we asked the owners if they would be open to having the tree removed and the ground excavated.

Even though it was already dead, the ancient tree was sort of a showpiece on the property, a beacon of the past looming alone in the field. I wasn't sure if they would want it removed, and I could certainly appreciate why. To their credit, though, both Glenda and Steve agreed to it, without any hesitation. They wanted answers more than a dead tree.

The next morning, we had a lot of heavy excavation equipment on-site to rip the tree out of the ground. It wasn't a major undertaking; after digging around the tree, all the excavator operator had to do was push the giant metal claw against the trunk and drive forward. As I watched things get underway, I felt a pang of loss mixed with a wave of excitement.

As a lover of the old and decaying, I found something stunningly beautiful about this gray tree with its bark cracked open and its dead, brittle arms almost reaching out for help . . . especially since it was the only thing standing out on the land. And the stories it must have held . . . and more important, was it hiding any secrets underneath? After taking

Breaking ground to begin the process of removing the tree for our client

a few pictures to preserve its macabre beauty, I eagerly waited for it to be ripped from its earthly bounds.

As the excavator pushed forward, the tree's wood made moaning sounds akin to screams, then snapped in a cacophony of a thousand loud cracks. It just let go and fell to the ground it had so defiantly stood over for more than 150 years. If the curse was real and the lore behind it was true, then its removal should set the witch underneath it free and either let her pass on . . . or cause a spike in activity. Though I don't think any of us truly believed that would be the case, I think we all held our breath as the tree slammed to the ground, its brittle branches shattering everywhere. With our shovels, pickaxes, metal detectors, and boatloads of enthusiasm, Jay, Tango, and I attacked the divot in the ground, ready to find anything that lay below.

It had been a while since I'd played in the dirt, but the anticipation of sifting through to find a treasure under this tree reminded me of my childhood. Of course, the blisters that quickly formed on my fingers also reminded me that digging could be hard work and not always so fun. It also made me understand how every movie that's ever showed a character digging a perfectly rectangular six-foot hole with ease to bury someone is utter ridiculousness. Jay, Tango, and I dug all day and barely got down a few feet. It was pretty damn cold outside as well, which made the ground extra hard. Plus, we were constantly sifting through the dirt to make sure we didn't miss any detail. As we scooped and sifted, there was clearly an underlying nervousness among the three of us that we would find actual human bones . . . that was what we were looking for, after all.

After playing archaeologists for nearly two full days, we found a few railroad and cannon spikes, which were used to hold the weapon in place so that it didn't recoil when in use. Being that they were tied to the Civil War, the history buff in me thought these were really cool finds. Some time after, we uncovered some old cloth material. It was hard to tell if it came from pants, a shirt, a dress, or something else; it was so tattered that it was indistinguishable. We sprayed it with luminol and placed a black light on it—doing so would make any blood light up brightly through a process called chemiluminescence. And sure enough, the excavated cloth material lit up like a Christmas fir. The cadaver dogs had been right on the money—under that tree was bloody clothing.

• • •

None of us found any other evidence of human remains—we dug down only about four feet—but it's certainly possible that there could have been

Steve digging at the tree site
PHOTO BY DAVE TANGO

something farther below. The bloody clothing had to have belonged to a person, as cadaver dogs would only pick up on human scents. Could it have been a bloody rag from an injured farmer, or was it a part of the witch's clothing and her bones were yet to be discovered?

Though we really wanted to go deeper, we had only a few days left before our next case—we seriously had to wrap up the Biglerville investigation, as we'd already fallen behind by almost two weeks. The police investigation and having to dig up the tree had not been on our investigation's agenda. In fact, it pushed our shooting schedule back to the point where we had to film and investigate for an extra week. In a nice instance of a network and a production company caring about people over profit, the powers that be let us keep filming and do whatever was necessary for the case. It was truly amazing to be supported in getting the police involved, calling in for construction equipment, and taking our time to chase down any leads, all in the service of helping our clients. We were led down a rabbit hole we weren't expecting to find and thankfully everyone pitched in to help solve the mystery.

Before we left Glenda and Steve, we offered to fill in the hole and plant some grass, or to even make it a pond for them. They asked us to just leave it open for them to investigate further before they decided whether they wanted to plant a new tree. Since I haven't heard anything from them at this point, I can only assume they never found any other remains.

Our investigation in Biglerville was intense, unique, and certainly a learning experience. In the end, I think we were able to rule out that it was a witch who had been haunting Glenda and Steve; more likely it was an old couple who loved their property and simply didn't want to leave it. They might have been crotchety and believed in antiquated stereotypes of what men and women should and shouldn't do, but I don't think they ever meant any harm or that they were evil or menacing.

As for the children in the barn . . . honestly, I'm not sure where they came from. Our extensive research couldn't locate any records of children being raised there, but of course they could have visited the location or predated the current structure and modern recordkeeping. If I had to guess, I'd speculate that perhaps an item that some child was attached to was stored inside the barn.

In talking to them, Glenda and Steve also realized that they'd had a miscommunication. Steve believed that the paranormal activity was driving a wedge into their marriage, while Glenda thought it was helping them bond and become closer. After realizing this, they joined forces to overcome whatever was haunting their lives and their property.

They say that people who go through a harrowing experience to- gether have a lifelong connection because of it . . . some people even fall in love over a shared traumatic experience. Dealing with witches and old cranky spirits is a bonding experience, for sure. Even though this could have hurt Glenda and Steve's relationship, I think the investigation might have been exactly what they needed. Along with some additional help from the local investigation team, I believe the couple were able to settle in and finally make their house a home, one that was theirs . . . even if it still had a few stubborn previous owners watching over them.

A WEEK WITH THE LAWLESS
SPIRITS OF TOMBSTONE

BIRD CAGE THEATRE

—

TOMBSTONE, AZ

BUILT IN 1881

The saloon doors swung open on rusty hinges, making a clattering noise as a stranger strutted in. No one inside turned to look; instead, they were more focused on enjoying their drinks, playing their card games, and eyeing the saloon girls who fluttered about in their short, frilly dresses. The stranger's metal spurs clinked on the wooden floors, resounding almost in step with the upright piano that was being played vigorously near the stage. The long, skinny theater hall, every inch dripping in brown colors, was filled with cigarette smoke and the stench of men who hadn't seen a bath in weeks. On the small performing area, at the dead end of the room, a woman danced out of sync with the upbeat music.

Suddenly, all hell broke loose. The stranger pulled out a gun and fired five rounds toward those seated around the card table. People screamed and ran for cover. Glass shattered, tables flipped over, and within moments two bodies lay on the floor, covered in blood. Amazingly, less than twenty minutes later the dead had been relocated to the back alley, the music had resumed, and everyone went about their business as bartenders mopped up new pools of red blotches that soaked the floor. All in all, it was just another day at the Bird Cage Theatre in Tombstone, Arizona.

In the heyday of the late-nineteenth-century Wild West, the Bird Cage was the epitome of the classic western saloon. From 1881 to 1889, "the wildest, wickedest night spot between Basin Street and the Barbary Coast" (as described by the New York Times) stayed open twenty-four hours a day, 365 days a year. Legend has it that twenty-six people were murdered throughout the saloon's history and even while the killings ensued, employees kept pouring drinks, cleaning up spilled blood, and moving bodies outside, all so the nonstop drinking and gambling could continue undisturbed.

With over 140 bullet holes still lodged inside its walls, the Bird Cage remains standing and fully intact. However, instead of serving up drinks, debauchery, and fistfights, it now serves as a museum about the Old West. The stories those walls saw and the legendary characters who visited the

The Bird Cage Theatre during the Tombstone mining boom
LIBRARY OF CONGRESS PUBLIC DOMAIN ARCHIVE

saloon—*Doc Holliday and Bat Masterson, to name a couple—are already enough to make the place an iconic spot. But it's the spirits trapped there who bring in the paranormal tourists. Visitors and employees alike claim they have seen phantasmal prostitutes and spectral men in cowboy hats walking the floors. Many say they have been pushed or touched when no one was around, heard piano music despite nothing playing inside the establishment, or seen a visor-wearing man in black pacing across the stage. These consistent accounts have effectively made the Bird Cage the most haunted location in the "Town Too Tough to Die."*

• • •

The first time I crossed over the border into Tombstone, I instantly thought of *Back to The Future III*, when Marty McFly travels to Hill Valley in 1885 to save Doc Brown. It likely popped into my head not only because *Back to the Future* was one of my favorite film series when I was growing up but also because Tombstone made me feel like I'd been suddenly transported back in time. One minute I'm driving through modern-day Arizona, then I take a turn and *"Great Scott, Marty!"* I'm suddenly in the Wild West, as if there were a line on the road that threw me through a wormhole.

Tombstone is so picturesque and authentic that it makes you want to buy a pair of cowboy boots and a ten-gallon hat (which many stores in the town sell for that very reason). All of Main Street is set up just like it was in the cowboy days—only horses and buggies are allowed on the dirt roads, and paid actors stroll around in period clothing while street performers with large handlebar mustaches entertain with classic musical and sideshow acts. When I went, there was one guy with a banjo playing old tunes, a man juggling knives, and even outlaws and cowboys wandering around and playing up their parts. Hell, the legendary O.K. Corral was right down the road; I thought that at any moment I might bump into Val Kilmer and Kurt Russell. Because everything is so authentic, right down to dirt roads and horses, it's hard not to feel like you're really in the Wild West.

With Tombstone being a mecca for family road trippers and vacationers, I was a bit surprised that the area was still a bit wild. In fact, during my visit I saw not one but *two* people stabbed in front of me—*legitimately* stabbed. I had seen incidents like that during my days as a police officer; it wasn't something I expected to witness in my civilian life, let alone twice in one incident. Outside one bar, I saw a guy wearing a cowboy hat standing over a man and screaming, "I'll stab you again if you get up!" A few seconds later, another man stumbled out of a bar clenching his stomach, with blood dripping down his hands. In the background, I heard a person yell, "Jim's been stabbed again. Call the cops!" Hearing the guy yell "again" made me laugh, even though it was a serious situation. The way he said it was so casual, like someone had knocked over a drink for the umpteenth time. It was surreal, to say the least.

After talking to some local police officers, I learned that Tombstone had a massive methamphetamine epidemic at the time, but the junkies and dealers typically stayed on the outskirts of town. The fights I witnessed were fisticuffs, albeit more violent than I had seen elsewhere. That's not a comment on the city; it's more of an observation that a place renowned for its fighting and shootouts still exudes that vibe to this day.

Despite seeing such unsettling incidents, neither the team nor I ever once felt in any personal danger. I loved Tombstone and would go back in a second. We were so comfortable there that one night the crew lugged some equipment to the desert on the edge of town and projected the comedy *What About Bob?* onto the side of a mountain. It was magical, watching one of my favorite nineties movies under the stars . . . until it suddenly dawned on all of us that we were sitting on desert dirt, home to a plethora of venomous creatures. Peering into the shadows, we envisioned a multitude of things just skittering about: snakes, spiders, lizards, you name it. Of course, it was mostly just our minds overreacting, but we did see two scorpions, commonplace for the area but enough to make us pack up and hightail it out of there.

. . .

Based on my years of paranormal investigating, I half-jokingly came up with the motto "If it has a gift shop, it's not haunted." So many of the locations we've visited have had merchandise outlets because the people running them viewed the unexplained as a marketing opportunity. Then there have been the countless places where the activity was little to nonexistent, yet they'd still have the gift shops selling T-shirts, cups, keychains, and more to promote their supposed haunting. Hey, I get it. There's big money in paranormal tourism. Keeping any small business afloat is hard, so I understand the need to market and make extra money on merchandise. However, it's been my experience that the locations whose owners scream, "We're haunted!" the loudest are the *least* active places.

My theory had long been that if a location was making money off such claims, its owners would push whatever they had seen as real and stretch the truth to keep building the story. In my early years with TAPS, this thought process held true time and again. Over the years, though, as the field expanded, gift shops became far more common. It's hard to stay open from merely selling tickets for tours, so almost all the hot spots now have a merch angle. That includes even my favorite places, so my slogan is no longer quite so cut and dried. However, the Bird Cage Theatre was one of the first locations I visited that changed my way of thinking on the subject; it not only has a *great* gift shop, but in my opinion, the place is very much paranormally active.

On the other hand, if a location makes money based *only* on its paranormal claims, that should give you pause. I can't tell you how many people mention to me that a place is "the most haunted location in the city/country/world," yet they've never even been there. We can do our research and be fascinated by the stories that a location generates, but until you experience something there for yourself, assume it isn't haunted. Think about it like this: How many times have you had a friend or family member say, "You have to try this restaurant; it's the greatest place I've ever eaten at"? Then you go there, try it . . . and you think the food was just okay or outright sucked. It's the same thinking with my profession and haunted locations, but without the tiramisu.

Another issue I always face is that when anything gets billed as "the most haunted," people go in *expecting* to experience something. That creates a tricky situation of automatically thinking anything that happens there must be a paranormal occurrence. I've watched this happen during public hunts and even with some overzealous investigators. Having paranormal enthusiasts and avid viewers join me in my work is usually a blast, but seeing the inexperienced go in with the wrong mentality can really hinder the investigation. One time, a few of us sat in a circle inside an old building. It was pitch-black, and at one point I leaned back and accidentally brushed the wall, knocking some crumbling cement chips to the ground. As it was dark and no one could see what happened, I heard audible gasps when the pebbles bounced on the floor, echoing in the silence. Before I could even apologize, people were shouting out theories and claiming it was a ghost named Richard who was known for throwing pebbles at guests.

I let them go on for a bit, hoping someone would try to debunk what we'd heard; instead, the group went along with the idea that they had just "experienced" something. One by one, they started calling out to Richard, hoping he would respond. After a few seconds, I leaned back and made the sound again, then quickly apologized and took credit for making the noise. Some were disappointed, but others began arguing that the first noise I made was different and that it *had* to be Richard. It just goes to show that sometimes the need to find proof is much stronger than the truth itself. That kind of thinking can really hurt our community.

Ultimately, until we have a hundred-percent scientific way to prove the paranormal exists, it's in everyone's best interest to investigate and gather evidence rather than blindly believe. It's vital for the paranormal community to offer proof and solid facts over assumptions and baseless conviction. Even when it comes to writing this book, regardless of any evidence and personal experiences I cite about a location, I implore anyone to not just assume it is haunted; go there and find out for yourself.

• • •

Before I even walked in, I was in love with the Bird Cage Theatre because of its rich background. Being inside, though . . . everything was so well-preserved, from the bullet holes in the walls to the original card tables. Knowing that the real Doc Holliday sat on those very chairs and had a drink gave me chills.

History oozed out of every inch of the place. Even if there had been no activity, the location itself would have been worth the visit (and little did I know at the time that I would not be disappointed).

The paranormal stories we'd been told ran the gamut of the usual accounts TAPS hears about in many of the places we visit. The most consistent one we heard about, though, was also the most intriguing: an apparition of a woman ascending and descending the staircase. Guests and staff claimed to have seen the woman's entire body and face, and the same description was reported multiple times. The second most consistent activity reported was of a shadowlike figure on the first floor and in the basement areas.

Consistency with claims helps tip the odds in our favor, and if there is frequency, we have better chances of experiencing it ourselves. An individualized claim, regardless of whether it's true, is more difficult to focus an investigation around. On the other hand, hearing numerous,

The Bird Cage Theatre interior, with the
original piano and balcony boxes
LIBRARY OF CONGRESS PUBLIC DOMAIN ARCHIVE

separate statements that support one another's stories provides me with more credible details on which to concentrate. This is especially true when the reports come from both patrons and employees. If the stories come from only one source, it's harder to determine if there's an ulterior motive at play, or perhaps just some overzealous imagination.

Most of the time, a claim comes from one person. It's very rare for two people to experience something simultaneously, because a lot of people either work separately or are home alone for the experience. Quiet and solitude mean not having your attention divided elsewhere, allowing your brain to focus more and easily notice things around you. A singular experience gives us something to look into, but it isn't something we can corroborate. That's one of the reasons our team members never investigate alone. We make sure to always have a partner with us. And it's not just a matter of safety; if two people see, hear, or experience the same thing, then we know with less doubt it was real and not a trick of one person's mind. The only time we allow someone to hunt alone is if the area being investigated is completely covered by cameras and another team member is watching from the command center.

Of course, while that's our rule of thumb, I admit that on very rare occasions I have broken it myself. If I do investigate alone, however, I always get permission beforehand to be at the location, then check the area out during daylight to address any potential safety concerns. I make sure someone knows where I am and carry a cell phone at all times. Typically, if I'm going alone, I'm doing it for myself and my own experiences. Sometimes I'll try out new techniques, and other times I prefer the silence and peaceful calm that a location provides me. I realize, though, that if I ever happen upon some amazing evidence during one of my solo hunts, it'll be hard to present to anyone, because there's no one to confirm my personal experience. At the end of the day, partnering up with someone is always the better option.

It's also a huge help to substantiate claims if we can find some historical data that correlates with the reported activity. If people state they heard piano music coming from inside a place like the Bird Cage, we know it makes logical sense since the theater always had an upright piano.

However, if I am told that music came from a hospital room, it would be hard to line up the history with the claim. That isn't to say it couldn't be true, but it just takes away one more layer of evidence for us to work with.

• • •

After noting all the reported stories, we set up inside the theater and started our investigation that very evening. I began by walking through the main bar; it was dark, and the floorboards creaked like they were

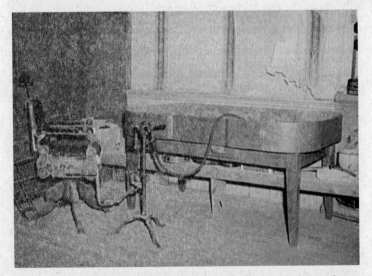

The original dice table and gambling chair still on display at the Bird Cage Theatre
LIBRARY OF CONGRESS PUBLIC DOMAIN ARCHIVE

stretching after a lazy nap in the Southwest sunshine. The room smelled smoky and slightly damp even though the air was as dry as paper. I imagined what the saloon had looked like back in its heyday. Of course, all my imagery of the Wild West comes from old photos, movies, and TV shows, so the faces I saw sitting around the tables and by the bar were all glossy, Hollywood figures either smoothing lace trim over strained cleavage or peering over yellowed playing cards while gnashing their strong, stubbly jawlines. It was thrilling to be inside a location that had inspired the set designs for so many of my beloved movies.

At one point, I walked over to the stage and looked just below the lip of the wooden platform. Right there, nestled inside the wood, were three bullet holes. A small note card beneath them explained that a drunk cowboy got angry during one of the shows and shot at an actor, thankfully with bad aim. I knelt and looked into the holes; I could see the flat brass back of each bullet. Taking my finger, I touched the wood and felt the circular indentations. I remember thinking how amazing it was that, more than a century after a real cowboy had loaded his gun and shot toward the stage, I was here examining the outcome. Even more incredible, at least in my mind, was that in all this time no one had ever patched up the holes; in fact, they were part of the attraction.

Another team member called to me from the other side of the room, jostling my train of thought. I walked over and we started talking, only to be interrupted by a loud slapping noise that echoed behind us. It seemed way out of place in the dusty silence, so we took a quick look around for the origin point. The only thing we found was a wire on the floor. Normally, we're incredibly careful about securing our equipment and making sure that no one can trip over anything. Having camerapeople walk around backwards in pitch black is dangerous enough; a stray wire or electrical cable could lead to catastrophe. The wire could have caused the noise, though it was almost impossible for it to have come loose and fallen.

More often than not, Murphy's Law is our enemy, and our cameras are usually facing the wrong way when something happens during a hunt. In this instance, our cameras were actually pointed right at the cables, albeit in the background of the shot. Normally, we check all the recordings after the investigation, but in this instance, we wanted answers, so we grabbed the footage to look at it right then. In the video, we saw that the cable had been hung over an old-school brass fire alarm bell, the kind with a striker arm that slams against it and sounds the alarm. The circular bell was affixed to a wall, so the wire had been hung over it to keep it off the floor. The cord went behind the bell and rested on the striker arm that came out of the wall, a good four inches lower than the lip of the brass.

We just assumed the wire had slid off somehow, but what the video revealed made our jaws drop: The footage shows the two of us investigating, and behind us you can see the wire actually "whip" up and over, completely on its own. Half a second later, as the wire slams down onto the floor, you see us jump and spin around in reaction to the sound.

Could the cable falling have been a natural occurrence, or was there some sort of consciousness or energy behind it? I watched the video many times, yet I couldn't see a way that the cord could have come undone on its own—*something* had to have helped it unwrap. I even wrapped the wire around the bell again, then tugged on it to see if it would fall—it wouldn't budge. If someone tripped on it or just tried to yank it off the bell, they would have also ripped everything from the wall. The only way the cord could have fallen was if someone grabbed it and whipped it hard, getting it to jump over the lip.

After experiencing something like that, we always snap on our recorders and ask questions out loud to try to catch an EVP, posing different inquiries in the hopes of getting whatever aided its movement to speak up. (Nowadays we keep the voice recorders constantly recording during the entire investigation—digital technology has progressed, so we don't have to worry about wasting storage and can record almost endlessly.) Sadly, we got nothing from those sessions, but that doesn't change my opinion. Until someone can explain how it was physically possible for it to happen the way it did, the wire coming off the bell was most likely the result of paranormal activity.

• • •

Later that night, on the theater's main floor, I kept hearing an odd noise that I couldn't place. It was faint, flapping, and at first reminded me of a baseball card hitting the spokes on a bicycle wheel. After I heard it a few more times, though, it sounded more like someone was slowly thumbing through one of those old flip-books, where the pages create the optical illusion of a little cartoon dancing around. Another investigator suggested that the noise resembled that of a deck of cards being shuffled. *Bingo*: that was *exactly* the sound I'd heard, and with the heavy amount of gambling that had taken place inside the theater, of course it made perfect sense.

Hearing this card-shuffling noise fascinated me. I needed to find the source. We looked everywhere to determine what might be making the sound—perhaps it was something caught in the wind, or a piece of paper stuck inside an air vent? There's usually a very rational explanation, but if we can't find one, then we can consider the activity to be paranormal in nature. With this particular sound, we just couldn't find anything in the room that could have been causing it.

While Tango and I strained our ears to pick up on the card-shuffling noise again, we heard faint music. It was way off in the distance, tinny, and almost mechanical, with a lot of high clangs. It was almost indistinguishable, but it was clearly music coming from the theater—and heard as a shared experience. We initially brushed it off as a sound from the outside, but as a precaution, we radioed everyone on the walkies to confirm our suspicions. And I'm glad that we did—everyone came back with the same response: There was *no* music playing outside.

Though Tango and I caught only mere snippets of the orchestral fluttering after that, the team's replies had certainly piqued our interest. When we later did our analysis and boosted the audio levels a bit, we discovered that it was calliope music, the kind of melody that might stream from inside an old saloon. This realization was super exciting, as it confirmed without a doubt that we had experienced something and, best of all, caught it on a recording.

It's important to point out that we may boost an audio level or enhance an image for better analysis and confirmation, but when it's time to present our findings to a client we *always* play whatever we captured at the level or size at which we captured it. This way, the client has something that's genuine and uncompromised. A TV show will do it to improve the home audience experience (especially since viewers don't have the opportunity to listen to something repeatedly with headphones), but we *never* boost anything for a client. That's even more reason why we were thrilled that our recordings, even at their fainter levels, had clearly captured the sounds of old-timey music.

There's a long-winded concept called the Stone Tape Theory that explains disembodied sounds. The idea is that objects made of stone, wood, and other porous surfaces can be "imprinted" with traumatic events that occurred regularly around them. They "pick up" and hold on to those sounds, much like a video or audio tape recorder, and play them back when the setting or moment is right or when something disturbs the stone, like an earthquake or a demolition. And sometimes they'll do so on a loop—hence why people might hear the same saying or sound or music in a particular place. It imprints on the location and gets played back every now and then. Sometimes we're fortunate enough to catch it.

Personally, I love the idea of this theory. The thought that a location can also be traumatized and hold on to a moment like a recording, or that something had occurred so much in one spot that the structure absorbed it . . . it's sort of a romantic idea. In addition to multiple books written on the subject, there was even a theatrical play that became a BBC special (and the origin of its name) focusing on this concept. Unfortunately, from a scientific standpoint, it doesn't hold much water. As you know by now, I try to disprove first, and when it comes to theories I look at the science. Even though this hypothesis has been around for decades, there's simply no science to definitively prove, let alone give hope, that this could happen. Right now, it's simply a fun idea that provides no plausibility. (However, I'm hardly ready to rule out any possibility of future discoveries that can support the theory.)

• • •

Though we live in a rapidly advancing society where technology jumps by leaps and bounds, we still hardly understand the paranormal world and the causes behind the phenomena we experience. Hearing small sounds in a room might seem minor, but it's really a complex and fascinating experience we cannot yet explain. With the Bird Cage Theatre, were we hearing sounds trapped in time within an old saloon hall, repeating themselves on an endless loop and unconscious that we even existed? Was an intelligent spirit trying to communicate with us? Unfortunately, we just don't know yet, but that's *precisely* why I do this: to have these experiences, to document them, and, we hope, to one day solve the mysteries of the unknown.

Trying to learn how and why things happen is one of the motivations that keeps me going. The idea of discovering new and enthralling things, of moving closer to finding answers, provides me with such excitement and joy that I know I'll keep investigating for as long as I live. Don't misunderstand . . . I get a thrill from *all* my investigations. Yet the Bird Cage Theatre was one of those rare locations that filled me with so much happiness I felt like I was about to burst.

Unfortunately, my euphoric feeling regarding our investigation didn't last very long. After leaving the Bird Cage, I had an experience on the road that will forever haunt my memory.

• • •

With our investigation wrapped up, Tango and I took our equipment van out of Tombstone and down the long stretches of a lonesome hot and dry highway through the night. Let me tell you, your brain can go numb when riding through perfectly straight, endless periods of blackness. There's no steering, no maneuvering; you just have to stay awake and keep the wheel steady so you don't veer off the road. For me, it feels like I'm driving through purgatory, and if you've ever been in an area like Tombstone, then you understand precisely what I mean. Once that sun goes down, the world completely disappears. All you can see is a sliver of road gleaned from your headlights' pyramid of vision, and the ominous glow from your dashboard reflecting on a passenger's face. It was late. We hadn't seen a single car for over an hour, and our hopes of finding a diner dwindled with every mile marker. Tango and I were truly alone in the middle of nowhere.

Thinking about the case, our experiences, and our upcoming road trip, we drove in silence. The radio was off, and neither Tango nor I had any conversation left in us, which was fine with me. I simply kept my eyes ahead, watching the yellow line flash by, thinking about nothing in particular. Tango shared the same calm, mindless mood as he watched the darkness pass us.

That's when I noticed a giant red smear in the middle of the road.

The smudge snapped me out of my daze, and I instantly sat up and paid closer attention. I assumed some animal had been hit, so I was on high alert to avoid whatever unfortunate wounded critter I was about to come upon. I started to slow down as the red smear got darker and thicker. Tango was also fully awake by this point, and an eerie, nervous silence floated between us. Blood is blood, but the two of us began to think that this trail was looking too dark and thick to belong to an unfortunate animal.

Several moments later, we came upon some long, yellowed orange and white tubes. Some were bunched up, and a few appeared stretched and snapped in various places. I pressed softly on the brake, slowing to a crawl. Neither Tango nor I needed to let each the know that we were seeing intestines in front of us.

The van crept soundlessly past the torn guts. I did my best to maneuver around them, as I was terrified of defiling anything further. It was like we had stumbled into one of those graphic driving safety videos from the 1970s, the ones they used to show in schools to scare students in the hopes of making them better drivers. I stopped thinking about the guts, though, once I saw an image that will forever haunt me: a human being's hairy torso . . . and *just* a torso. This moment, while so brief, is frozen in my mind like some awful slideshow that I can't escape. Though I may go months without thinking about it, every now and then the horrible scene inevitably pops back into my mind as if to say, "Hey, don't forget about me."

I was an EMT in my early twenties, then a cop, so I got used to seeing all sorts of horrific accidents. But witnessing *this*, in such a creepy, desolate setting, was so unexpected that it made my stomach turn. I could only stare at the decimated midsection of a man who must have been alive only minutes before. Then Tango broke the silence with a terrified mutter to get my attention—there was a pair of legs on the other side of the road. There was no clothing on them; just a nude human pelvis and limbs. I couldn't think. My mind just shifted into autopilot while I cautiously wove the car around all the gore. I considered getting out to help. Yet I realized that there was absolutely nothing at this point that Tango or I could do other than traumatize ourselves even further.

Without realizing it, I had stopped the van just past the horrible scene, now all behind us, no longer illuminated by the headlights. Those human remains sat in the pitch black, which made everything seem even more terrifying. Finally, Tango and I broke our silence and had a frantic conversation about searching for other victims, but at the same time we were positively shaken.

"Where was his head, Steve?" Tango asked.

I could only respond with, "Where was his *clothing*?"

This fearful situation had reached a boiling point for the two of us. Perhaps it was from the shock and my mind scrambling for a way to process everything, but I couldn't help but start to envision that Tango and I were stuck in some twisted novel that Stephen King was writing.

Rocketing back to reality, we decided that the best thing to do was keep driving and call the police. I stepped on the gas pedal and glanced back, somewhat hoping that nothing would emerge from the darkness to chase us. I kept my eyes locked on my rearview mirror, watching the glowing red from my taillights until it all but disappeared. Tango got on his phone and dialed 911. He alerted the authorities to what we had seen and gave them the mile marker—they thanked us for the information and said someone would be on the way. (I'm not proud to admit this, but I was quietly thankful that they didn't ask us to stay put.) Tango ended the call, and the silence enveloped us again. We drove without speaking for what seemed like hours, still held captive by the horrible tableau we had just witnessed.

• • •

All these years later, I still feel guilty for not stopping and getting out. Sometimes I just have to remind myself that there really was nothing in the world I could have done. And for the record, Tango and I never found out who the man was, why he was in the middle of nowhere, or why his body had no clothing. And perhaps worst of all, how could someone have hit him and then driven off?

It didn't occur to me until much later that since the victim was headless, it was likely that he had met an unfortunate end somewhere else and the body was dumped there and hit by a passing vehicle afterward. This lack of information makes the experience a terrifying mystery—an unsolved case that my mind will never be able to get over. I've even done my own research to see if I could find any news articles that might be connected, but I've come up with nothing. At the same time, I don't necessarily want to put a face to the body, because then the gore I came upon would become even more real—it would become a person who had a name and a life snuffed out all too soon.

In the paranormal world, we deal with the dead and beyond on a daily basis; in a way, death is all that the job is about. At times, though, we forget that the "ghosts" we seek were once human beings, with families, love lives, jobs, and dreams. They were a part of our society. It's easy to let this fact slip our minds when we're busy listening for unexpected sounds or trying to capture something during an investigation, but we can't forget that they were people. Respecting that the spirit we're trying to communicate with was at one time a living person is vital to our field. We might be chasing the dead, but they were once alive . . . and one day, we too will be on the other side.

Every day, we walk a thin tightrope between this world and whatever comes after. In a split second, your life can be over, just like that unfortunate man in the road. It's a morbid thought, but we need to step back and think about that from time to time. When we forget how fragile life is, we tend to stop enjoying and appreciating what we have. No matter how hard things are or how bad they can get, we are *alive*, able to do great things and experience amazing wonders.

Though I wish I'd never seen that body, I'm also thankful that I did. I keep that incident in my arsenal of memories to help me get over tiny things that bug me. It's a reminder that life is fleeting, and that we shouldn't ever sweat the small stuff. Most importantly, it encourages me to enjoy and be thankful for every beautiful moment of every beautiful day . . . as you never know when it could all be over.

THEY NEVER LEFT

MYRTLES PLANTATION
—
ST. FRANCISVILLE, LA
BUILT 1796

Near the end of the eighteenth century, General David Bradford acquired 650 acres of land on Bayou Sara (then a Spanish colony) and built the first structures around what would become the Myrtles Plantation. Originally called Laurel Grove, the property served as a private hideout for Bradford until he was pardoned by President John Adams for his role in the Whiskey Rebellion (in which farmers and distillers fought the government over a tax on whiskey sales). Once cleared, he moved his family down to the property and the working life of the plantation began. Over the next three decades, the plantation ran without issue until it was sold to Ruffin Gray Stirling in 1834. The Stirling family expanded the house, doubling its size, and changed the name of the plantation to Myrtles, based on the large number of flowering bushes called crepe myrtles that grew in the vicinity.

The Myrtles Plantation remained standing after the American Civil War, though it was robbed of almost all its furnishings and expensive accessories. With slavery abolished and the family's fortune lost in worthless

Confederate currency, the Stirlings hired a lawyer, William Winter, to manage the plantation. Though Winter was able to pull the Stirlings out of bankruptcy, he could not save himself—in 1871, while Winter taught a Sunday school lesson in the parlor, a man on a horse rode up to the house and called Winter outside, then fatally shot him and fled. The crime was never solved, and the residence once again fell on hard times. Over the next hundred years, the property changed hands repeatedly until it was finally converted into a bed-and-breakfast in the late 1970s.

The Myrtles' stunning beauty and charm remain intact to this day, making it too easy to forget that, like all plantations, it was built on the backs of enslaved people who were brutalized and suffered beyond imagination. For human beings to be regarded as "property," beaten, and forced to work their entire lives under horrid conditions, all for rich, white plantation owners to enjoy lives of luxury, was an atrocity and nightmare that will forever stain the history of our country. The Myrtles' current owners, who use the land as a resort, certainly aren't to blame, but the history can never be forgotten. And where there is pain and suffering, there are souls who remain behind.

There's no telling how many people died at the Myrtles Plantation, or how many souls still remain on the property. However, activity there is considered to be so commonplace that the plantation is frequently referred to as one of the most haunted homes in America. Almost every possible paranormal happening has allegedly occurred at the Myrtles, including items disappearing, the inexplicable sounds of footsteps on stairs, odd scents materializing, and cold spots suddenly manifesting.

There have also been separate reports of more than twelve ghosts who frequent the grounds, with the most well-documented among them being "Chloe," a young enslaved woman who lived on the property. What is as-

sumed to be Chloe's specter has been photographed numerous times, even verified by credible sources such as National Geographic, which stated that one particular photo "contained what appeared to be an apparition of an enslaved girl"; most recently, in 2019, she appeared as a reflection on a window behind a group that had been taking a picture. The reasons for the hauntings, whether they be the spirits of tortured souls like Chloe, the ghosts of those in the burial ground, or the lives of those who were murdered there, remain unknown. What we do know is that a location of such violence and cruelty is full of consistent paranormal activity.

• • •

Driving up to the Myrtles Plantation, I remember being instantly taken with its beauty—the weeping, waving oak trees covered in Spanish moss—along with the warm, sticky air.

Front entrance of Myrtles Plantation
JUDY LACHANCE

But the visual allure quickly wore off and my gut twisted. It was hard to appreciate the majestic landscape when all I could think of were those who were forced against their will to maintain it, to make the road I was driving on, and to plant and take care of the stunning property. They made this place what it was, and the thought of how horribly they were treated while doing so was something I had a hard time overlooking. As a New Englander, just the word *plantation* makes me uncomfortable. When I was a child, the only time I heard that word was in history class, when the teacher talked about the enslaved. It just wasn't a term we heard in any other context.

Once I was fully on the property, I inhaled deeply and took in the outside of the main house. It truly was gorgeous . . . full of southern charm. Yet, as soon as someone said, "The enslaved shacks are over there," it was like a bucket of ice-cold water had been thrown on me, washing away anything positive there. I've been on countless battlefields and inside asylums where humans were treated in horrendous ways, but the thought of being *owned* by someone and inhumanely forced to work for them against your will for the rest of your life . . . it made my heart ache more than just about anything at any other place I've ever visited.

Be that as it was, I had to remind myself that I was at the Myrtles to do a job. I had to face the history and use it as part of my investigation, meaning I also had to put my personal disdain aside and get to work.

• • •

After hearing all of the accounts and picking the best locations to set up equipment, I had an hour or so before sundown. Having heard about Chloe, an active spirit who likes to be in pictures, I wanted to do a little more research so I could possibly establish contact with her. I walked around and read all the historic markers on the property, then went to my room and set up my laptop.

Chloe's story was truly heart-wrenching. She was a house servant, a job that was highly desired by enslaved people, as it wasn't as torturous and physical as working in the fields. Chloe had to endure other forms of harrowing abuse, however. First, the enslaver, Judge Clark Woodruff, physically abused and took advantage of her repeatedly. When she worried that he might grow weary of her and send her out to work in the fields, Chloe began eavesdropping on conversations to hear any mentions of her name. She was eventually discovered, and Woodruff cut off her ear as punishment for having the audacity to listen in on her enslavers' private discussions. From that point, she'd wear a green turban to cover up her mutilation. Not long after, Chloe made a cake sprinkled with oleander plant leaves, hoping that their toxicity might make the family sick enough that they'd need her to remain in the house and care for them. Unfortunately, the poisonous cake killed Woodruff's wife and two daughters. After learning what happened, the other enslaved people feared Chloe's deeds would result in violent reprisals from Woodruff, who hadn't eaten the cake that evening. They dragged Chloe outside and hanged her themselves.

This powerful, terrifying, and moving story is abundant on the internet and has been recounted in sad whispers to guests for decades. The Myrtles sells postcards with Chloe's ghostly image, and its website has an entire page of information dedicated to her. However, based on our research, there's no *official* documentation to prove any of the story. There are no records of a Chloe ever living or working on the property (which isn't to say there wasn't one; records of the enslaved weren't often well detailed, if they were even kept at all). Plus, the Woodruffs had a daughter and a *son*, and it's documented that they perished from yellow fever a year after their mother had died. Beyond the plantation owners' real names, not a single other fact can be proven or even assumed. Historical documents reveal the truth . . . the legend of Chloe is simply not based in fact.

For an investigator, one of the hardest things to do is separate the myths from reality. Unfortunately, the truth isn't quite as exciting as the legends we may tell or hear (in a few rare cases, it has been the opposite). But this story of Chloe—actively promoted at the Myrtles Plantation—is a prime example as to why it's vital that those in my line of work do the research and learn the real details before starting an investigation. If you truly believe a false narrative, it will hamper every aspect of your investigation and taint your findings. There has been more than one occasion when I've watched someone build an entire experience based on a fake story that they truly believed. Doing that gives all paranormal investigators and clients a bad reputation. I cannot emphasize this enough: Do your research and fact-check. Truth first, *always*. It might not be as fun, but it's better to be right and to respect the real spirits on a property than to chase a legend. Perpetuating false stories and histories does no good to anyone.

Fiction spreads faster and stains deeper than the truth. The story of Chloe has caught fire, with reality shows, documentaries, and other outlets covering it. Her legend is told during tours, merchandise with her name on it is sold in stores, and various websites dedicate entire pages to her tale. Now, I will admit that there can also be a downside to researching and learning true history. If you find out that a person died or suffered something horrific at a location, you might automatically assume that any paranormal activity is attributed to that person, when it could be someone or something else entirely that's causing the incident. Again, it puts you, the investigator, in a situation where you could be calling out to the wrong entity, which will only hinder your work. The best thing you can do is try the names you gather from your research but also ask "who" is there as well . . . let the entity speak up for itself.

If there's one thing that the Myrtles does offer in abundance, it's fantastic photographic evidence. Even *National Geographic* verified that an image of what appears to be the ghost of an enslaved girl—allegedly Chloe—had not been tampered with in any way. There's also the intriguing photo of her spirit appearing inside the reflection of a window, behind a teacher and some students. It's an incredibly clear image of a woman dressed in antebellum-style clothing; you can even see the details on her dress as well as her full facial features. It's an astounding picture that I can see why people find mesmerizing . . . though honestly, I always take photographic evidence with a grain of salt, especially one that is just a reflection. Why wouldn't the spirit be in the photo proper instead of just the reflection?

I like to think that most people are aboveboard, and that they truly find and capture things in an honest way. However, if I don't personally take the photo or I'm not there to see it taken, I simply cannot trust such an image. Sure, they can be interesting and certainly creepy at times, but photos are often misinterpreted; a smudge or blur can absolutely look like a ghost. Remember, our brains *want* to see things they understand. Any time something has a familiar shape or structure, our minds quickly jump to what it *should* be. Think about when you were a kid looking at a cloud—you'd quickly shout out what it resembled, even if it was vaguely similar at best; it's the mind's way of processing information.

This phenomenon of assigning meaning to random shapes and images is called pareidolia, but in the field we commonly call it matrixing. When you're on the lookout for a ghost and find an anomaly within a photo you took, your mind will quickly race to figure out what it is. Most of the time, your mind will perceive shapes to be familiar objects like humans, animals, cars, and other things we see on a regular basis. That's especially true if someone else sees the image; they're going to point out what they see, making it even more defined in our minds.

Worse than misinterpretation, photos have been manipulated since their very inception. Back in the 1860s, getting a photograph was extremely rare and expensive; to common folk, this new medium of capturing someone's image with a camera was practically regarded as magic. Then photographers started playing around with exposures and different techniques, and they learned that images could be made to appear as "ghosts." They started using this trick to manipulate and take advantage of people desperately looking to connect with a lost loved one. With that, "ghost photography" was born, and it became extremely popular. In one scenario, photos taken during séances (which were so common back then, it became a normal activity on a first date) would show ectoplasm leaving a medium's body (this was often achieved by ingesting and then regurgitating cheesecloth), thereby "proving" the existence of spirits. The most popular scam, though, was having a portrait session with people who hoped a loved one would appear in the picture with them; of course, most of the time, their loved one would magically appear.

William Mumler, who is credited as the inventor of ghost photography, became so popular in the 1860s that famous people flocked to have portraits taken by him. Even Mary Todd Lincoln sat for a photograph, and wouldn't you know it, good ol' Honest Abe appeared right behind her, his hands lovingly on her shoulders. Eventually, however, not-so-honest Mumler's "ability" to bring back the dead through his photography was brought into question, and before long he was put on trial for fraud. Famed circus founder P. T. Barnum would testify against Mumler and accuse him of faking the images for profit. The renowned showman even hired someone to create a ghost photo of Lincoln standing alongside Barnum, thereby demonstrating to the court how easy it was to manipulate photography. Though Mumler was ultimately acquitted because there wasn't enough incontrovertible proof he was ripping people off, Barnum's testimony provided enough damning evidence to expose the process as all fakery.

By 1875, officials of the Ghost Club (a paranormal team that existed well over 150 years ago) examined more than six hundred ghost photos. They claimed that fewer than a dozen of them *could* be real, and even then they couldn't confirm their authenticity. Nevertheless, ghost photography's popularity continued to skyrocket through the rest of the century and beyond. It wasn't until consumers began buying cameras to take their own photos that the "art form" slowly slipped away. Yet people still catch spirits regularly on camera, and in today's digital world, anyone with even a slightly elevated level of computer skills can create incredibly convincing ghost photos. What can be manipulated now is endless, not to mention the recent influence of artificial intelligence. In addition, cameras are flawed. As good as digital is, if you move too fast while taking a photo or the light is hitting something just right, you're guaranteed to capture things that seem unexplainable. Always question and investigate first and believe last.

The thought of capturing a definitive image of a ghost is beyond exciting, and it's something I'll always hope for. Ultimately, though, in all my years of paranormal investigation, I've never seen a photo that I believed was a hundred percent real. It would be almost impossible to say definitively that one was genuine. I've caught inexplicable things in incredibly compelling photographs, but that doesn't mean they were ghosts. And again, unless I'm the one taking the photo, it's impossible for me to authenticate it. Regrettably, almost every famous photo of a ghost throughout history has been disproved, and the ones that haven't been can't be proven real either. The images being touted at the Myrtles Plantation are fantastic and absolutely *could* be real; unfortunately, I personally can't verify them.

• • •

The team started off its investigation inside the main house of the Myrtles Plantation. Earlier on, the manager pointed out to us that the chandelier hanging in the entrance was made of Baccarat crystal and weighed over three hundred pounds. It was certainly gorgeous and lavish, but it was the area's stained-glass windows that really caught my attention. We were told the windows had very specific etchings written in French as well as a French cross, all of which had been put there to ward off evil. Knowing that a proprietor had crafted and incorporated something into their home to repel the supernatural is an important fact when investigating, as it can give us valuable clues about the mind-set of the original owners. Such a discovery also allows us to understand that those who lived there actually feared something unnatural coming into their home so deeply that they felt the need to drive it away. Did the owners incorporate these repellents into their home because they feared karmic retribution, whether human or supernatural, for the atrocities of enslavement they had committed? Or were they afraid of something else?

Throughout time, superstition has been a constant in paranormal investigation. Everyone has a little bit of it in them, whether it's avoiding breaking glass, not walking under a ladder, or not letting a black cat cross your path. Almost all of us have something we don't do because a fear was handed down to us through the years. Every walk of life has its own bizarre beliefs that make people feel better. In my field, I've encountered everything from mummified cats in walls to fend off evil spirits to putting shoes under floorboards to help with fertility and, yes, to also ward off evil (it amazes me how a shoe not only can stop evil but also can get someone pregnant). Though I might not believe in such superstitions, plenty of people do. Respecting those beliefs and the spirit who might have had faith in them is important, especially if the suspected ghost lived before the twentieth century, when superstitions carried far more weight in the general population.

Though the Myrtles' owners might have felt a need to keep unwanted forces at bay, I decided to start my investigation *outside* the house, where much of the property's real-life evil took place. One of our original team members went with me to start, but he was quickly called back regarding a camera he'd forgotten to set up earlier in the evening, leaving me to explore alone.

The night sky was crystal clear—I could see stars for miles. There was a constant cacophony of insects and other animals making their nightly calls. Walking among trees with Spanish moss dripping off them like old sheets blowing in the wind was breathtaking . . . and more than a bit creepy. Not because of the possibility of ghosts, but because I was in Louisiana, where there are snakes, alligators, giant spiders, and the awful chiggers that live in the Spanish moss—with those, if you brush up against them, you'll get bites that lead to a nasty rash. Besides all those horrific things, there are other ungodly creatures I can't bring myself to write about because they freak me out so much.

This is the exact spot where I encountered the shadow phenomena.
JUDY LACHANCE

The cabins used for housing the enslaved
JUDY LACHANCE

Unfortunately, the beautiful night sky wasn't providing enough illumination around the darkness surrounding this remote plantation. Even with my flashlight on, it was borderline impossible to see if anything could be slithering up next to me.

The swaying tree moss was also playing tricks with my eyes, causing movement in my peripheral vision that took getting used to. It was at that point when I started to feel like someone was close by watching me, and while that feeling might not always be paranormal, it put me on a higher alert than usual. I shined my flashlight around and was still alone, so I shut it off and started to speak out loud, saying, "Well, I guess there's no one here." Seconds later, a human figure peeked out from behind a nearby tree. The outline of the figure was all in shadows.

By the time I turned my flashlight on again and illuminated the spot, the figure was already gone. As I started searching for it, I noticed more dark shadows in the distance, darting in and out around the trees. It was like they wanted to play some odd game of flashlight tag, and they were not off the mark.

Of course, if they were from the time period we were expecting, they wouldn't know what a flashlight was, so they could have simply been startled by seeing one. It was overwhelming; when I shined my light at them, they'd vanish. After several minutes, the shadows appeared to grow weary of the game and didn't return. What I found amazing was that they were not shadows—they were corporeal black masses that moved fluidly on their own.

Alone once again in the dark, with the symphony of hated insects serenading me, I took a moment to look up at the stars and realized how damn lucky I was. At the time, this was only the second season of *Ghost Hunters*, so the traveling and opportunities of getting to investigate places that would have been off-limits to me a few years earlier were still over-whelming, and I had no clue how long it would last. Taking a deep breath, the mossy smells tingling my nose, I thanked the universe for my great fortune. Because not only was I getting to live the dream of investigating the paranormal for a living but I also had just played hide-and-seek with a shadowy humanoid figure. All these years later, I have seen many similar figures, but none that behaved like the ones at the Myrtles Plantation. It was truly an experience that I will remember for the rest of my life.

• • •

My evening encounter with the shadows outside was the most significant thing to happen to me at the Myrtles, but it certainly wasn't the only extraordinary thing that occurred during the investigation.

Among the most fascinating pieces of footage caught by one of our cameras was that of a classic brass lamp sliding across a table inside one of the shacks on the property. The lamp moved at an incredibly slow pace—almost five minutes to shift over about two feet—which somehow made the footage even more mesmerizing to watch. It's also important to note that the furniture had a doily-style tablecloth; it's relevant because when Jay and Grant tried to re-create the lamp's movement by pulling on its cord, the cloth would just bunch up. That's something that *didn't* happen in the video.

This is another situation where the "why" must be considered. Lights wouldn't have existed when the shacks were occupied, so why would a spirit concentrate so hard on moving something like a lamp, and in such a subtle manner? Was there any motivation behind it? I doubt we'll ever find out, but it remains a rather curious incident, and great evidence of *something* otherworldly interacting with our environment.

The stairs at the entrance of the main house also provided us with some very interesting footage. We had a camera focusing down the steps leading to the front door, and the imagery showed us what appeared to be a person getting up from the ground outside the door. It very clearly looked like someone had been on their hands and knees, then just stood up. Our records and footage confirmed that no one on the team or among the property's staff was out there at that time. That incident, along with the moving table lamp and the playful shadows I met, made for an incredibly interesting investigation. I wouldn't go so far as to say that the property is the most haunted place in the world . . . but there's definitely something very unusual going on around there.

The Myrtles Plantation is a mix of scenic beauty with a horrific, condemnable past that forces us to confront a terrible, blemished period

Our cameras caught the shadowlike figure moving
right in front of these entry doors.
JUDY LACHANCE

in our country's history. Though it was an intriguing place to investigate, I really hope that more people will visit the grounds to learn about the events that happened there and not so much for the ghosts. The sorrow and stories of those who suffered at Myrtles deserve to be told and remembered, and not just promoted and treated as part of a paranormal investigation.

BLINDED BY THE LIGHT

ST. AUGUSTINE LIGHTHOUSE
—

ST. AUGUSTINE, FL
OPENED 1874

When fog blankets an ocean, visibility becomes impossible. At times it can be so thick you can hardly see your hand in front of your face. For centuries, fog was also deadly—ships would run into the shoreline and entire crews would drown, with safety only yards, if not mere feet, away. When proper lighthouse structures came into existence toward the end of the seventeenth century, they were considered a godsend. Not only did they warn ships of potential harm but they also guided seafarers safely home.

For nearly five centuries, a structure has stood over Florida's rocky coast in the quaint seaside town of St. Augustine. At first it was Spanish lookout towers that warned of approaching threats. Around the mid-1700s, the first lighthouse was built on the site, where it shined its watchful eye for over a hundred years. Beach erosion and a changing landscape prompted the construction of a new 165-foot black-and-white lighthouse in 1874. In the nearly 150 years since first casting its powerful beam onto the endless ocean, the current watchtower has remained a vital fixture for the local community and countless seafarers.

St. Augustine Lighthouse in 1936
THE LIBRARY OF CONGRESS PUBLIC DOMAIN

Until recently, lighthouses required round-the-clock care, meaning someone had to live on the premises and maintain the facilities at all times. A lighthouse keeper would religiously monitor everything, as the burning lard (eventually kerosene and oil) had to be constantly replenished and the light cleaned and maintained; lives depended greatly on the keepers' diligence. To keep an ever-watchful eye on their light, keepers typically lived on the grounds in a small house nearby. Some would reside there with their families, but most lived alone and in near isolation. It wasn't until electricity made its way to the shore in the 1920s that things changed.

Monitoring the lighthouse went from three lightkeepers splitting daily shifts down to two, then to one. Eventually, the light became fully automated and only weekly maintenance checks were required.

Over the past century and a half, the St. Augustine Lighthouse has endured numerous wars, a constant threat of pirates, earthquakes, hurricanes, and even arson. Yet the watchtower and its shoreline have also seen their fair share of tragedy. Arguably, the saddest documented story in the structure's history occurred in 1873. Hezekiah H. Pittee, the superintendent overseeing the new tower's construction, had allowed his three daughters, Mary, Eliza, and Carrie, and an unidentified local girl to play with an old wooden cart on a rail system that was used to transport building materials from supply ships to the site. The four girls would ride inside the cart to see how far they could make it glide toward the water. One fateful day, the cart rolled too close to the rock ledge and it tipped over. The children were hurled into the water, where Mary, Eliza, and the unnamed girl drowned. This horrific tragedy marred the creation of Pittee's lighthouse . . . and seemingly tied the children's spirits to the land.

One of the most common paranormal occurrences experienced by both the lighthouse staff and its visitors is hearing raucous children laughing. Doors and windows that are closed and locked are later discovered open or unlocked, as if someone is playing a game. Toys in the gift shop seem to move and are displaced, particularly music boxes. On numerous occasions, these delicate toys will also pop open on their own and start to play a soft melody, as if someone were staring at it in wonder. Being that the gift shop is connected to the old lightkeeper's quarters, could the children still feel at home there?

Fourteen years before these deaths, another had occurred. The keeper of the original lighthouse, Joseph Andreu, was adding a fresh coat of paint to the structure when he lost his balance and fell more than a hundred feet to his untimely demise. In recent years, several workers have claimed to hear a scream through the shore's strong winds that sounded like a man falling. Others have seen a young woman in period clothing often gazing out of the lighthouse's upper windows, possibly looking out to sea and waiting for a long-lost love to return. There are numerous reports of phantom smells as well, particularly one of cigars inside the lightkeeper's house, where former keeper Peter Rasmusson smoked daily.

As with the children, most of the activity around the lighthouse seems to be harmless. However, there have also been accounts of a darker entity, one whom some call the Man in Blue, who seems to try to chase people who are inside the lighthouse. And though there are no official records, there are tales of a lighthouse keeper who found the solitude of the job too much to handle and hung himself inside the echoing stairwell, only to be found days later when the light had burned out. Could this be the mysterious Man in Blue? One keeper was so disturbed by a spirit who pursued him up the stairs, only to appear above him and run him back down, that he quit the job and never came back. Similar tales have been abundant, with consistent claims of a dark figure looking over the long spiral staircase, as if it's watching those who enter.

The lighthouse tower, looking down from the fifth platform
JASON NELSON

Even without the misfortunes that have become recorded history, add in the hundreds of years of *undocumented deaths associated with the aforementioned wars, slavery, pirate attacks, prisoners, and natural disasters and there is no knowing how many tragedies have occurred on these grounds . . . or which are responsible for the mysterious activities currently taking place.*

• • •

In my opinion, St. Augustine is one of the most gorgeous cities not only in Florida but in all of America. I've fallen so in love with the municipality and its stunning lighthouse that I've gone there at least eight times now to investigate . . . which, admittedly, always turns into a minivacation. It certainly doesn't hurt that it's only two hours away from my favorite place, Walt Disney World, or that it's by the ocean and offers great food. On more than one occasion, I've rented a scooter and zipped around the streets to take in the sights, including the countless pirate-themed locations that I love. Complete with its cobblestone streets, the entire city has an old New Orleans–meets–Key West feel with a little *Pirates of the Caribbean* sprinkled on top. It's also steeped in history and full of life . . . and death.

If there hadn't been a haunted lighthouse in town, I might never have even visited St. Augustine. In fact, the first time the TAPS team went to visit the city was to investigate a few different locations. After investigating an old hospital and jail, we lost a third location for a few reasons. After we had been there for a while, word got around that we were in St. Augustine and fans started to come to our hotel in droves. Also, ironically, every person we ran into kept assuming we were in town to investigate the lighthouse. Having heard so much about it, we headed over there and asked the owners if we could investigate the facility. Before I knew what was happening, we had the location on our schedule and in our van's GPS.

When we first arrived in town, I had seen the stunning behemoth with its stark white and black rotating stripes and red cap—it looked like it belonged on a postcard. Once we officially had it on the agenda, though, it no longer appeared picturesque but like some demented barbershop pole swirling to taunt me, because I knew I would have to be there at night, going up its winding staircase.

From my hotel room about half a mile away, sure enough, the beauty was gone—the structure was ominous. I imagined it spinning while some creepy music played, lightning crackling over the ocean in the distance.

Even though I was terrified of the climb, I was excited for what could happen at the lighthouse . . . well, what could happen on the ground level at least. In my extensive catalog of phobias (spiders, airplanes, driving over high bridges, et cetera), acrophobia—a fear of heights—is highlighted, dog-eared, and slapped with a huge WARNING label. How this fear started I'm not sure. I have no memories of a scary or traumatic incident with heights; it's just always been there. I'm sure that I could pinpoint the reason after a thousand hours of expensive therapy sessions, but in the end, that wouldn't change the fact that it's something I will never get over. Therefore, the thought of walking up a constantly winding 219-step staircase so I could be in a tight space overlooking everything from more than 165 feet in the air made my head jittery.

Modern photograph of the
St. Augustine Lighthouse tower
JASON NELSON

Even now, after all these years and many visits later, I get a little panicked just thinking about climbing those stairs.

My overwhelming sense of dread was amplified by the fact that one of the ghosts who supposedly haunt the location was a man who fell to his death from the very structure we were going to investigate. For me, the math was painfully simple: *Falling + Death = Rationalized Fear.* Hearing that tale was like adding gas to a nightmare-fueled fire that already raged inside my head. Thankfully, the fire didn't have to rage very long, as there wasn't much time to anticipate what might happen during the investigation . . . especially since we were never supposed to be there in the first place.

• • •

That afternoon, I decided to stop trying to see the watchtower through my window and took a nap. Unfortunately, I kept dreaming of falling from the top of the evil monstrosity that awaited me, so I woke up more tired than rested. When it was time to leave, I knew I would go, but part of me really wanted to find a reason not to go (it wasn't planned, after all). With various excuses running through my head, I found myself on autopilot and taking the elevator downstairs to leave. My eyes were closed as I tried to focus my thoughts when the elevator door opened . . . and I suddenly heard cheering. I had to do a double take at the number of fans who were in the hotel lobby—there was an entire group camping out like they were waiting for a concert. Within seconds, I was swarmed. I wasn't ready for this, but it was a welcome distraction from the persistant fear that pervaded my head.

Mind you, all this happened right when *Ghost Hunters* was reaching a new level of popularity; we were suddenly thrust into the limelight as the new "hot thing." Because word of our production being in town had spread, St. Augustine was teeming with paranormal fans. I spent nearly twenty minutes getting my photo taken with people before I could get out of the lobby, and when I got to the van it was surrounded by even more fans. This was all new to me at the time, so I found it a bit overwhelming and confusing that complete strangers wanted to meet *me*. But the constant attention continued to take me out of the moment regarding where I was going and what we were about to do. While I would never skip an investigation, no matter how strong the fear, I honestly think that this was the closest I ever came to having one win out—I desperately wanted to make up an excuse and drive the other way.

After driving just a few minutes, I pulled into the lighthouse parking lot and saw how damn big 165 feet really is. Getting out of the van, I stupidly forced myself to look up. My head started to spin with fear. I tried slowing my breath and did my best to admire the lighthouse's beauty. It didn't work.

Then I focused on the team briefing we'd had earlier, during which we'd talked about the location and what we were hoping to accomplish with the claims. I was pretty relieved to find out that most of the accounts centered around other area structures and not necessarily the lighthouse; it gave me some hope that I wouldn't have to spend too much time inside the beaconing nightmare. There were only a few claims of a male spirit chasing someone up and down the stairs, and we didn't find much validity in them. We even considered putting cameras inside the lighthouse, figuring it wouldn't hurt, and I'm so glad that we did— some of the best evidence of my time in the field was caught inside that spiraling tower of terror.

• • •

During our pre-investigation discussion, I was relieved to hear that Jay and Grant wanted to do the lighthouse first; I would be doing the lightkeeper's house, delaying my inevitable visit to the tower. Everyone on the team knew of my fear of heights, but they always respected it and didn't push or mock me about it, which is why I'm sure Jay and Grant volunteered to go to the lighthouse, in order to give me time to work on my fear. Given the all clear, I walked around the keeper's house and used my thermal camera but didn't find much there. Next, I headed to the outside grounds, where numerous experiences with the children reportedly occurred. Again, I came up empty. That meant it was time to swap locations with Jay and Grant, going to the damn lighthouse itself.

Steeling myself, I walked inside and looked up with my flashlight. The spiraling staircase disappeared into blackness. It was like peering into the inverted pit of hell. I felt faint, but the cameras were on and I had a job to do, so I did my best not to show how hard it was for me to breathe. Fortunately, after only two landings, where I paused to compose myself, I heard footsteps going up the stairs. Without a thought, I chased after them, trying to catch the phantom noise. Before I knew it, I was a full flight off the ground. This wasn't too surprising, as I could definitely handle a few flights, but at that moment it still felt like a triumph. Slowly making my way to the second-flight landing (I was incredibly thankful that there were landings at each level where I could find my legs; most lighthouses don't have them), I suddenly heard the noise below me. Shocked, I chased it back down.

No sooner had I made it back downstairs when I heard *above* me, as clear as day, loud footsteps again marching up the stairs. Once more, I ran up and gave chase, and like before, the sounds suddenly materialized below me. It was as if something was playing a game of cat and mouse. I wondered if it was just holding still while I climbed upstairs past it, before it would race back down. It was absolutely thrilling, playing this supernatural sport with disembodied footsteps. To this day, it was one of the top experiences of my life. However, it was nothing compared to the other evidence we'd soon collect in this location.

When the team later reviewed the audio, we discovered that we'd caught an EVP of a woman yelling, "*Help me!*" Unlike most EVPs, which can sound muffled and be hard to decipher, this one was extremely loud. But there were no stories or documented history that had a woman ever being harmed in the lighthouse. It was an odd finding but still incredibly clear evidence.

Then we watched the video footage. I think I felt my heart backflip for joy when I saw a shadowy mass dart around the inside of the lighthouse railings. It was faster than I think any human could move. The shadow had a fluidity and grace that reminded me of the Dementors from the Harry Potter books—black and wispy, with a liquid, smooth grace as it shot around. It was so unlike anything I had seen before—truly other-worldly. And it was about to get even better.

We had positioned a night vision camera to face straight up the spiraling staircase, and it caught probably some of the best evidence I have ever witnessed. Jay and Grant were walking up the stairs and got about halfway to the top when a shadow—one that was clearly shaped like a person—leaned over the railing. The shadow was about five levels above them, and it was looking down, as if trying to see where Jay and Grant were. After a second or two, it disappeared from our camera view, then resurfaced and peered over the railing again a few moments later, this time from two levels higher. When the shadow leaned over that second time, it became even more evident that it was a human shape. After looking down for a few seconds longer, it vanished again, this time moving to the left. Thinking about it now, all these years later, gives me chills. Was that dark mass the thing that had been playing games with me? Was it the Man in Blue? Whatever it was, I remain grateful that it showed itself to us that night.

• • •

When you're shooting for a TV show, you learn to find a balance between making friends with the crew and completely ignoring them while you're filming. On *Ghost Hunters*, we've been incredibly lucky to have great crews and producers who let us maintain a lot of control. If we told them there couldn't be too many people in a room or we needed them to back out so we could try something on our own, they'd always listen. Any activity that TAPS records is done so with equipment that is personally set up, monitored, and examined. The production crew, meanwhile, is hyper-focused only on filming us, staying out of the way, and keeping silent, so they typically don't experience much on the paranormal end, if anything. I've had things happen right in front of me that were so clear and apparent, yet the camera operator didn't notice it because they had their headphones on or their face buried in a monitor, making sure that they got what was needed.

That night inside the St. Augustine Lighthouse, however, members of the film crew truly had their own inexplicable experiences. I remember one of them telling us that he saw something that looked green and was moving all on its own, floating free and high in the air and emanating from the tower itself, where no one or nothing could possibly be. He said he felt the blood run out of his face and a fear unlike anything he had ever imagined surge through his body. He just dropped everything he was doing in the lighthouse, ran outside, and refused to go back in or even go to the lightkeeper's quarters that night. He was so adamant when he told us, "I love my job and all of you, but I will quit before going back in there again." It could have been the most fearful that I'd ever seen a person. Whatever he saw frightened him so badly that he was ready to leave his dream job in television.

Another time while investigating there, our sound engineer heard someone walk right past him and up the stairs, even though there was no one around him. He insisted that the movement had been so clear, he could feel the vibration of each footstep and the concussive force produced by whatever it was moving quickly by him. It terrified him to the point where he too became resistant about staying inside the lighthouse.

As immensely talented as these two crew members were, they both eventually left the *Ghost Hunters* production, and I think the lighthouse encounters might have had something to do with it—they simply no longer wanted any part of what we did on a daily basis. That is the true testament of a location's activity.

• • •

A few years later, I visited St. Augustine again with our spin-off show *Ghost Hunters Academy*, where we trained new and potential investigators. This time I was looking forward to going back to the lighthouse rather than feeling full of angst . . . though I still had no intention of going any higher than three floors up, as I wasn't the person doing the investigation. After filming one night, I went and found Grace, one of the heads of the lighthouse facility, to say good night before she locked up. As I turned to leave, she stopped me and said, "Steve, I know you can do it. Why don't you go to the top with me? If you do, I'll let you go *inside* the light." A part of me wanted to laugh out loud and start walking right past her, but I knew that going inside the lantern room—the area that houses the lighthouse lens—was forbidden and something so few people ever get to do. You already know that I'm all about unique life experiences, and this seemed like as good a reason as any to fight my overwhelming fear of heights. So, before I could talk myself out of it, I gripped the railing tighter and marched upward, with Grace encouraging me every step of the way.

Keeping my head down, I moved robotically up the stairs, completely surprised with myself. I could feel my thighs and calves burning from the long climb, but I didn't dare stop; I worried that if I took any kind of break, the courage I had mustered would vanish. I might even become so paralyzed with fear that I'd find myself stuck where I was, too afraid to do anything. So, I kept going forward on my seemingly endless climb, my legs feeling like a wobbly Slinky working in reverse. It made me appreciate how, back in the day, lightkeepers had to carry heavy buckets of sloshing oil all the way up these stairs three times a day, every day. If they could do that, then I could walk up *once* to see the light.

I doubt Mount Everest could have been a harder climb for me, but I finally reached the very top, where a door awaited. Grace quickly opened it and let me step inside. The entire lantern room was made with thick, intricately carved glass, so there was no chance that I could fall out. Actually, it felt like a pretty normal room, aside from the blinding light that kept spinning around. Knowing that I couldn't fall, I took a deep breath and looked up. There in front of me was what looked like the world's largest crystal . . . double my height and two hay barrels' width around. Though I was still sucking air after the long climb, I couldn't help but hold my breath at that moment. I felt like some medieval warrior who had finally found the magical gemstone that would save his village, the music swelling and wind heroically blowing my hair (at least what was outside my baseball cap). Each time the light spun around, I closed my eyes and bowed my head to avoid the blinding beacon.

"Turn around, Steve," Grace said. I was so in awe of the massive light that I didn't even realize how high up I was. As I turned, I was slammed with the beauty outside. Water was all around, and the land far below looked miniscule, like that town diorama in *Beetlejuice*. The moon was almost full and shining on the water in a glorious, mysterious way. As I had always been so afraid of heights, such sights were incredibly rare for me. It was almost indescribable . . . especially since I was able to truly enjoy what I was seeing.

After I took in the sights, a sense of pride came over me, but it was quickly killed by the realization that I had to walk back down soon. I turned back to the magnificent light behind me, thinking my journey was done, when Grace asked, "Are you ready?" I thought she was asking if I was going to head back down, and I was admittedly a bit sad about that. But then, with a gentle flick of her wrist, she pointed at the spinning light. I hadn't noticed it before, but there was a gap in the glass that acted like a moving doorway.

"You have to time it just right, wait for the light to pass, then hop in." She said this like it was nothing, even though earlier that night I'd heard how the light would cost over a quarter of a million dollars to replace. As I ignored the thought of accidentally destroying this historic and incredibly important lens, and the fact that I could be crushed to death, heroic music flooded back into my thoughts and I readied myself to jump in at the right time. I felt like I was about to enter a new dimension.

Holding the railing with one hand, I watched as the giant light, the lens of which was taller than me, spun around at a perfect, consistent pace; it was like looking at the inner workings of a massive clock, only this one glowed hot with intense illumination. Hesitant, I ducked my head, stepped over the lip, and timed my approach. It was nerve-racking to know that if I got it wrong, not only would I get smooshed and fall face-first into a burning-hot bulb the size of a seedless watermelon but I might also destroy a piece of local history. Counting in my head, I watched the light spin past and took two quick steps into the center. Cue theme music.

Grace stood on the platform behind me, and the world disappeared. The sounds of the wind, the crashing ocean waves below . . . everything gone. All I could see was this brilliant ball of light rocket around me as if I were the center of its orbit. Sharp, stunning angles of glass were on all sides, like being inside a kaleidoscope. For a moment, my film-obsessed mind thought of General Zod getting banished to the Phantom Zone in *Superman: The Movie*.

Finally, a serenity washed over me as I looked out to the world through a fractured lens. Thoughts of all the lives this light had saved and those who took care of it flooded my mind. Yet just as fast as those thoughts came, they disappeared. My mind was calm and all I could think about was being in the moment. The surreal beauty and uniqueness enveloped me so warmly that I forgot all time and space around me. I was in a moment of pure reverence that remains incomparable to anything else I have ever done . . . a moment that I would have never experienced if I hadn't fought against my deepest fear.

I looked at Grace as she nodded for me to come back out. She was beaming because she truly understood the mind-blowing nature of being inside the display. I had to be precise with my exit, which was harder this time for some reason, but when I finally got out, my eyes were watery. I momentarily grasped on to Grace and thanked her. "Congratulations, Steve," she said. "You're one of only a handful of people to ever be *inside* the St. Augustine Lighthouse lens." I smiled big, the rush still washing over me.

"Ready to go outside on the balcony to get a clear view?" Grace asked, as if I were suddenly cured of acrophobia. Though I was still smiling, I shook my head in an emphatic *no*. I had done enough! And if you think I'm now about to share a poignant moment in which I tell you how I overcame my fear of heights, you are sadly mistaken. And going back down the lighthouse stairs was worse than coming up—I kept envisioning myself falling forward and tumbling down to ground level. Sorry, but as amazing and worthwhile as this experience was, it was still business as usual inside my head.

Be that as it may, the paranormal and personal experiences I've gone through at the St. Augustine Lighthouse have been profound and, I daresay, life-changing. It's also one of the few places that I can say is truly haunted. But I won't be going past the fourth floor again—if there are ghosts somewhere on a higher level of the lighthouse, *they* can come down and see *me*.

After my terrifying journey, I couldn't help but think once again about the lightkeepers who made that monumental trek so many times. As paranormal investigators, we talk about getting attached to locations, and lighthouses are a perfect example. They seem to be hot spots for the paranormal, and I believe that is because of the bond the keepers

A LIFE WITH GHOSTS

have with these illuminated towers. It is not just a job to them—it's their personality, it becomes their persona in the community, and with them living there twenty-four hours a day, it is their life. Being so melded with the place they take care of for years is certain to create a bond with the locations they oversee. How could it not? It makes sense that a spirit would be looking over the railing down at us at St. Augustine, because the ghost of a lightkeeper would have been doing his normal tasks and curious, if not defensive, about who was coming into his lighthouse.

The bonds we have to locations, people, and items are some of the things that seem to keep spirits attached or coming back to the physical world. They tend to become so important to us that we can't let them go and hold on as much as we can (that is, if these haunting conscious spirits are coming back with intent and not a natural occurrence or a residual impression left behind). I've often wondered, when I eventually pass on, will there be a place that my ethereal being will find its way to? While I have a home and places I love dearly, like my parents' house, I have been on the move for decades. More than 80 percent of my time is spent traveling all over the country. If my spirit was to go to the place that I'm the happiest, he would probably go to Disney World, but if that's how this all works, I would expect Disney to be one of the most haunted places in the world.

On the opposite side, we have tragedy that seems to bond people to locations, like the stories of the spirits of the little children who died tragically, playing on the land where the gift shop was eventually built. While I personally didn't experience any activity from them, they could still be there, having lost their lives in the water nearby. Sometimes that's enough of a reason to stick around. While it may be a movie trope, the "unfinished business" theory holds true in real life.

While we strive to find evidence, we are also left to ponder the "why" a ghost is in a particular location. Perhaps one day we'll have an answer to these questions and we'll finally know why some spirts get stuck in, imprinted on, or choose to stay (or return) in certain locations. With St. Augustine, I like to think that the lightkeeper is just doing his job, making sure the place is safe and running right. And if there are any child spirits remaining, I hope they know people like me are wondering if they are okay wherever they are.

SOMETIMES IT'S WHEN
YOU LEAST EXPECT IT

BUCKSTEEP MANOR

—

WASHINGTON, MA

BUILT 1897

Unlike many of the other locations I refer to in this book, which are associated with torturous, painful histories, Bucksteep Manor has a simple past. Built on top of Washington Mountain at the turn of the twentieth century for George F. Crane, a wealthy New York attorney, this massive estate with its three-hundred-plus acres of preserved wilderness was a private residence for many years. The property was designed to resemble an estate that Crane had once visited in England—the stone architecture of the chapel is reminiscent of a grand castle, though slightly out of place in Massachusetts. The main lodge, on the other hand, with its redwood paneling, fits right in. Set in the heart of the Berkshires, a popular vacation destination known for its hiking trails, world-class music, and arts festivals in the summer and colorful foliage in the fall, Bucksteep Manor quickly became renowned for its luxurious private parties and for breeding some of the finest thoroughbred horses in the country.

Shortly after its construction in 1897, the Crane family had a church erected near the entrance to Bucksteep's grounds. With the importance of religion strong in their family, this structure allowed them to make the property a private compound that didn't require anyone to leave. When Crane passed away, Rudolph Sacco, a former judge, and his family purchased the land and turned it into a wildlife resort, using the main house as a lodge. Small inns were built on the land, as it boasted fishing, hunting, and other recreational activities to lure visitors. Bucksteep became a New England favorite for weddings in the warm season and skiing in the winter.

However, as the land and structures became an area of business where employees worked daily and guests often frequented, the paranormal claims began. Over the years, staff and visitors alike have consistently reported sightings of a man in long brown robes who strongly resembles a monk.

The Bucksteep Manor chapel,
visible from the road

Unlike the spirits who seem to haunt one specific location, this apparition has been seen across the entire property, from the lawn to inside the church to all the way up to the numerous rooms throughout the main house. In the lodge, female employees claim to have had their hair gently stroked or pulled while they're down in the basement; others talk of being touched or gripped with the vibe of an unseen entity watching them. Is the monk responsible for these experiences, or could it be the work of someone else who's strongly connected to the property's history?

• • •

Nestled in a thick pocket of woods in the heart of New England, Bucksteep Manor, with its picturesque European structure and a one-hundred-year-old church on its grounds, is the perfect setting for a sappy Hallmark movie. When we were called in to investigate the property, it was like a dream come true—Bucksteep was only a little over an hour from where I lived, and it wasn't often that I got to do an investigation and then be able to go home and sleep in my own bed.

Even though it was close by, I had never been to Bucksteep, nor had I ever heard much about the place. As I am an investigator, people constantly relate stories to me about locations being haunted. I thought I would have heard so much more about Bucksteep, all things considered, but I could only recall the briefest of mentions over the years. Never hearing anything about an allegedly haunted place right near my home didn't bode well for the investigation.

The New England–themed backdrop was just like all the towns I grew up around. Unlike the massive, abandoned buildings I was used to investigating, Bucksteep was quaint, as it was just a large house, so

Front view of the now-abandoned
Bucksteep Manor

The view from the entrance driveway

setting up was rather easy and a welcome break from the multilevel, institutionalized structures I usually had to work within.

It was also a welcome break to investigate in a place that had electricity, heat, and a comfortable ambience. Close to home, cozy setting . . . if there was paranormal activity, this location would be a perfect treat.

To better understand what we might be dealing with, we spoke with the manor's chef, Heather, who told us all about her experiences, which for her were rather intense. One night, while looking for some supplies in the basement, she suddenly felt an overwhelming sense of fear . . . as if she was not alone and someone was about to attack her, so much that she threw a knife into a darkened crawl space. Eerily, the knife made no noise when it landed. It was an intriguing story, but honestly, I was way more intrigued about Heather's offer to make me the best filet mignon I'd ever had after our investigation. That alone was enough motivation to get me going.

Our investigation of Bucksteep turned out to be a complete bust, with none of us experiencing anything and most claims being disproved. Not only that, but because of crappy timing, we finished our investigation in the morning and I never got the steak. No paranormal experiences and no fine dining made for a dual disappointment of epic proportions. This lack of experiences helped me understand why I had never heard stories about the location.

• • •

When you're in the dark and intently looking for ghosts, every little sound, every flicker of light, and every change of temperature can get your heart racing. It's important that we always calmly examine these occurrences and figure out what could cause them, one by one. Anything that we encountered at Bucksteep, from scratching noises to a few thermal hits, was almost instantly revealed as wires moving in the wind or wild animals. The closest thing to an experience I had there was feeling a church pew vibrate. I easily dismissed even that—it could have been just in my mind or caused by anything, like a furnace kicking on. By the end of the investigation, we were ready to move on, as the activity wasn't showing itself to us.

I have never been so wrong in my life.

When I say a place isn't haunted, it doesn't mean there isn't anything there. It only means that I thoroughly investigated but found nothing to indicate paranormal activity during my investigation. Not all activity is consistent and not all spirits are outgoing. There could be ghosts every-where, but they may not want to be found. Honestly, if I had been a very shy person when I was alive, I think I would stay hidden if a bunch of strangers set up cameras everywhere and started yelling for "Ghost Steve" to come out. Besides, even if a spirit wanted to bring attention to itself or call out, we have no understanding of how difficult communication is for them.

Investigations can also take a lot of time. As noted earlier, when we're at a location for an episode, what the audience sees on television is the edited accumulation of multiple days of our investigation. When we're not televising our investigation of a place, we may spend months, even *years*, looking into that location—we may frequently visit the place and keep recordings going even when we're not there in the hopes of catching something. In a way, you can think of investigating like metal detecting—you might search an old battlefield a dozen times and find nothing but junk. Then, on your umpteenth visit there, you find the belt buckle of a legendary general. That first time you didn't find anything, you could have easily declared that the place doesn't have any artifacts, when all along there was a true gem out there that you just kept missing.

It can be very difficult to properly determine whether a location is haunted. I know I can be a little stringent when deciding whether a place is haunted. There are many places that allege to be haunted, but what's the basis for those claims? I can't just assume a haunting because someone says so. If I spend a few nights or a week at a location and experience nothing, we tend to move on to a new location that has a higher rate of occurrence. It does not mean that the place isn't haunted—it just means that I didn't find anything during my time there that would require us to stay longer. One of the first cases I ever did had me investigating for over two months before we found our first piece of evidence. Taking your time pays off, but in most instances, we can only dedicate so much time to non-activity. There could still be something there, but it's no longer productive for me to keep looking into it when there are many other clients who need help. Of course, before ever moving on, we'll do our best to get as many answers for the client as possible so they feel comfortable in the location. After we investigated Bucksteep Manor, the team's initial opinion was that most of the claims could be explained by natural occurrences. In that respect, I take some solace in knowing that I wasn't the only one who was way off the mark about that place.

$$\bullet\ \bullet\ \bullet$$

Throughout my time investigating the unexplained, I've captured countless EVPs, heard many disembodied sounds and voices, been touched by unseen hands, and witnessed objects moving on their own. And while I have seen human shapes and silhouettes, I have never seen a full-body apparition or a ghost. Some of my contemporaries have had intimate and intense experiences where they saw or interacted with ghosts; a few even claim to see them on a regular basis. A part of me feels a little jealous whenever I hear about this good fortune—if I ever saw an entire ghost right before my eyes, my paranormal ambitions would be realized. It's the ultimate proof of what I have always chased. Seeing a full-body apparition in front of me would confirm my own beliefs that something is here with us.

I might not have seen a full-body apparition yet; however, what I experienced at Bucksteep was the equivalent for me, and the most profound paranormal experience of my life. It made all the years chasing the unknown pay off in one fell swoop.

At times, chasing the paranormal can be emotionally draining, especially when you don't catch anything for a long period. Bucksteep Manor was just that . . . endless days of long, hard work that resulted in no solid answers for our client. It was a letdown to find out that the old lodge wasn't active and that most of the reported experiences there could be solved with a bit of investigating. So, without thinking anything more about it, we packed up and left. The next day, Tango and I went over the evidence . . . and found virtually nothing. We were both disappointed but not surprised. After talking about it for a bit, we decided to do something we almost never did—go back to the location. Since we were so close and had nothing scheduled that night, we planned on setting up the static cameras and letting them record. We wouldn't do a full investigation—we would just let the cameras run in the hope that we might catch something for our clients, as they were having a hard time keeping the restaurant staffed. If nothing came of it, it would be no big deal.

We arrived back at Bucksteep about seven that evening. The owner was gracious enough to come and let us in, but he promptly left—we could tell he wasn't too happy at having to drive all the way there during the off-season just to unlock the place and then leave, but he was still kind enough to do it for us. Before he left, he made us promise to shut all the lights off and to lock everything up, as he didn't plan on coming back for a few weeks. We agreed and thanked him profusely for letting us return.

Tango and I quickly set up a handful of cameras, doing our best to put them in the same locations as before, and pressed RECORD. Then we sat in the lobby and killed time on our laptops while the cameras did their thing. We didn't go exploring, as we wanted to keep the footage as uncontaminated as possible. We let the cameras run in the hopes that we would capture something that could get the clients more answers.

By predawn, Tango and I decided we had enough footage, turned off the DVR system and computers, and started to pack up. We couldn't help but notice how eerily quiet everything was. Usually, having a full crew and their equipment at work creates some ambient noise; with just the two of us, however, something felt off. I also started to feel like something was watching us, but I quickly chalked it up to it being so quiet when we were used to more people rushing around at the end of an investigation.

Once we stored everything away and loaded the van, we just had to go back inside to get our personal items, shut off the lights, and lock up. As we grabbed our bags, Tango and I started hearing voices in the ballroom. At first, we figured that someone had come in without us noticing . . . possibly the owner forgot something? Regardless, we stayed silent and tried to listen, hoping that it wasn't an intruder. The noise we heard started off as light chatter, but then it evolved into party sounds, complete with clinking glasses and silverware pinging against plates. The sound gradually grew louder, like someone was turning up the volume as slowly as possible. Tango locked eyes with me—both of us immediately understood that this was *not* an intruder.

We walked together quickly but silently toward the banquet hall. In a lot of cases that I've had with disembodied voices and phantom sounds, they'd stop as soon as you approached or walked near them. Yet, when the two of us entered the ballroom, our flashlights bouncing around the darkened emptiness . . . the sounds of laughter, like at a lively dinner party, got even *louder*. There was no one and nothing in the room, yet Tango and I felt like we were in the middle of a packed dance floor at a large reception. The noise level was equivalent to at least fifteen to twenty people—we could hear very distinct human voices, but there were so many of them that it was hard to hear any clear words. It was like being in a crowd with noises everywhere, but you can't really hear any one particular thing, as all the sounds are mashed together in a jumble. We even tried shouting over the noise, but it proved pointless; it was almost deafening and confusing.

Tango and I ran back to the lobby and tried to figure out what to do next. All our gear was in the van, and by the time we got anything the sounds might have stopped. Not only that, but the sun was coming up in less than an hour. If we weren't on the road soon, we wouldn't be able to get sleep before our next investigation (and that's a really big deal—TV shoots run on a supertight schedule, plus the production crew and our TAPS teammates were counting on us to be on time). With our options being so limited, we decided to investigate without equipment in the hopes of just experiencing whatever we could in the room.

Stepping only a few feet back into the ballroom—I think because we both wanted the safety of the lobby behind us—Tango and I listened to the voices in astonishment. None of them had stopped talking. It was a mind-blowing experience, but without our equipment in hand, there wasn't much we could do. Neither of us had encountered anything remotely like it in our lives. We were surrounded by voices inside a ballroom, like those bone-chilling final moments in *The Shining*, with Jack Torrance at the Overlook Hotel's New Year's Eve party. It was eerie, exhilarating, and so shocking that it threw us off our game.

As we worked to decipher the voices and hear what they were talking about (hoping it would let us pinpoint an era of origin), I noticed that the kitchen light was glaring from the other end of the banquet hall. I could have sworn we had shut it off. With the voices being so loud, I had to shout over to Tango that we had to turn off the light, but more important, we had to make sure the back door was locked before we left, so we might as well walk through the ballroom noise and do so. A part of me wanted to just leave it all be and apologize for forgetting, but the owner was kind enough to let us use the facility again . . . and we didn't want to say we were too scared of ghosts to lock up!

As you've read throughout this book, I've been inside the creepiest, most haunted places in the country, sometimes completely alone—hell, I've been shut inside a morgue locker. My point is, I don't scare easily when it comes to the paranormal. Yet that night, Tango and I were absolutely, full-on freaking out as we shuffled across the ballroom through a crowd that wasn't there. With each step we took, some voices came closer and others moved away. I was so badly shaken, whether it was from fear or exhilaration, I dug my fingers into Tango's shoulder. Looking back,

The side entrance that Tango and I had to lock
before leaving

it's a little bewildering to me that the moment I had always hoped for had finally arrived, yet primal fear took over and I didn't know how to handle the situation.

Inside the kitchen, we could still hear the paranormal party raging in the banquet hall. Thankfully, Tango and I could also hear each other a bit more, though we were both a little too stunned to say much. But before I could even speak, every pot and pan unexpectedly began slamming into one another. The noise was deafening, as if a dozen ghostly cooks had decided to take up the cymbals right then and there. The two of us looked wildly around as now *everything* had started shaking. Pans on the counter jumped. Ladles fell off their hooks and bounced around like they were in a massive earthquake. Pots in the sink trembled like kernels of corn about to pop . . . every damn piece of cookware was moving. Along with the party noise in the other room, we couldn't hear anything again.

I think this moment may have been the first time in my paranormal career that I felt pure terror and panic wash over me. Maybe it was my survival instinct working overtime, but something in my subconscious urged me to grab hold of Tango and bury my face in his shoulder as we started to move quicker. Thankfully, he had the foresight to lock the door as we bolted out of the kitchen. The two of us darted through the banquet hall, hanging on to each other for dear life. The party sounds were louder than ever and we could still hear the pots clanging in the kitchen, though at that moment none of it mattered. "*Just keep going!*" Tango roared. He didn't have to tell me twice.

As soon as we reached the lobby, we checked on each other, grabbed our bags, and stood looking at each other in awe. And that's when the sounds, all of them, immediately stopped. I could hear one pot rolling far off in the distance, but that was only for a few seconds before the building went dead. Other than our rapid breathing, there was no noise. The two of us exchanged glances, walked outside, and sucked in the cool Massachusetts air as we watched the sun come up. After several long moments of silence, we burst out a series of rapid-fire sentences, trying to make sense of everything that had just happened.

• • •

I'll freely admit that if I read everything I just mentioned here in a book, I would have a hard time believing it all. I investigate for a living, but as I mentioned, I believe only in what I can see and experience for myself. Tango and I reminisce about that night at Bucksteep Manor several times a year, as if we need to make sure that what happened to us was real. And every time, we still can't believe it. We also have a laugh over the fact that that the two of us had actually debated going back into the building to clean up the massive mess in the kitchen (we decided not to). I can't imagine what the owner must have thought when he walked in and saw the kitchen trashed and no food cooked. Amazingly, we never heard from him, which makes me wonder if that had happened before and he was used to the mess.

Being unable to record what happened that night is one of the most frustrating regrets of my life. All I can do as an investigator is take comfort in knowing that I had the experience with someone I trust who can corroborate everything. It was truly the only paranormal experience that ever frightened us out of our skins, and we went through it together. Sometimes we talk about how it felt like a scene in a horror movie; other times we engage in a long philosophical discussion as to what it could have been. Whatever it was, it was definitely powerful enough to cause things to move violently. A part of me even wonders if it was something that happened spontaneously, regardless of us being there, or if it was just trying to invite us to its party.

There's no history of pain, death, or great tragedy, or stories of love lost at Bucksteep Manor that I could find; could the voices we heard have been celebratory spirits, or the playback of a past event? The talking made me think it was residual, but the pots seemed like an intelligent act, as that only started when we walked into the kitchen and stopped when we were leaving the building. Was everything the work of only one powerful spirit, or dozens of them? Why would they want us out so badly? Were they just trying to get our attention? What if they didn't even know we were there and all that activity would have happened at that moment anyway? There are just so many questions that Tango and I will endlessly debate.

Unfortunately, Bucksteep Manor closed its doors not long after we were there. Financial troubles shut the place down. The property now sits in a legal limbo while the new owners try to get it back on its feet. I tell you, if it weren't off-limits, I would be begging the owners to set up a long-term investigation there, but that isn't an option in the foreseeable future. Sadly it is currently condemned. If it ever does reopen, though, and the building is still intact, I'll be there on opening day to talk to the new owners about conducting another investigation, and wondering what might be waiting for me inside.

AFTERWORD
LIFE, DEATH, AND WHAT'S NEXT

In 1847, while working at an obstetric department in Vienna, Austria, Dr. Ignaz Semmelweis implemented a new policy that he believed would reduce the absurdly high mortality rates suffered by pregnant women during childbirth. He had developed his theory after making one change in his own medical procedures and seeing a drastic drop in the number of patient deaths. Semmelweis's results were incredible—the mortality rate for pregnant women delivered by doctors at his hospital alone had plummeted from 18 percent to 2 percent. However, his peers, insulted by Semmelweis's arrogance and aggressive nature, belittled his theory. After years of frustration, Semmelweis's mental health deteriorated; his persistent claims that his idea could save countless lives prompted several of his fellow physicians to lure him to visit a public insane asylum and examine a patient with them. When they arrived there, though, Semmelweis was beaten, locked away, and deemed insane for his ludicrous talk. Two weeks later, he died from his injuries.

The controversial idea that eventually resulted in Dr. Semmelweis's death? He postulated that *washing one's hands*, before and after treating patients, could save lives. He soon extended his proposals to include washing surgical tools as well, which reduced mortality rates even further. Back then, it was common for a doctor to cut up a cadaver, without gloves, to determine a cause of death, then proceed with examining and treating their next living patient after using only a dirty rag to clean their hands and instruments. Semmelweis had no concept of infectious disease transmission when he made his theory; he simply believed in what he was doing because he saw effective results. It's almost universally understood today that hand-washing is the easiest way to prevent contracting germs and getting sick. Yet back then, doctors, who were considered the smartest people of the time, laughed at this preposterous notion.

Personally, I believe that the paranormal field has now moved a few steps past the phase of being laughed at. At least in our line of work, the TAPS team and others who have experienced supernatural sightings no longer have to worry about being deemed insane for believing and ending up in an asylum like poor Ignaz Semmelweis. There are now millions of people around the world who believe in the paranormal and thousands who actively participate in similar investigations and research.

Of course, we're still a long way off from proving our theories and understanding them on a scientific level. Until we can, I like to use a phrase when talking about the paranormal that I learned from Dr. Qilin Dai, a physicist whom I once worked with, who explained wind to me: "You could argue that wind doesn't exist because you can't see it. However, we see and measure the effects of wind, so we *know* it exists." In the paranormal world, I've seen things move, heard disembodied voices, sniffed up phantom smells, and much more. I can't prove that ghosts exist yet, but I certainly can *see* the effects and the results . . . just like Dr. Semmelweis.

Thankfully, in my own lifetime, I've gone from having to hide my passion for the peculiar, fearing being misunderstood or embarrassed, to being recognized everywhere I go as an expert in the field. That's a massive leap for someone who was once a shy teenager worried about telling people he wanted to find ghosts. Twenty years ago, when there were no ghost-hunting TV shows, only a small selection of books, and very few teams, we were an outside fringe. Now we're an established part of the mainstream culture. We have dozens of ghost-related reality and scripted shows, not to mention the many books and paranormal teams in almost every town in the world.

To know that I've been a part of that growth, even if in an ancillary way, fills me with a sense of humbling gratitude that I cannot measure, especially since it was never my goal to do any of that. I was just a kid who wanted answers to my own questions, and I got lucky by surrounding myself with the right people at the right time. Sometimes life works that way. Seneca, a Roman philosopher, said, "Luck is what happens when preparation meets opportunity." My life has certainly been like that: I studied, practiced, and prepared, and then luck opened a door for me and I walked through.

And I'm *far* from done. I'm only in my forties. If I have it my way, I have at least another few decades of investigating ahead of me. With the growth of our field and technology advancing at such a rapid pace, I couldn't be more excited about seeing what the future holds for the paranormal world. I've witnessed such massive growth in the last twenty years, and I can't even imagine what I'll see next. Maybe the questions that I and so many like me have always asked will finally be answered, or maybe I'll find myself with even more questions to ponder. But that's what I find thrilling about the paranormal: the mysteries and the chance to solve them.

My career has been well documented in front of a camera lens. This book was my effort to go a bit deeper than a show could, to peel back the onion and see the layers of my experiences on a more personal level. My goal was never to change people's minds or talk anyone into doing their own investigating. I simply wanted to write about some of the most frightening and fun locations that I've ever visited, and to give readers my thoughts and insights on what I experienced. In a small way, I also hope this book honors the memories of the people who died or suffered such horrible atrocities in so many of these places.

Whether or not I've successfully achieved any of those goals, I leave that for you to decide. And although this book was a labor of love that took me down memory lane and back to several of my favorite "haunts," it's a mere drop in the bucket. I've done well over a thousand investigations, and picking only a handful for this book was incredibly difficult. Plus, the experiences you've read about here only scratch the surface of those that I've yet to share.

When I was a teenager reading *ESP, Hauntings and Poltergeists: A Parapsychologist's Handbook* over and over again, I didn't fully grasp or appreciate the impact it would have on my life. All these years later, I understand how that book guided my obsession into quite an offbeat career. Granted, my book is very different from Loyd Auerbach's, which I still consider to be required reading. However, if just one person perusing these pages has gotten something out of them—be it educational, inspirational, or simply entertaining—then writing down my experiences here has been well worth the time and effort.

Whatever happens next in the paranormal world and with myself, the one thing I know for certain is that I'll continue investigating until I find the answers that I've always sought—who am I kidding, even if I find the answers, I'll keep on investigating, because it is the most intoxicating thing in the world to me. But if I don't get answers in my own lifetime, I hope when I slip over to the other side I'll discover for myself what's truly there. Regardless of what comes first, I also know I'll have countless more experiences that I'll look forward to sharing with my colleagues, paranormal enthusiasts . . . and anyone who just likes to hear a good, spooky tale. Thanks for reading about some of my paranormal adventures; I can't wait to tell you about where my adventures take me next.

Steve Gonsalves
2023

ACKNOWLEDGMENTS

This book took many years to write and it went through a few transformations, and I couldn't have done any of it alone. I owe a tremendous debt of gratitude to many people for making it possible:

To all of my *Ghost Hunters* crew and TAPS team members past and present: I'm so thankful that our lives have intertwined. This book is only possible because of the adventures we've been on together.

Jason Hawes: Without your friendship, love, and support, most of the stories in this book would not have happened. Thank you for kicking the door open for all of us.

Dave Tango: My best friend, my most trusted companion. My life is better because you're in it. Thank you for everything. I love you.

Grant Wilson: Thank you for the trust and guidance. We had so much fun in the early days of TAPS and *Ghost Hunters*.

Kris Williams: I'm so happy to call you a friend. You're one of the best people out there. Thank you for keeping me on my toes for all these years.

Amy Bruni: We have a friendship that I'm not sure I deserve but am so grateful to have! Thank you, Amy. I'll see you at Disney!

ACKNOWLEDGMENTS

Adam Berry: You're one of my favorite people and a dear friend. Thank you for being in my life and for the sing-alongs.

Shari DeBenedetti: Your unwavering commitment to the team and always being there in the best ways says a lot about the person you are. Here's to many more years investigating together.

Dustin Pari: I'm constantly blown away by your selflessness and commitment to helping other people overcome life's toughest moments. Fifteen years later and you still haven't gotten me to like circus peanuts.

Ken Robert: When we became friends at fourteen and bonded over a shared love of music, horror, and all things strange and unusual, I didn't know you would become a lifelong best friend. Those early days of going to see the Warrens together and staying up most nights entrenched in the paranormal set in motion the path that my life would eventually take me on.

Pilgrim Media: Thank you for believing in us and turning our hobby into a TV show, and for all of the opportunities that have come with it. What a ride it's been.

Mike Aloisi: I can't imagine anyone else I'd want to write this book with. Thank you for believing in it and guiding me all the way to the finish line. Most of all, thank you for being my friend the whole way.

My gratitude to Alec Shankman, Jared Thompson, and David Doerrer at A3 Artists Agency. David, thank you for finding this book a great home!

Thanks to Ping Pong Productions for being such great partners with *Ghost Nation*.

To all of my friends at Travel Channel and Discovery Plus: Thank you for giving me such amazing opportunities and the adventures of a lifetime.

ACKNOWLEDGMENTS

SyFy channel: Thank you for taking a chance and giving us our first home.

Thanks to everyone at Simon & Schuster, especially the Gallery Books division and my editor, Ed Schlesinger. Ed, thank you for your patience and kindness. Working with you has made this experience an absolute pleasure, and I can't thank you enough in this short paragraph.

To my entire family, for all their love and support: This book might be called *A Life with Ghosts*, but it's a life with family whom I cherish.

I would like to end this with a sincere and deep thank-you to all of the viewers, fans, paranormal investigators, enthusiasts, ghost hunters, historians, researchers, scientists, curators, librarians, and clerks who have supported me, been there, or helped me over the years. Without each one of you, none of this is possible—you will always have my gratitude, love, and respect!

INDEX

NOTE: Page references in *italics* refer to photos

ABOUT THE AUTHORS

STEVE GONSALVES has been a public speaker and educator about paranormal phenomena for more than two decades. As a main cast member of the hit television series *Ghost Hunters* as well as *Ghost Hunters Live*, *Ghost Hunters Academy*, and *Ghost Nation*, he helped pave the way for a worldwide paranormal explosion. Gonsalves started his work in paranormal studies at a very young age and has investigated more than 1,500 reportedly haunted locations. He had the privilege of working closely with Ed and Lorraine Warren, paranormal pioneers and the inspiration for the *Conjuring* movie series, as well as Dr. William G. Roll (*Poltergeist*). Along with his multiple appearances on a variety of television, radio, and paranormal series, Gonsalves executive produced and codirected the popular documentary series *The House in Between*. He lives with his cat, Fleur, in Massachusetts.

MICHAEL ALOISI is the author of more than a dozen books, including the official biographies of film legends Tom Savini and Kane Hodder. Michael has also written several novels, including *Mr. Bluestick* and *Pieces* (cowritten with Rebecca Rowland). Under his pen name, Michael

Gore, he has released three horror short story collections, including *Do Not Open* and *Skeletons in the Attic*. His books have been adapted into a reality show and a documentary film, and they have been translated into several languages. With a BFA in film directing and an MFA in creative writing, Michael teaches filmmaking classes, and he lives in Massachusetts with his wife and children.